Samuel Willenberg

Revolt in Treblinka

First published in Hebrew as:
Mered be-Treblinka, Israel Ministry of Defense, Tel Aviv, 1986

First published in English as:
Surviving Treblinka, Basil Blackwell, Oxford and New York, 1989

First published in Spanish as:
Rebelion en Treblinka, La Semana Publications, Jerusalem, 1988

First published in Polish as:
Bunt w Treblince, Res Publica, Warsaw, 1991

Current printing:
Revolt in Treblinka, 1992

REVOLT IN TREBLINKA
Samuel Willenberg
Jerusalem, Israel
Tel. 02 — 63 73 26

Żydowski Instytut Historyczny
00-090 Warszawa
ul. Tłomackie 3/5
Tel. 27 92 21

Contents

...So be it, we are already accustomed to death,
and it makes no impression on us.
If any of us survives, he will tread the earth like
a creature from another planet — because only by a miracle
or by an error will he survive.

Emanuel Ringelblum
Warsaw Ghetto, 1.1.1943

GENERAL PLAN

TREBLINKA
EXTERMINATION CAMP

EXTERMINATION CAMP

SORTING AREA

THE ASSEMBLY AND UNDRESSING AREA (YARD)

ROLL-CALL GROUNDS

ADMINISTRATION WING AND STAFF LIVING QUARTERS

To Labour Camp Treblinka →

← To Treblinka railway station

Plan drawn up by Samuel Willenberg

KEY TO GENERAL PLAN OF CAMP

TREBLINKA EXTERMINATION CAMP – GENERAL PLAN

1 The railway track and the platform (ramp).

2 A small wooden sign attached to the gate, with an arrow indicating the direction of Bialystok and Wolkowysk.

3 A long barrack with a large painted inscription 'OBERMAJDAN'. On this outer wall a fake clock and on the barrack door the inscription 'CASH'; a locked door with an inscription: 'To the first class waiting room'; a locked door with an inscription 'To the second class waiting hall'; a locked door with an inscription 'To the third class waiting hall'. The barrack served as a storeroom for more valuable objects taken away from the victims.

THE ASSEMBLY AND UNDRESSING AREA (YARD)

4 On left, the women's barrack, where they had to undress. At the end of the barrack, behind a partition-wall worked the barbers. Behind the women's barrack – a sorting place for bottles and kitchen appliances ('Flaschensortieren').

5 On right, a barrack serving as storeroom. It also served as prisoners' night quarters until the escape of four of them.

X A well.

7 Path to the gas chambers.

SORTING AREA

6 'Lazarett' – execution site.

3 Two barracks where more valuable objects were stored. On the wall facing the ramp were signs for deceiving the victims.

12 Five-metre high wall.

ADMINISTRATION WING AND STAFF LIVING QUARTERS

15 Stables and pigsty.

16 Bakery.

17 Barrack containing: Ukrainian women's quarters; dental clinic of the SS men and Ukrainians; general clinic of the SS men and Ukrainians; room of the 'Goldjuden'.

18 Barracks of the Ukrainian guards.

19 Zoo ('Tiergarten').

20 SS men barracks connected by a corridor with the armory.

21 The armoured car.

22 Chairs on which relaxed the SS men. Above them were sun shades.

23 Ukrainians' guardroom.

24 Administration rooms, including the quarters of the camp commander Stangel.

25 Garage.

26 Gasoline and lubricating oil depot.

27 Timber yard.

28 Vegetable garden.

29 Watchtowers.

30 Anti-tank obstacles.

31 Barbed wire camouflaged by pine branches.

32 Main entrance gate.

33 Latrines.

34 Railway track.

EXTERMINATION CAMP

8 Ten new gas chambers; three old, small gas chambers.

9 Burial pits.

10 Rails on which victims' bodies were cremated.

11 Barrack prisoners' living quarters.

ROLL-CALL GROUNDS

33 Latrines.

BARRACK – PRISONERS' LIVING QUARTERS

13 On left, barrack; kitchen; capos' and specialists ('Hofjuden'); tailor and furrier shop; next to the window stood the painter's easel, carpentry and locksmith's shop; smithy.

14 On right – barrack divided into latrines, washroom and on its sides prisoners' living quarters.

Prologue

April in Israel, a clear, calm spring morning: streets basking in the warm rays of the sun, the aroma of citrus flowers, heavy traffic. I must get to work. Sitting with my wife and my daughter in the car, I grow irate as the trip drags on. Then a siren splits the air. Everything – cars, trucks, buses – comes to a stop. Drivers and passengers step into the street, where they stand in taut silence. More distant sirens echo. Their wail blankets the entire country. They augur the beginning of Holocaust Day: a minute of silence for the memory of six million murdered Jews. I look at my wife, my daughter, the people around me. A sudden fog has come over them. Cars, buildings, people have vanished. Green silhouettes appear before my eyes: a dense forest. I peer through a small grating laced with barbed wire; it belongs to a railroad freight car. I hear the clicking of wheels and feel the train jounce. The light of early dawn filters in...

I

En Route to the Unknown

We sat on the floor of the car, arm in arm, shoulder to shoulder, leg to leg. Total silence reigned, as if the universe had frozen over. Anxious faces. Where were we headed? What awaited us?

I reflected on scenes out of the past – my happy youth, a serene family home... Suddenly it was all very far away, part of another world, just a beautiful dream. I worried about Mother, Father, my sisters. What had become of them? Momentarily my concern for their well-being tumbled into a terrible despair: if only it were all done with! Now and then I imagined that the surrounding reality was but a daydream, a nothingness; that at any moment I would wake up free and full of *joie de vivre*. But the clicking wheels jarred me back to earth, to the events of the past few days.

I had woken the previous morning to the sound of drummers marching through the streets of the Opatow ghetto, awakening its 7,000 Jews. I was disoriented. It was 4:00 a.m. It soon became clear: the Germans were about to expel the Jews and liquidate the ghetto. But where were they sending us?

Squadrons of SS materialized in the ghetto streets, greeted every-where with howls of despair. The Germans cursed, threatened, prodded: "Get up, get out, get moving!" Finally they dragged people out of their homes. Out the Jews went, doubled over. Their belongings were now limited to what they could load onto their backs.

We were herded into the vast market square, the crowd growing with each passing moment. Many shuffled along in total resignation, as if guessing that the world of their past was irrevocably gone. We were lined up in ranks of five. Now the guards reached into the mass of people and pulled out several dozen Jews: these would dismantle the ghetto once it was no longer needed. Jewish militiamen and *Judenrat* members, together with their families, were taken aside as well. Houses were searched; perhaps some Jews had thought to hide something. The sick and elderly who could not march were shot then and there.

We stood there a few hours. Then we were taken on a grueling eighteen-kilometer mass march to a railroad junction. Some could not cope with the ordeal. When the armed guards noticed such a Jew, they surrounded him, took him out of line, pressed him face down into a ditch beside the road, pushed a rifle barrel to his head and pulled the trigger. With each shot, a shattered skull sent a fountain of blood splashing onto the earth.

Discipline in the ranks was essential, any violation of order being resolved with gunfire. Our Ukrainian guards brought a supply of wooden shoes; any Jew seen wearing fine high boots was stripped of them and given wooden shoes in exchange.

At twilight we reached the tracks, on which a train of standard cattle cars awaited. With curses and murderous beatings they shoved 120 Jews into each car. I was pushed roughly to the little grated window of one of these cars. Night passed; mist rose from the swamps. By the light of dawn we beheld green fields, rivers and lakes, a forest on the horizon. Gleaming sunbeams lent the forest a reddish hue which, to this day, I see only as so grey-blue.

It was a lovely autumn morning. As the train slowed and then, shuddering, lurched from one track to another, the crushed travellers asked each other if anyone had seen a station. Another moment, and we indeed pulled into a little depot. One of the platforms bore a sign: Siedlce. People were standing there, waiting for a train. We overheard their greeting: "Jews, they're going to make you into soap!"

Total silence reigned in the car, our faces reflecting acquiescence and profound sorrow. Berger, a pious Jew with a clipped beard, touched me: "You see, Samek? You wanted to join the partisans, to fight... On whose side? With these people – who hate us as badly as the Germans do? You said I should send my children into the forest for hiding. With whom should they hide? With these people – who'd murder us or turn us over to the Germans at the first opportunity for a bottle of vodka? Look, you were on the Aryan side. Did anyone help you? What happened to your two sisters, who looked like perfect Aryans? Wasn't it the Poles who handed them to the Germans? The Poles are happy about what's happening to us, about how we're being expelled, who knows where to..." His head dropped; he returned to his family.

We had come to a stop. On the track opposite us stood a train just like ours, its passengers crushing one another in an attempt to peer through its tiny, barbed-wire grilles. They were from Warsaw.

Our train inched forward again, now stopping at another platform. Here we noticed several railroad workers, a few SS men and another sign: Treblinka.

Again the train stopped. Now it lurched backward. The cars rocked violently. Through the grating I saw that most of the train had been left behind at the station. Only a few cars, ours included, were being pushed slowly onto a siding. The train inched into a dense forest, nearly touching the trees. Then some huts burst into view, beside the track in the forest. Immediately behind them stood a huge pile of shoes; people milled about, this way and that, in the pile and around it. Suddenly we were entering a clearing – a camp enclosed in barbed wire. The train approached a wooden structure. A narrow strip of land along the track broadened into a platform of sorts. We saw SS men walking around everywhere, armed with whips. Black-uniformed Ukrainian sentries stood beside the fence and alongside the hut, each bearing a loaded, cocked rifle. Ten meters away stood Jews, in civilian dress with blue armbands, holding brooms. The train stopped. The door opened with a clatter. Black uniforms pounced upon us and, shouting wildly in Russian and Ukrainian, ordered us out of the train.

The platform filled with a mob of human beings – families carrying all their meager possessions on their backs, mothers embracing sobbing children, crying people seeking one another out.

We were herded to an open gate in the middle of the fence, prodded with rifle butts and cries of "*Schnell! Schnell!* – Move it!". An armed

Ukrainian stood at the gate; inside stood a man with a red band about his forearm. He looked Jewish to me. He ordered the men to walk to the right, and the women to the left.

I found myself in a yard about thirty meters wide, with huts on either side. In front of the hut to the right was a well. The entire yard was enclosed by a fence of dry, brown-green bushes.

I took position within a herd of men at the edge of the hut. A group of some fifteen Jews, all with red armbands, ordered us to sit on the ground, take off our shoes and tie them together by the laces.

A young fellow in high boots, a windbreaker and a colorful neckerchief approached us with bits of thread in hand. He looked familiar. Where might we have met? I asked him, and began to list off cities where I had lived: Warsaw, Opatow, Czestochowa... At the sound of latter, he interrupted me:

"From Czestochowa? What's your name?" He looked at me with curiosity. Tension rose.

"Samek Willenberg."

"It's you, Samek? Tell them you're a 'builder'!"

He stepped away from me and continued handing out bits of thread. Looking around, I saw that all the new arrivals were taking off their shoes and tying them together with thread. I conformed. SS men then ordered us to strip: *"Alles herunter! – Everything off!"*

Across the yard were some of the women, standing in front of a wood hut which was too small to admit them all. They, too, had undressed. We observed those who were inside through a peephole in the wall of the hut. The clothing and bundles we had brought were strewn on the ground. A horrible stench filled the air.

The men began to undress, their faces reflecting a dread and terror which mounted from moment to moment. Ukrainians and SS spurred us on with shouts of *"Schnell, schnell!"*. An SS man came up to me and roared *"Wo ist der Maurer? –* Where's the builder?". I struggled to my feet, straightened to a stiff attention and unbuttoned my shirt, displaying a dirty, multicolored linen smock which had belonged to my father, a painter. I had donned this garment during the expulsion to keep myself warm. The SS man kicked me in the rear and propelled me into the hut.

My eyes adjusted slowly to the gloom inside. I looked around, and found I was alone. I peered through a peephole in effort to see what was going on in the yard. Our packages and bundles of clothes covered the ground like a technicolor carpet. The men, totally naked, were pushed brutally through an opening in the fence of bushes. The yard emptied. The women, too, were gone.

Suddenly some fifty men returned to the yard from the group which had just vanished. Under a rain of beatings, they gathered piles of rags and deposited them behind the hut. They repeated the process several times, helped by their guards on each occasion with wild bawls and cruel beatings. When the yard was totally clean, an armed Ukrainian propelled the entire group of men into my section of the hut and ordered them to sit on the floor. Their faces bore the welts of whiplashes; their eyes oozed blood, and their bodies were masses of red bruises. The Ukrainian standing beside them aimed his rifle and stared at them dispassionately. I spotted some familiar faces: Lolek Burstein, who had escaped from the Warsaw Ghetto to Opatow, and, beside him, Heniek Goldman, clutching his father. Their eyes mirrored fright, dread and despair. They did not know what awaited them. Neither, of course, did I.

A little later we heard new voices. Another train had arrived, and the howls of "Everything off!" began anew. My company of fifty naked men was taken out of the hut. Again, under the Ukrainian's supervision, they began to gather the rags newly strewn across the yard. As I watched through the knothole, the whole drama was reenacted. The naked men vanished at the edge of the hut, and the women were pushed in. Now and then someone shouted a phrase which I did not yet understand: "*Grosse Packe!* – a big package!"

The rag contingent returned to the hut, again under the Ukrainian's supervision. This time the men were more severely beaten. Noses dripped blood; bodies were one great bruise. "Samek", Lolek yelled, his face a mask of blood, "they're murdering us!" Hopelessly he asked me: "What will become of us?" No one had an answer. There I stood, the only one in clothes, the only man not to have been beaten. I had left only my shoes in the yard. Now an SS man threw the door open and approached the party of tortured, bleeding men. For the third time he ordered them to gather and deposit rags. Out they went again, shoved by the Ukrainians and the SS. This time, however, they did not return. They were taken away, as the men of previous transports had been, finally vanishing through the gate in the fence. Deathly silence reigned in the empty, clean yard.

A few minutes later my childhood friend Alfred Boehm entered the hut. Alfred, German-born, had moved to our town of Czestochowa as a child in the 1930s with his Polish-born parents and little sister, when Hitler was expelling all Jews of Polish extraction who had settled in Germany. One could identify them by their perceptible German accent, which they could not shake off even after several years in Poland.

Alfred and I had became friends after Polish thugs had attacked us on my street (his rudimentary Polish and foreign accent grated on their ears). I was several years older than him, and was known as someone who knew how to hit back. After a few rounds with the local thugs in his defense, they stopped assailing him. How well I remember his family – his mother, his short, fat father, and his little sister, whom he protected from the young hooligans.

Had I arrived alone? he asked. And what of my family? I told him that my parents were on the "Aryan side" – outside the ghetto – that my sisters had been arrested in Czestochowa, and that I did not know what had become of them. Yes, I had reached Treblinka alone. It was a kind of suicide on my part; once my sisters had been arrested, I saw no further point in lying low by means of false "Aryan" documents. I had returned to the Opatow ghetto and waited for the expulsion...

"Me, too", Alfred said. "I'm the only one here now. I came here with the whole family – my mother, father, sisters. They've all been murdered."

We exchanged speechless glances of despair and anguish; we embraced and burst into tears. We recalled our lives together in Czestochowa, on Fabryczna Street, the rough cobblestone avenue, Mr. Roziewicz's yard. We recalled ice-skating in the winter, bicycle--riding in the summer. We recalled the needle factory, and how we met each morning on the way to school. He would lead his sister to kindergarten by the hand.

Here we were, in this hut in Treblinka. A different world: piles of multicolor rags on the floor; pajamas and towels strewn about; razors and mirrors, forks and spoons jammed between the boards and planks; cups of various colors and shapes resting on the boards. Signs of human habitation.

It was incomprehensible. Alfred and I were alone in the hut. Enveloped in all this color, I asked: "What's going on here? Where am I?"

"Don't you know?"

"I can guess. When I was on the Aryan side I heard rumors..."

Alfred gave me a pitying look. Spreading his arms wide as if presenting me his empire, he said: "Samek, you're in the Treblinka death camp..."

Incredibly horrible thoughts crossed my mind with lightning speed. Indeed. So everything we had heard on the Aryan side, and had not wanted to believe, was true. All the Poles who had showered us with catcalls about our being made into soap, about our being headed for extermination in gas chambers – everything we could not accept as the truth – were right. The little Polish children who had shouted "They'll make you into soap!" as our train passed knew more than we did, more than we had wanted to know. It could not be. Even today I refuse to believe it.

"Samek", said Alfred, "I didn't believe it at first either, until I realized what's happening here. This is an efficient, top-of-the-line, well-oiled death factory. All the men, after they undress, are taken to the neighboring camp, past the sand bank, on the run. That's the *Teutlager* – the 'death camp'. There they are stuffed into gas chambers. After they've been gassed, the bodies are thrown into deep pits, and when one pit is filled, they dig new ones. They're buried, town after town, together. The elderly, the sick, the children who might not be able to run to the gas chambers fast enough – these are taken aside for 'personal treatment'. They're put into a hut at the edge of our camp, where they undress without imagining what's awaiting them. At the other side of the hut they go out onto a bank of earth, and they're ordered to sit down on the edge. At the bottom of the bank they see a large pit where there's an 'eternal flame' which consumes an endless supply of corpses. Then they realize what's up. But the horror doesn't last long, because the Ukrainian who's always on duty there shoots them from behind and pushes the bodies in, right on top of the rest. Somebody's always on duty down there to receive the new material and add it to the burning heap.

"You see, Samek, you were privileged in being taken out of the transport. Everyone else marched to the gas chambers on a path the Germans call the *Himmelstrasse* – the 'Road to Heaven'. We call it Death Avenue. That's how it is, Samek. Now we've got to try to hold on." From under the blankets he pulled out a pair of large boots, which I laced over my bare feet, and we walked out.

We crossed the empty, clean yard to the platform. There we found people, standing in strange attire, lined up in ranks of five facing the kitchen. We joined them and marched to the gate from the platform to the forest, the same forest beside which I had been traveling several hours earlier.

Of the several huts in the forest area, one was a mess hall. Lunch: a thick soup, well-cooked and delicious. Astoundingly, Treblinka's food was better than that available to us in the ghetto. What I did not know at the time was that Jews from various countries had reached Treblinka with superb delicacies in their packs. After they had gone to the gas chambers, their foodstuffs remained in the transport yard; the Germans put them away for our nourishment.

I raised a spoonful of egg barley which had undoubtedly been prepared by a worried Jewish housewife, perhaps with her last few coins. Rich in oil and eggs, it had a high caloric value. Someone was supposed to have used this nourishment to hold out a little longer somewhere in the East, where it was thought he was going.

Alfred introduced me to a Jewish engineer from Lodz who was *Kapo* of a *Baukommando* – head of a builders' brigade – and the man responsible for the hut where Alfred lived. Alfred tried to have me quartered in the same hut, and I was very satisfied to see that he succeeded.

I spent half the next day at kitchen duty.

Evening roll call took place on the wide part of the platform, between the tracks and the fence with its intertwined pine branches.

Standing with our backs to the fence, we could see a hut which seemed to vanish into the forest to our right, and another hut parallel to the platform to our left. SS men stood on the platform along the tracks. After they had counted us, we were surrounded by black-uniformed Ukrainian guards, whose field caps bore an emblem of a skull. These marched us to supper. On the way, Alfred offered me his canteen and advised me to obtain as much coffee as possible. Since water was in short supply in Treblinka, it was best to drink only a little coffee during supper and take the rest with us. After dinner, the *Baumeister* – the "foreman" of our builders' brigade – whistled at us, ordering us to line up in fives beside the kitchen. The *Wachmanner* – sentries – surrounded us and, rifles aimed in our direction, marched us back. Again we set out for the platform, crossed it, moved across the transport yard and paraded into the hut where I had been before.

There I turned to the *Baumeister* and asked if he had recorded me on his list of prisoners; I had been separated from the transport as a "builder", I reminded him. He looked at me with a contemptuous smile: "'Builder?' For what? For whom? You're naive. We don't need builders here and we don't have any. Here there's nothing at all. No life, either. You're in Treblinka, the biggest shithole of a camp there is. Did you notice that they didn't shave our heads? No one gives a damn about it. This isn't a labor camp or a concentration camp; it's simply one giant extermination camp, a genocide operation. No one cares how you look, because it doesn't matter if they murder you with or without the hair on your head. Of course, you want to know how we get along here. You came here from Czestochowa as part of a transport. Just before you came, the Germans gunned down most of the prisoners who used to sort the clothing of the ones they'd murdered before in the gas chambers. They took lots of men from our transport in order to fill the depleted quota, and they organized us into something resembling a camp. But don't fool yourself: it's not a camp at all, but one big death factory. Up to now, everything was chaos, madness here: they shot people, murdered people, sent them to the gas chambers. Now the Germans have knocked a little order into things."

"Does that mean", I broke in, "that they're exterminating people more efficiently now?"

"Call it what you want. The only reason there are lots of Czestochowa people here is that they were the first transport to arrive after the massacre of prisoners like ourselves, who were held here only for a very short time. It looks like they'll keep us, too, for a very short time. Size it up for yourself: it's been two weeks, and we're the *Sonderkommando* – the 'special forces' of Treblinka."

His thorough briefing complete, he patted me on the shoulder affectionately, as if in consolation, and walked on.

In the hut, Alfred gestured at a rudimentary bed of multicolored rags and said that it was available; the prisoner who had slept there yesterday had been killed during the day. Settling down there, I suddenly noticed that the entire hut was illuminated with little flickering candles, stuck by prisoners onto wooden stools which had been hidden in the bedding during the day. Most of the people in the hut were arranging their beds. Others, myself included, took out empty metal tins of canned food. We cut three triangular openings in the top of each tin, inserted candle butts and wads of cotton into the holes, and ignited them. We set the clay pots which we had received from the veteran inmates of the hut on these "burners", and began cooking our own dinner – a mixture of egg barley, cocoa, sugar and oil, which represented our only true meal of the day.

The burning candles generated a thick layer of smoke which hid my more distant hutmates from view. Nevertheless, a familiar voice reached my ears, as if from a great distance – a voice which triggered a flood of memories, a voice I had often heard years ago and which had never left my subconscious. Why was it so familiar? "Are you Samek Willenberg of Czestochowa?" it said.

I saw a tall, bespectacled figure with greyish hair approaching me slowly, stepping around the multicolored beds and the prisoners who occupied most of them.

"Willenberg, is it you? What of your parents and all your family?"

"Who are you, sir?" I asked.

"I'm your teacher."

In the gloom I discerned the pleasant face of my history teacher, Professor Merring, who fixed his slightly walleyed gaze on me. Those eyes and that gaze had terrorized me while I was a pupil in the low elementary grades, although he was a friend of my father's and a frequent guest in our home. Here, again, was that gaze – in this multicolored hut with its twinkling candles. The two of us, prisoners in pajamas and robes, fell into each other's arms. We were as if alone, oblivious to everything around us.

Someone tugged at my leg: Alfred, trying to jerk me back to reality. Professor Merring sat down on my bed, clutched my hand and inquired about my family's fate. Father, I told him, had fled Opatow, where he had been painting the synagogue before the war broke out. Polish acquaintances had provided him with Aryan papers in the name of one Karol Baltazar Penkoslawsky, and he had fled in the direction of Warsaw.

"You speak beautiful Polish", Professor Merring remarked.

"Sir Professor", I replied, "this is how we spoke at home."

"Have you gone mad, to address me that way now? Forget all the titles."

"I shall find that a little hard, after so many years. Please forgive me if I slip."

I asked him about himself and his family. His voice quivering and his eyes filling with tears, he informed me that his wife had perished here, in Treblinka. I remembered her well, and can see this wonderful woman in my imagination to this day. Before marrying Professor Merring, she had been my Polish teacher in the lower elementary grades.

"My little daughter reached Treblinka with us, too, and they wiped her out as well. They left me quite alone. They separated me from the transport, and I've become a prisoner in this death factory. Here, Samek, you are a witness to the murder of the entire Jewish people. Let me make it clear that I, as a former teacher, am viewing this as a historian." Again looking at me with that gaze which had frightened me so when he was speaking to me from his podium, Merring clasped my hand and whispered: "Willenberg, you've got to live! You've got to break out of here."

I looked at him in disbelief. What was he talking about? What did he want from me? Escape, from here? I, who had just arrived, who had not yet sized up the terrible situation for myself?

"You look Aryan; you have a good accent. Nothing about you gives you away as a Jew. You've got to escape from here and tell the world what you've seen and what you haven't yet seen. That will be your duty."

I looked at the professor uncomprehendingly. He returned to his bed.

Another prisoner, garbed in a colorful pair of Chinese pajamas, approached me just as Merring vanished. "Don't you remember me?" he asked.

"Who are you?"

"Harry Gershonovitz's father."

"Where is Harry?"

"On the Aryan side. My wife and I were transported from Czestochowa."

He asked me about my family, and I told my story once again. Thus it happened many times, because almost everyone there was from Czestochowa.

I certainly remembered my friend Harry. He was a *sabra*, born in Palestine. His family had emigrated to Poland in the late 1920s, and we became schoolmates.

As I talked with Harry's father, I noticed some pails standing beside the door of the hut. "These are our toilets – only for urinating. Since we're not allowed out of the hut at night, we try not to stink up the place – so we use the pails only when we can't hold it in."

I looked around the hut: the bedding on the floor, the twinkling candles, the multicolored rags, the prisoners' clothing. One never had to wash his clothes in Treblinka; you just picked up some more from the limitless supply in the yard.

A partition of velvet drapes of all colors hung in a corner. Behind it were the living quarters of Galewski, the camp *Kommandant*. His privileges included a bed, a small table, and a servant – Alfred. Galewski had attained his position by sheer chance, apparently due to his mighty, impressive physique and fluent German. It was one of those unusual things, like my being separated from the transport.

The candles died out. Alfred snuffed out my last wick. Though everyone appeared to be falling asleep, I could not join them; I could not understand how sleep was possible under such conditions.

It was still utterly dark when a sharp whistle sent me flying from my pile of rags. The hut hummed with voices. Prisoners leaped from their multicolored beds, dressed and prepared to go. People gulped down the remains of last night's dinner and headed for the unlit yard. *En route* the *Wachmanner* who guarded the hut let us go to the latrine around the back. The outhouse, fenced in with barbed wire, was made of boards arranged in a ladder-like pattern atop a deep pit filled with excrement. A prisoner would sit astride the ladder as its pieces shuddered, harboring a constant fear of falling into the stinking pit. The *Wachmanner* stood guard outside.

As dawn broke, we lined up in fives in front of the hut. The engineer responsible for the block made sure no one was missing, and reported the number of men he found to an SS officer. The latter counted us again, and then repeated the word *tzetele* (Yiddish for "note") several times. Though I did not understand the term, I noticed that the *Baumeister* was handing him a note bearing the names of several prisoners. By order of the officer, we marched in fives, all 150 of us, toward the kitchen, covered from every direction by armed Ukrainians. I stood at the kitchen door, where we were given coffee and bread; there I met the inmates of other huts, including many acquaintances from Czestochowa.

2

The Sorting Yard

After a "breakfast" of watery, miserable coffee, we lined up again in fives according to block. From afar we caught the sound of Russian marching songs. The noise grew in intensity. From the forest behind the barbed-wire fence a group of some 50 Ukrainians materialized, marching in straight rows and bearing rifles. The camp and block *Kommandants* now ordered us to march to the railroad platform. There we were surrounded by Ukrainians – and by SS officers who complemented the guards' work with their whips.

Having mounted the platform, we lined up along the fence. Each block *Kommandant* announced the results of his rollcall to an SS man – the one who, the previous day, had asked me if I were a "builder". Someone had told me his name: Kiwe. This done, we marched to a large yard behind our hut, which was cluttered from one end to the other with soaring mountains of shoes, clothing, suitcases and other luggage. These rose to a multicolored height of some ten meters. Around them were thousands of open suitcases, their locks broken, and their owners' names smeared on them in oil paint.

I was taken to a *Vorarbeiter* – a prisoner selected as "foreman". This was a Czech Jew who had arrived in a transport from Theresienstadt, and his work instructions boiled down to one word: "Sort!". This involved scouring the mountain of objects for eyeglasses, spoons, shavers, watches, cigarette cases and other personal effects, and placing them in suitcases according to type. Our contingent also sorted clothing, shoes and bedding, which we laid on the ground on sheets of different colors. We were to search every object we picked up painstakingly – emptying the pockets, removing every indication of manufacturer or owner, and squeezing each bit of clothing in case diamonds, gold coins or paper money were sewn inside.

The *Vorarbeiter* continued: "No name is to leave this place. Everything must go out nameless, so that no one every discovers the origin of these shitty rags. Get it? Now, get to work fast before I whip you." On the latter point he immediately proved himself a man of his word – if only to make the correct impression.

Like peddlars in a Persian market who trumpet praise of their wares, the *Vorarbeiters* and the *Kapos* shouted "*Arbeiten, arbeiten! Schneller!* – Work, work! Faster!" Their roars reverberated across the vast yard. Like everyone else, I worked at breakneck speed. Anything I picked up had to be sorted not only by type of cloth but even by quality. Worthless rags were thrown onto special white sheets, tied into bundles and lugged to open storage areas in the middle of the yard. These white bundles stretched in piles for hundreds of meters, resulting in "streets" of a sort, eerie avenues lined with piles of coats, jackets, dresses and other garments. At a murderous pace, accompanied with the mad cries of the *Vorarbeiters*, we worked and sorted all these personal effects. Now and then we found various documents – birth certificates, passports, money, family photos, letters from relatives, diplomas, university degrees, professional certificates, doctors' licenses.

I sorted eyeglasses, knives, spoons, pots, scissors, stuffing them like everyone else into suitcases at my side. Bent double, we worked like madmen. Suddenly, as if by order, the *Vorarbeiters* began to scream "*koirem, koirem!*" – a vulgarization of a term from the Hebrew liturgy meaning "bend over" – and everyone began working even more frantically. We tossed the belongings of murdered Jews into the air, producing the impression of swift progress. We were all aware of the reason for this urgency.

Just then a tall SS officer strode from the hut into the yard, dressed with great aplomb in a uniform well-tailored to his athletic body, with gleaming high boots, and a soft cloth cap bearing a skining skull emblem set at a jaunty angle. His face was full, his lips sensuous and smirking in ridicule; his head was poised coquettishly yet imperially. With the look of Caesar he surveyed the yard and approached the prisoners. The *Kapo*, *Oberkapo* and *Vorarbeiters* raced over to him, snapped to attention and took off their caps in submission. Their faces radiated emotions of surrender – and excitement. They knew how dearly he loved this scene. The work was being expedited swiftly, they barked. The SS officer smirked at them, shifted his weight from one gleaming booted leg to the other, like a circus horse or an over-the-hill ballet dancer. While looking at the *Vorarbeiters*, he gestured with a leather-gloved hand at one of the toiling prisoners. The latter began to perform a variety of strange acrobatic motions in an effort to achieve maximum speed in sorting the jackets of the murdered and arranging them in nice, even rows. The SS man, however, was not amused by all these efforts. With a barely perceptible motion, he ordered him to approach. The bespectacled prisoner drew near, cringing – whereupon the SS officer, gathered his full, massive weight and struck him, threw him to the ground and kicked him.

Beside him stood a beautiful Saint Bernard dog. This species is the epitome of humane virtue. He is known for trudging into the snowy Alps, a bottle of rum about his neck, and rescuing people freezing to death in the snow. So I recalled from illustrations in books of children's legends. This particular animal, however, had been painstakingly trained by his master to be as wild a monster as his master was. The dog would leap upon prisoners and tear away chunks of their flesh, with a special preference for genitals. Now, too, dog and master toyed with this prisoner, who, at first, writhed in terror. As the master rained blows of fist and boot, the dog bit and gnawed at what had become a corpse. I was in fact witnessing a pair of bloodthirsty, demonic creatures. Suddenly the SS officer let up, folded his arms across his chest Napoleonically, turned his back, and mounted the pile of clothing and underwear which represented the earthly remains of the murdered Jews. Summoning his dog, he now began to indulge in a characteristic game: drawing his handgun, aiming it slowly and carefully at the men at work, and shooting. His success depended on his mood...

At times the spectacle ended in mere terror. Sometimes, however, the outcome was different: the wounded prisoner would collapse, fall on the pile of clothes and stain them with his blood. The others would continue working, maintaining silence, gagging, muscles slack with terror.

Fellow prisoners explained the background of this performance. The SS officer, known as Lalka – "doll" in Polish (his real hame was Kurt Franz) – was on the verge of promotion to the rank of captain (he was merely a lieutenant, *Oberfuhrer* in the SS, at the time). Though all the SS men were extreme sadists and difficult to rank in that regard, Lalka was definitely one of the worst.

Lalka quickly grew bored, and walked away in search of lighter entertainment. He turned toward the latrine with the prancing steps of a pimp – or an inhuman monster – and, from a certain distance, began shooting between the legs of the men seated there. After each volley, he would race toward the outhouse to check the results; then, with a courteous smile, he would order his victim to get to work. When the miserable quarry turned around to do Lalka's bidding, the officer would shoot him in the back or the head, leaving the corpse where it fell.

As the *Vorarbeiters* shrieked and barked, we heard a whistle: Kiwe had come. Then, a few minutes later, we heard another whistle – an approaching train. It was 7:00 a.m., and a new transport was arriving.

A long hut and a fence stood between ourselves and the train. As people stepped out of the freight cars, SS men in pursuit, we heard them shouting, crying, calling out to one another. Suddenly a group of naked men burst into the yard – exactly as in my transport. Their function, too, was the same: they scoured the yard for clothes and packages, as their overseers urged them on with whip lashings and cries of *"Schnell, Schnell!"*. Now they came to our yard and cleaned it. This was the procedure by which these miserable, tortured souls raced to their death. They had to erase any sign of what had happened here, lest the trap malfunction and enable the next transport to guess at its predecessor's fate. Thus, too, they kept the yard clean and tidy. A moment later, the racket of an engine reached us from afar.

"Now they poison the people with gas", I was told with terrifying simplicity. "With gas made by a diesel engine."

Clothing covered the yard, in huge piles arranged parallel to the hut. At the edge of the yard 150 meters away stood the fence with its intertwined pine branches. An opening in this fence was marked by a Red Cross flag.

The *Vorarbeiter* ordered me to collect the papers, documents and photographs which had accumulated after the clothes were sorted. Following his instructions, I wrapped the wad of papers in a sheet and strode to the hole in the brown-green fence. Passing through, I walked along a narrow trail between two high fences camouflaged with branches. Finally I reached a little room camouflaged at every angle; even some benches along the walls were covered with red velvet rugs. Elderly and crippled men sat on the benches, and a *Kapo* wearing a white apron and a Red Cross armband stood in the middle of the room. He turned to the oldsters and, with great deference, asked them to undress for a medical examination. His tone of voice kindled a spark of hope and trust in these prisoners, impressions which they shared with one another while undressing with the help of a prisoner nicknamed "the Cat." Finally they sat down, withered and shivering with cold.

Noticing that the scene was being observed, the *Kapo* ordered me to leave at once through a door to the right. As I obeyed, however, I found a wall of shrubbery in my way; to circumvent it, I turned left and climbed to the top of a raised bank of sand. Ahead of me, a bored Ukrainian sentry sat on a little chair, clutching a rifle. Before him, down below, was a deep pit. At its bottom were heaps of corpses which had not yet been consumed by a fire burning under them. I stopped in my tracks, paralyzed with terror and fright. The sizzling, half-burnt cadavers emitted grinding and crackling sounds. The flames, once having enveloped them, either dissipated into little jets of smoke or reignited into a blaze which forced firewood and corpses into a devil's embrace. Here and there I could make out the torsos of men, women, or little children. The smell of burning flesh penetrated my nose and prompted a flow of tears.

I threw my documents as far as possible and turned around to escape this hell. Just then the old men began toddling up the 3–4 meter bank in front of me. Stepping hesitantly, they suddenly caught sight of the pit and its contents. Aware that they had stepped into a trap, the miserable souls tried to escape as best as their exhausted condition permitted. As they scattered across the little platform, however, the Ukrainians pumped bullets into their heads and shoved them into the pit. Those who yet lived but were utterly spent were forced to sit at the edge of the pit, where they were shot. Their bodies, oozing blood, were then rolled down the bank into the pit, augmenting its burning load.

Stunned by what I had seen, I climbed up the sand hill and there, behind the wood fence, noticed a sign bearing the ironically innocuous message "*Lazarett*" – field hospital in German, a device meant to mislead anyone who might resist Treblinka's designs for him.

I returned to my station in the sorting yard, empty sheet in hand. The *Vorarbeiter*, sneering, asked me whether I had done a good job of burning the papers I had taken away. When he saw the shock on my face, he patted me on the shoulder as a gesture of consolation and told me not to worry: in the end, all of us would end up there.

Toward sunset that day, I was ordered to finish my workday by hauling another bundle of papers – letters, photos and documents – to the *Lazarett*. The cleanliness-loving master race required us to have the entire camp spic-and-span by 6:00, with not a trace of anything remaining. We rushed to do their bidding: "*Sauber machen!* – Clean up! Clean up!" they screamed time and again. We lay blankets over the objects we had sorted during the day, and closed the suitcases to prevent spoilage, penetration of dirt – and theft on the part of our Ukrainian watchmen.

Back at the incineration pit, I hurled this second bundle of papers into the fire. Then two prisoners came through the gate, bearing a wire--frame stretcher on which an unconscious man lay. Behind them strode an Ukrainian, his rifle trained. The prisoners lowered their burden, lay him on the ground... and watched as the Ukrainian took aim and fired. The bullet struck the victim's head; he shuddered and lay still. Now the prisoners took up the corpse by its legs and shoulders, cast it forcibly into the incineration pit, and headed back to the railroad platform.

I thought that this most recent casualty had belonged to a transport and had tried to escape, whereupon he was caught and beaten senseless. My comrades, however, explained that he was an ordinary prisoner who had fallen ill. They'd drugged him to keep him from dying in agony; he had been shot in his sleep. Thus the curtain fell on another little human drama in Treblinka.

One warm autumn day, as I stood again at the base of the mountain of clothing and sorted rags – making sure no gold had been sewn into them and removing any indication of surnames or initials – the *Vorarbeiter* howled a warning: SS approaching! On this occasion, nothing came of it. Thus I spent day after day sorting clothes, always finding new photos, new faces which were no more. I opened sewn-up folds in the clothing to remove "piggies" (gold coins bearing the likeness of Czar Nikolai), rubles, dollars, currency notes, diamonds, and keepsakes treasured by generation after generation over centuries. All of this now spilled onto a yard in Treblinka, near Warsaw.

As an unfamiliar prisoner approached me, I took note of his yellow shoulder-band: *Goldjude*, literally "gold-Jew". These prisoners collected and sorted the gold, jewelry, money and valuables which reached the transport yard. As "skilled professionals", they functioned as a gold-sorters' detail or *"Kommando"*. Several of them, like the one who approached me now, would wander about the clothing yard and collect any valuables we had found in the clothing. *Goldjuden* were considered the elite of the prisoners. Their work was relatively tranquil; they sat in a closed, warm hut under the supervision of Suchomil, a German from Sudetenland who spoke good Czech and usually assigned this work to Czech Jews sent to Treblinka from Theresienstadt. Ordinary prisoners were not admitted to the hut where the *Goldjuden* did their work. They were better dressed than the other prisoners, going about in elegant coats, colorful scarves and leather gloves. They looked more like bankers than like prisoners, especially when carrying the briefcases where they stored the valuables they had found in the clothing of people who had just then been murdered.

The daily turnover was impressive: kilograms of gold and diamonds, thousands of gold watches, and millions of coins from all over the world, including China. We also found various securities and stock certificates from everywhere on earth. All these, together with family photographs, were incinerated. Thus it went, day after day.

After a while I felt myself incapable of sorting the plundered clothes of murdered Jews any longer. I arranged a meeting with Galewski, who promised me a position as warehouseman. My new job involved receiving checked and tied bundles of coats from the sorters, which I was to arrange on the ground between the transport yard and the sand bank at the edge of the camp. The pile grew ever higher.

One of the greatest advantages of my new position was its autonomy. I had no prodding *Vorarbeiter*; I arranged those thousands of coats in total silence. True, the job afforded no opportunity to converse with anyone (though this drawback was preferable to SS beatings and bullets in the sorting yard). Furthermore, I now had no access to food, which I had previously found in abundance in the sorted bundles. Now all I had was coats.

Certain prisoners, I discovered, specialized in various fields. For example, we had a fountain-pen expert named Kudlik. He always carried a concealed fountain pen of the very finest make, and he always knew when and to whom to give it (recipients were usually SS men or *Vorarbeiters*). On quite a few occasions I saw him extract a juicy sandwich from a camp official in exchange for a gold-nib model (which, in all likelihood, was filled with diamonds).

My personal Ukrainian guard, though allowed to beat me when necessary, could not otherwise approach me nor talk to me, let alone accept anything from me. The SS people kept a very close eye on the Ukrainians. They could not remain alone in the yard, where they might take something, and were not allowed to fraternize with prisoners. This put us at a certain advantage: we processed millions of dollars worth of goods, and the Ukrainians were reduced to begging for a few tidbits. They would exchange these handouts for money, and, when off-duty, would spend it on prostitutes and booze with the peasants near the camp. The whores were brought in especially for them from Warsaw. Sometimes our neighbors, the peasants, would lend the Ukrainians their daughters for a fistful of gold; the Ukrainians would often reward them for their generosity by infecting the lovely damsels with syphilis.

The *Wachmanner* who guarded us were Ukrainians who had served in the Red Army and had surrendered to the Germans. Though they were loyal apprentices and pupils of the Soviet regime, they remained – even after twenty-odd years of indoctrination – the same maniacal

Ukrainians they had been in the Czar's time. While they disliked Poles, Belorussians, Russians and Cossacks, they reserved a sizzling, boundless hatred for the Jews. The dispassionate murder of Jews was their great joy in life. Their cheeks sprouted wispy blond hair; they had the foreheads of beasts, and their every feature burned with hate. Their faces were wholly devoid of even a glitter of sense or humanity; they awoke only to the sound of wild screeching, and our tragic situation did such wonders for their temperament that they would pound their thighs in glee.

These monsters were entrusted with the responsibility of guarding and murdering us, and they fulfilled these duties with expertise and limitless strength. Without getting excited or batting an eye, they were capable of murdering hundreds of human beings at a time in the *Lazarett*. In between transports, one of them would sit quietly on a stool and peer into the pit, rifle across his lap, as the mass of corpses – our daily harvest of blood – burned below. Beside this sentry was his commander, an SS man with the rank of *Scharführer* (somewhere between corporal and sergeant). This man had a long, dark face, large buck teeth, black hair and mustache, and a perpetual laugh on his face. His uniform hung on him like on a coat hanger; his legs bowed backward like a rainbow. We called him Frankenstein. Directly in command of the *Lazarett*, he specialized in shooting Jews in the back of the head. When he was out of eyeshot, the Ukrainian would collar prisoners *en route* to the incinerator with papers and pocket any gold or dollars in their possession, throwing some cigarettes as payment. Explaining the transaction, he would stutter in crude, faltering Polish: "Throw money and I give you to eat."

One day, as I stood and conversed with Kurland, a *Wachmann* approached us and asked what we were talking about. Lest he think we had something to hide, I told him we were discussing which prostitute infected one more easily with syphilis – a blonde or a brunette. He looked at us and, with total circumspection – as if wishing to share a secret known only to himself, and as if he were an expert in venereal diseases – informed us in a hushed, serious whisper: "Brunette". I smiled at Kurland and said: "Well, you were right." When the *Wachmann* saw us turning to the gate leading out of the *Lazarett*, he began to beg in a whisper: How many zlotys would we pay him for half a liter of vodka and some bread? Making sure the coast was clear and no SS men were around, I threw him a $100 bill which he snatched and stuffed into his pocket. He gestured at a pile of sand beside the ditch around the *Lazarett*. As the Ukrainian moved away I "accidentally" dropped the sheet I was carrying, and when I bent over to pick it up a package "stuck" to it. The dangling sheet concealed my movements until I reached the yard and my place of work, where I hid the precious contents in the rags.

It was after work; all the prisoners had fallen asleep. Alfred and I opened the package, which was wrapped in paper and tied with string. We found vodka, cold meat and bread. Satiated, we mounted our rude beds, falling asleep immediately under the influence of drink and fatigue.

The next morning, the whistle of a locomotive augured the arrival of a new transport. This one was from Warsaw, and about fifteen men on board were spared extermination so as to reinforce our dwindling ranks. The little group included a young boy who had apparently appealed to one of the "Reds", who tried to spare him from death by gassing. The Red succeeded in attaching him to the detail of older men who worked in the transport yard. Shortly thereafter the camp *Kommandant*, Engineer Galewski, led the group to the sorting yard, where the newcomers were assigned to *Vorarbeiters* for work.

The youngster, redeemed, stood next to me, ashen with fright, and began to sort the rags. He was about thirteen, a typical Warsaw Ghetto child, though fair-skinned. He had come here with his mother; his father appeared to be alive in an *Oflag* in Germany (short for *Offizierlager*, a prison camp reserved for officers, as opposed to *Stalag*, where raw recruits and enlisted men were sent). His father had been an officer in the Polish army and was captured by the Germans in 1939. His name was Yezhik, I recall, and he spoke at length about his parents. Multicolored rags piled up behind him, and suitcases filled with valuables in front. Tears which had welled up in the eyes of this prematurely grown-up boy spilled down his slender face and moistened the strewn bags and suitcases.

The Czech Jewish *Vorarbeiter* from Theresienstadt cracked his whip in the air threateningly and barked: "*Schnell, schnell arbeiten!* – Work fast!" But he checked carefully all around to see if any SS were approaching, so as to warn us of the encroaching menace. He walked up to us, gave the sobbing child a tender and sensitive look, and, with a gesture of his eye hinted to me that I should take him under my wing; perhaps my own relative youth would help. I grabbed the boy's quivering chin firmly and said: "Relax, Yezhik. No one cries in this camp; they just hate." The sad, emaciated face began to brighten as I spoke; he tried to show that he understood me, that he was already grown up and our equal.

We immediately extracted clothes of his size from the pile, adding oversized high-cut shoes and a strange hat which gave him a grotesque appearance, like ours. We slipped a pair of pajamas and a towel for his nighttime use into the backpack which he carried over his shoulder. Suddenly transformed from a little boy into a man, he, together with us, became a witness to the annihilation of the Jewish people. One morning a prisoner named Yankele, who slept beside Yezhik, took me aside and, in concern, told me that he had heard suspicious noises during the night. Yezhik was masturbating, he was sure. Would I please warn the boy that the practice was unhealthy? I told Yankele that if it gave the boy pleasure, he might as well continue – it was one of the few pleasures we had left.

3

The Todeslager

It was a sun-drenched morning. Now, as every day, the *Vorarbeiters'* shouts reverberated across the yard as they spurred the prisoners to work. The pungent, nauseating stench of decomposing corpses wafted over the camp, penetrated our nostrils, filled our lungs and mantled our lips. From the railroad platform we heard the clatter of flanged wheels inching toward the camp. The first morning transport had arrived, loaded with the condemned who as yet had no idea of what awaited them here.

We toiled at sorting their belongings, laying sheets and empty suitcases all around and arranging and wrapping various objects from the towering piles. Sheets were reserved for foodstuffs – sugar, flour, grits and egg barley. Sometimes we found bread, butter and goosefat.

A line of prisoners, in pairs, bearing stretchers made of stout, strong branches, walked downhill from the pitched sand bank which separated our camp from the *Todeslager*. They were escorted by Ukrainians, their rifles aimed and cocked. The group approached us. The faces of the stretcher-bearers were black with dirt and soot; their clothing was torn, and even from afar they reeked of corpses.

One of them shouted: "*Yidn, getz essen!* – Jews, give us food! We're starving in the camp, and all around us – nothing but corpses!"

We loaded the bloody, stinking stretchers with food, bribing the guards with a wad of paper money to allow the prisoners to stay with us a little longer.

The ragged prisoner who had spoken before now explained: "Thirteen gas chambers are at work in the *Todeslager* now. Ivan, the Ukrainian guard, takes out his horseman's sword and hacks to bits anyone who tries to resist at the entrance. He amputates hands and slices up the bodies of naked people; he tears infants out of their mothers' arms and rips them in half. Sometimes he grabs them by the legs and smashes their heads against the wall. The guards set specially-trained dogs on defenseless, naked people; they bite and tear chunks out of their flesh. This is how they pack about four hundred people into each gas chamber. A diesel motor from a Soviet tank is started up, producing burning gas which is piped into the chambers. The man in charge of the motor is Ivan, the same brute who stuffed everyone into the gas chambers in the first place.

"Forty minutes later, we open the doors at the back end of the chambers to take the corpses out. They're still warm. They're all crushed into one great mass of meat, and we've got to pull them apart. We throw them on the ground, and then it's the turn of the prisoners known as 'dentists', who pull the gold teeth out of the corpses' mouths. After the gold hunt, we load the corpses onto the stretchers which you're filling with food now. We dump them into giant pits, where they are stacked in layers – with a layer of chlorine between each layer of corpses. A little later, the ground covering the pits begins to shake from the explosions caused by the fermenting bodies. SS men amuse themselves by throwing the working prisoners into the burial pits, where they sink into the mush of the decomposing, rotting flesh.

"We work on the run and at a killing pace, whipped all the while by the Germans and Ukrainians. Our team is supposed to have 200 men, but they've got to bring in new prisoners every day to keep us at full strength, because lots of us get killed or commit suicide." As one of the guards approached, our comrades parted from us. Carrying their stretchers as before – loaded this time with food – they disappeared through the gate leading to Death Avenue at the other side of the camp.

4

Konguretzky

I was working in the yard, sorting the clothes which had been brought in several hours previously by the naked men of the first morning transport. The entire cargo – clothes, bundles and suitcases – was piled up beside the outhouse next to the hut where I lived. With the mountain of rags in the background I saw Alfred racing toward me, clutching an armful of multicolored rags of his own. "Samek!" he shouted as he ran, finally dumping the load, "put this in the hut!".

I lifted his burden and found new pajamas. As noon approached, I scanned the yard and saw none of the SS whipmen. I leaped into the outhouse and ran from there to the transport yard, which was deserted at the time and illuminated with the warm sunbeams of autumn. Beside the hut stood several "Reds". The yard, and its attendant pair of huts, looked altogether innocent just then.

I opened the door and stepped inside, bumping into an iron stretcher beside the cot of Konguretzky of Czestochowa. On it, prostrate, lay Konguretzky. The camp doctors, Dr. Riback and Dr. Reislik, were tending him; the latter clutched an empty syringe. "Leave me alone", Konguretzky whispered. "I want to live."

"What are you saying? You want to live here, in Treblinka? You were sent here to die. By chance you got a stay of execution for a few hours or days, to make it easier for them to exterminate you. Do you want to be any better off than your family, which was poisoned with gas? Think of them and you'll be alright; you won't feel the injection when I administer it. Even if I don't give it to you, Mitte will wipe you out in the *Lazarett*. So what are we arguing about?" With this, Reislik pulled a needle from a leather case, loaded it in the syringe and tried to plunge it into the sick man.

Konguretzky began to struggle with Dr. Riback, who was trying to pin him down. Just then a group of prisoners entered the hut on afternoon break; the doctors walked out, leaving the patient behind. The next day Konguretzky went out to work, but he was found dead on his cot several weeks later.

5

Katzap

Alfred brought me a cap the day I reached Treblinka. He set it on my head and said seriously: "Be aware that this is one of the most essential items in the camp. It has many purposes. Take it off in front of any passing SS man. Wear it during lineup, and take it off when the block *Kommandant* is reporting to the Germans who command the huts and count their occupants. You'll hear them shouting "*Muetzen ab!* – hats off!" – over and over during lineup. When SS men come by, stand at attention, whip off your cap and report: "*Ich melde gehorsam* – I report in submission." I noticed that no prisoner, from *Kommandant* to rank-and-file, ever parted with his cap.

These cap games were sometimes tragic and sometimes virtually grotesque. The Germans insisted that we pound our thighs with the caps, and the gesture had to emit just the right sound. If the "thwack" we produced was not perfect as the Germans defined it, we had to practice the maneuver again, for hours on end if necessary. Upon the command "*Muetzen ab!*", prisoners removed caps with their right hand, brought them down to their thigh, and "thwack".

Only the camp *Kommandant* was exempt from this ritual. He would press his cap to his left shoulder, clutching with his free hand the whip which the Germans had issued him and which, in fact, he never used. He had another distinction: a red shoulder band identifying him as *Lageraeltester* – "Camp Elder".

The cap Alfred had provided me was several sizes too big, and would often slip down over my forehead and cover my eyes. Prisoners' attire in general was very eclectic: each man picked what he needed out of the clothing he had sorted, and each was dressed differently. To fend off the cold, most wore high-cut shoes and various and sundry caps. We did not have to shave our heads, and, by evening, enjoyed the services of professional barbers who owed their lives to this skill. Even here, we wanted to look right.

It was late autumn, and the chill was already irksome. One day, as I stood at the "summit" of a 4 m.-high mountain of coats which I was to arrange, I felt the cold wind cut me to the bone. I climbed down to bring over another pile of clothing, and found a brimless fur hat beside it. All my comrades had hats of one kind or another, of one color or another, all with brims. My discovery was apparently a genuine Russian hat of *karakul* – Persian lamb's wool – which had come in some transport from the east. I wore it breadthwise, allowing its fringes to protect the sides of my face as the Cossacks did. As I climbed my mountain with the new bundle, I heard cries of "Katzap, Katzap!" – Polish slange for a Russian – from my comrades below.

At the foothills of my mountain I saw the massive body of *Kapo* Rakowsky, his fat legs spread apart and whip in hand. "Katzap, you son of a bitch!" he roared. "Arrange those things right or the whole damned pile will collapse!"

Why had he called me this? I wondered. Just then he made the matter clear: "Can't you see for yourself? You look like a Russian!"

From that day on I was no longer Samek Willenberg. Even my most intimate comrades knew me simply as Katzap.

Alfred and I kept ourselves dressed in warm, clean clothes; we were apprehensive about getting sick in a camp where even a common cold represented mortal peril. Just the same, we tried not to be flashy.

6

Grodno

One night the door was suddenly and forcefully thrown open. A beam of light from an electric lantern probed cot after cot on the floor. A voice, roared at the door for *Kommandant* Galewski. It was Kiwe of the SS. The hut burst into life. Several prisoners lit their candles. Galewski, in pajamas, came out from his sleeping place behind the partition. Alfred helped him dress and lace his high-cut shoes. Kiwe, submachine gun in hand, headed for the transport yard and ordered Galewski to follow him at a run. Why had they come for our *Kommandant* in the middle of the night? Had they decided to do away with him? Merring argued that Kiwe would not have put himself out at such an hour just to kill Galewski; he had ample time during the day.

Something had apparently happened during the night. We heard the train whistles we knew so well, followed by dull noises drifting from the platform area. After a spell of quiet, we heard familiar voices – Ukrainians and SS men barking *"Schnell! Schnell!"*. We guessed that a new transport had arrived. This nighttime action was odd; transports had put in only by day thus far.

After awhile we heard voices behind the hut. Then Kiwe came on the scene, ordering people to strip. We heard shouts in German – "Smash! Kill!" – and rejoinders in Yiddish: "Help!" There was a shot, then another, then another. The cacophony outside now included the sound of running men. A machine gun burst into action. We heard a knock at our door. Several strong men pushed on it, finally forcing it in with a clatter. Someone entered. Though I could not identify the intruder in the dark, I sensed the presence of a prostrate figure between myself and my neighbor. I asked no questions. Outside, the shooting went on: single shots, volleys, groans of the wounded, screaming prey, cries of SS and Ukrainians. Treblinka was overtaken by uproar and terror. Several *Wachmanner* burst into the hut, armed with rifles, escorted by a whip-bearing *Kapo*, a brute named Kuba. They ordered us to stand on our beds. Up we stood, in our fashion-plate pajamas, as Kuba verified that no one escaping from the transport had taken refuge among us. He whipped several prisoners as he searched.

At daybreak we learned that a transport from Grodno had arrived during the night. The Jews had climbed out of the cattle cars and discovered what awaited them here. When they were ordered to strip, they attacked the SS men with knives and bottles, sparking a cruel battle. There were 2,000 people in the transport, including many women and children. In the end, of course, they were gunned down. The corpses were stretched out in the yard; three SS casualties were taken to hospital. When we came out of the hut in the morning, we saw bodies strewn between the rags and bundles, with a thin layer of wonderful, pristine white snow covering everything.

7

The Reverend

Evening came. We blew out our candles; whispered conversation still went on here and there. "Shut up," someone shouted from a distant corner, "let us sleep." I lay beside Alfred on my cot, but could not sleep. I could not shake off the events of the day. Though I was a Treblinka veteran of several days, I could not believe what I had seen.

To my left, on the floor, lay a man in colorful pajamas. He touched me gently and whispered: "Where are you from, sir?" I told him I had wandered around Poland with Aryan papers in attempt to find a hiding place for my family.

"I felt extremely safe while on the train, wherever I went. My mother and sisters were on the Aryan side in Czestochowa. But then disaster struck: the Poles turned my sisters in and had them arrested. I returned to Opatow. Despite my Aryan documents, I saw no reason to go on living. I lay in bed and waited for them to send me from the ghetto to the death camp."

"I came here too", said my neighbor.

"I know you were brought here. All of us were brought here. No one came here on his own."

"I came here with a group of children of Jewish origin, who were in fact Protestants."

I gazed at the man uncomprehendingly.

"What are you talking about? What children, what origin? Here we're all Jews. Only Jews are sent here."

"Yes, but I am a reverend in a Jewish-Protestant sect."

I stared at him, flabbergasted. He said it again: he was an evangelical minister of Jewish lineage.

"So you were brought here too, and you're sitting here with us in this shithole, without knowing how many days we've got to live?"

"I don't believe we'll ever get out of here", the reverend answered. "I came with a group of about twenty-five children of different origins. Some were Protestant, but most were of Jewish descent. Their parents had entrusted them to me in the hope that they would be saved by virtue of being Christian. Now I see how naive we were. They brought all of us here. My wife and two daughters, too, were exterminated here."

"Where did you arrive from?"

"I was resettled from Germany to Poland – Starachowice – in 1941. There I founded orphanages for homeless Jewish orphans, and set up a small church alongside."

"But none of this helped you, sir. You were brought here anyway. What is your work here?"

"I sort things, as you do. I stand at the other side of that tremendous pile, and as I work I observe in horror the results of Satan's doings."

"What Satan are you talking about?"

"Hitler, of course."

"So why the embellishment? It's enough to say 'Hitler'. Even though everything that happens here is one great lunacy, no one anywhere is reacting. Here they're systematically and efficiently exterminating the entire Jewish people. In all this madness the fact that you are a Protestant did not help you, sir. I am a nonbelieving Jew; you are a God-fearing Protestant. But here we are, all equal, all going in the same direction: to death. This is not like the Inquisition. Then the Jews could save their lives by accepting Catholicism. Here the German brutes annihilate us efficiently. It doesn't matter where you're from – Germany, France, or anywhere else in Europe; your descent – Jewish, or Catholic of Jewish origin – doesn't help either."

"But I'm a Protestant of Jewish descent", my new comrade broke in.

"Reverend, that doesn't matter. No one can say they're killing us here because of Communism, Socialism or Zionism. They're killing us just because we're Jews. There's only one thing I don't understand,

Reverend: how is it that the world is keeping its mouth shut, enabling them to wipe out an entire people? No one's fighting it; no one is offering any help! No one is thinking of blowing this camp to bits! They certainly know exactly what's happening here."

"For my part, I pray every day."

"You 'pray'? To whom do you pray?"

"You have to understand, I'm a believing Protestant."

"That means you pray to that Jew! Why, if Jesus were alive now he'd be together with us. We'd all meet here. Not that they care, you know, but it may be that we're all suffering here because of Jesus. They cannot forgive us for having given them Jesus. I don't care if you're a Jew of Protestant origin or a Protestant of Jewish origin: let's stop this talk and go to sleep."

I turned my back on the reverend and fell asleep at once.

He approached me the next day during rollcall and fixed his blue, quiet eyes on me. They radiated such goodness of heart. Then he extended me his gentle hand, as a priest might when blessing his flock from the pulpit, and said: "I ask your forgiveness. I did not want to offend you."

"You made me angry last night, sir."

"For good reason, perhaps. But, as you know, I'm alone... I have no one."

"Everyone's alone here", I replied.

"I talk to no one here. At the end of my work, I go back to my bed, to the hut and to my gloomy thoughts. You are good to talk with, sir. I enjoy conversing with you and listening to you. I would greatly like to stay on good terms with you. And we occupy neighboring beds, after all. We can be friends during the few days we have yet to live."

He looked at me like a beaten dog – a man in his forties, a lonely man among others, thirsty for friendship. Surrounded by *Wachmanner*, we marched to the kitchen.

8

Siedlce

It was a sunny autumn morning. I clambered about on the pile, arranging bundles of coats and scouting the area cautiously for approaching SS men. It would not be wise to get caught taking a break. Sheltered from the chill by the heap of coats, I looked into the transport yard. It was absolutely empty. A mountain of shoes rose several meters in the air alongside my pile, near the fence which separated the transport yard from the sorting yard. The prisoners who worked in this yard, sorting shoes and arranging them in pairs, were known as "shoemakers". Beside them was an SS man named Zepp, who provided work incentives with a whip a meter and a half long. With veins taut and protruding from his red neck – the result of prolonged yelling – he would roar hoarsely: "*Schnell, schnell!* – Work, work fast, lazy bums!". With this added to the constant background thunder of *Vorarbeiters* and other SS men, work went on at its usual pace.

Suddenly a lengthy train whistle heralded the arrival of a new transport. SS men raced into the sorting yard and, whips cracking, herded the prisoners onto the platform. The Ukrainians followed, rifles in hand, lining up in two ranks and creating a double wall between the platform and the *Lazarett*. We reached the platform just as the railroad cars crashed threateningly to a stop at the platform. Several "Reds" joined us; they were hitched like horses to a two--wheeled wagon laden with blankets for us – one for every two prisoners. The "Blues" were there, too, as usual. The train stood.

Normally, the voices of a transport reached us from afar through
the little grated windows of the freight cars with their barbed
wire. Curious, frightened faces always looked out at us. This
time we were greeted by deathly silence. Not a voice, not a face
greeted us. Everyone fell silent, including the SS. The *Vorarbeiters*
were the first to open their mouths, ordering us to load the
bundles we had sorted previously onto the train. They, like us,
believed the train had arrived empty for the purpose of picking
up these objects. Mitte ordered us to open the cars. As the
door of the first car began to slide open, the hand of a child
fell out. Suddenly we saw that the cars were filled with corpses
– adults intermingled with children, all totally naked, one compressed
mass of dead human flesh. They had clearly been beaten and
shot to death.

The Ukrainians behind us began to pound us with whips and rifle
butts, yelling "Schnell, schnell!" Only now did I realize why we had
been provided with blankets. We were ordered to haul the corpses
from the freight cars to the *Lazarett*. We decided to separate the
tangle of naked corpses into individual bodies, which we loaded onto
the blankets and dragged toward the *Lazarett*. The Ukrainians beat
us cruelly as we went. Laden with the blankets and their cargo, we
could not protect our faces.

Reaching the *Lazarett*, we threw the corpses as far as possible and
ran back for more; again the Ukrainians pounded our unprotected
bodies and faces with rifles and whips. The SS man, Zepp, continued
to howl hoarsely, the veins of his neck taut and his face red as that
of a drunk. The whip he clutched was a custom job produced by the
Hofjuden ("court Jews", i.e. Jewish artisans who worked for the
Germans in the camp). Now, discovering that we had thrown the
corpses round the sides of the pit instead of having piled them up,
he lashed at us with force. Instead of creating one pile, we had left
half-empty areas! By order of the Ukrainians and the SS, we now
rearranged the corpses neatly and lit fires at the base of the pile. Often
we had to tread on bodies as we stepped around the fire. I lifted my
eyes to a heaven with which I had no relationship and in which I had
no faith. Overhead I saw a lovely autumn morning, illuminated by

sun – and, at my feet, a mounting heap of corpses. The reverend, Alfred and other comrades ran past bearing corpses. Some tried to pull children's bodies from the pile; these weighed less and improved one's chances of avoiding further beatings. Fate was laughing at us, I thought. Here's what we've come to: looking for children's corpses to make things easier for ourselves. Prisoners of Treblinka.

Even as we emptied twenty cattle cars, another twenty pulled up at the platform. These, too, were full of bodies. Again there were the brutal beatings of the Ukrainians and the SS men, and the hell began anew. We were bruised from head to toe. Our teeth were knocked loose from rifle blows which the *Wachmanner* aimed right at our faces. I had a salty taste in my mouth. Alfred, running beside me, shouted: "Katzap, Katzap, you're bleeding from the mouth!" Again we emptied the cars of corpses, only corpses. In several hours, we hauled 6,000-7,000 of them to the *Lazarett*.

We learned that the transport had come from Siedlce, a town about 60 kilometers from Treblinka. The Jews there had apparently known their destination and mounted a resistance. Shot and plundered by the SS, they ended up in the *Lazarett* and their clothing and personal effects were sold to peddlers for money which would go for booze. In place of the booty, old rags were loaded into two freight cars. The SS had to make sure there was no discrepancy between the original and the "new" weight. Treblinka's SS contingent fumed over having lost the booty: how could one SS man deceive another? It was highway robbery, they screamed. Who had given them permission to plunder Treblinka's corpses *en route*? Those were meant to be plundered in Treblinka, not near Siedlce!

Mitte of the SS, enraged, struck people right and left. It was not right, he told *Kommandant* Galewski; it was a dirty thing to do. They mustn't murder *en route*; they had to get the transport to Treblinka alive. Exterminating them is our job, he said. Neither could they be allowed to steal. The SS in Treblinka did not steal, he pointed out; they merely claimed the possessions permitted them by law.

Human law and justice were very strange in this world. As the fire over the *Lazarett* lit up the entire area, thousands of corpses of Siedlce's Jews burned.

9

The Arrest of My Sisters in Czestochowa

Alfred and I placed little folding wooden chairs on our bench-beds. These were brought by German Jews who believed they had been resettled in Poland so as to continue living. We lit candles and stuck them to one of the chairs which served as a table. This apparatus immediately attracted comrades lying nearby.

We ate our bread and bacon, taking care not to be seen. We shared our fare with Merring, who ate in small portions, a hand over his mouth. He did not look healthy of late; he was stooped, aged. His condition worried me. The reverend was seated to my left. Alfred and I sat on our bench-cots, which we had not yet made into beds for the night. All participants in this royal feast ate slowly, savoring the bacon and the fresh village bread. It was very cold in the hut; drops of water spattered on us from the planks which served as the hut's ceiling and roof. Snow on the roof melted drop by drop because of the heat generated by the breathing of several hundred prisoners.

Gershonowitz, seated between Professor Merring and Alfred, asked me if I had been in Czestochowa after the expulsion. I told him I had reached Czestochowa in October with my mother and sisters. My mother's friend, Elizabeth Stolz, with whom she had reached Poland before World War II, lived there. Elizabeth was a Protestant Pole who hated Russians and Germans, and called anyone she did not like "Bolsheviks". She was a towering, impressive woman, a vivacious blue-eyed brunette. Talking with her parents, I learned Elizabeth was already on her second husband ("but Jewish", her father always added with a smile). The husband I knew had been born Jewish, and belonged to a family which had once been very wealthy – and which now had only a mansion whose debts exceeded its value. Just the same, everyone in Czestochowa called it "Grossman's Palace". Grossman, truth be told, had converted to Catholicism, but he never set foot in a church – just as he had never previously set foot in a synagogue.

Because Father was very well-known in Czestochowa, he did not join us. He arranged forged documents identifying him as a Christian with the name of Karol Baltazar Penkoslawski and went to Warsaw. We reached Czestochowa in the afternoon from the Opatow ghetto, where we had lived since fleeing Warsaw after the war broke out. The Grossman family no longer lived in its mansion. Though he had converted, Grossman was Jewish in the Germans' eyes, and he took to hiding like any other Jew. Ella took up residence as a subtenant in a room on Kosciuszko Avenue, and from her we received the address of a flat where rooms could be had for one month at low rent.

To reach the flat which was in a house near the Jasna Gora Monastery, the holiest place in Poland for Catholics, one climbed a stone staircase and crossed a dark, moldy corridor that reeked of cooked cabbage. The apartment was owned by an old woman, a religious fanatic, who rented rooms to pilgrims who had come to pray to the holy Madonna. Wartime had not been kind to the pilgrim traffic. Thus, by paying one month's minimal rent in advance, we obtained a small room with three beds and a large number of holy pictures. The central room in the flat was the kitchen; three doors led from it to three rooms – two already tenanted.

After the landlady had shut the door, we sat down on the beds; only then did we realize the tension we had lived under all this time. Mother, eyes shut, did not say a word, but her face reflected our tragic situation. Overnight my grown sister, Itta, had become "Hella", as registered in her new forged birth certificate; five-year-old Tamara had likewise become Zosia, and I had turned from Samek into Ignacy.

For our forged birth certificates we were indebted to a Polish road engineer from Opatow who had also procured the papers for my father. My mother had her original Russian birth certificate from home, in her maiden name: Maniefa Popow, a Pravoslav (Russian

Orthodox). When the war broke out, my father attached it to a piece of cloth — not only to keep it intact but to conceal addresses and signatures which attested that Maniefa Popow had actually dwelled in the town of Bielsko in 1919.

My sister Itta broke the silence which had overtaken us all by beginning to arrange our meager baggage, which consisted entirely of little suitcases.

We entered the kitchen and surveyed its contents with curiosity. Just then, a door leading to the adjacent room opened, and there stood a girl in a lovely, light dress. Despite the smile on her round face, her gaze bored into us as if she wanted to examine our innards. This inspection lasted for only a split-second; then she approached my sister with light steps and said with a smile: "It'll be much nicer here now the delightful pilgrims have come, because once Mass in the Jasna Gora Convent was over I had no one to talk with except for..." And she nodded at the landlady, a woman in a filthy houserobe who was tending the large kitchen stove. She extended her hand to me, too, and, in her quiet voice, introduced herself as Irena Gourska. As I grasped her little hand, I introduced myself for the first time by my new name: Ignacy Popow.

Irena took Itta and Tamara to the public park that afternoon. While they were gone, Mother and I stayed in the room and pondered the future and how we might make a living, since our money was dwindling before our eyes. We decided that the two of us would go to Opatow, visit our flat, and remove everything of value which, when sold, might provide us with money for our most basic needs.

We set out for Opatow the next day, making the trip uneventfully and returning a day later to Czestochowa. We stopped *en route* at a grocery store, bought a little food and some chocolate for little Tamara; then, laden with packages, we headed for Jasna Gora and our new home. We entered the entrance corridor and knocked on the door impatiently. The landlady pulled the door open, blocked our access and announced that the girls were not at home. Mother asked if they had gone for a walk. The answer: they had been arrested by the police for being Jewish. The tenant in the second room had been arrested too. With this, she slammed the door in our faces.

There we stood, stunned and helpless, in the dark, putrid corridor. Suddenly it was clear that I had lost my two sisters, and Mother, her two daughters. We looked at each other in mute despair, and, at a loss where to go and to whom to turn, set out, with no fixed destination. We walked to the park between Jasna Gora and the town, where we sat down in a secluded corner. Each of us was a mass of despair and pain. I embraced Mother and felt her tears pouring onto my cheek. Thus we sat for a long time. Mother stirred first. She had to get to Ella, she said: perhaps she would help us. She had many influential acquaintances in Czestochowa; surely they would do something to free the girls.

"As for you", said Mother, "get out of here, out of this accursed city. Right now. You look like a typical Aryan. You can wander around freely everywhere in Poland, and you can certainly find somewhere to live. Just remember you've got to be very careful. I... if I can't get Itta and Tamara out of jail, I'll join them and go wherever they go."

I held her tight, dried her tears, and whispered: "Mother, Mother. You still have what to live for!" I made her swear not to carry out her vow. "Try to get the girls out, but remember you've got a son somewhere out there." A final kiss, and we parted. I strode out of the park, following side streets to the railroad station.

Once at the station, I stood beside one of the columns and watched what was happening. At the gate leading to the platform, beside the ticket-checker, stood a black-uniformed German policeman who was sizing up every passerby. I smelled the danger, walked out of the station and turned onto the boulevard. The street was lined on the right with coils of barbed wire. Along it sat some policemen; behind it was a void and a deathly silence. It was a lifeless, motionless place, something like a photograph in which everyone has "frozen". All I noticed was a thick layer of yellow-red leaves which covered the streets and sidewalks like tombstones. The Jews who had dwelled there had been packed off to Treblinka.

Approaching City Hall, I came upon a crowd. As I moved closer I was engulfed by a mass of enraged men and women, faces red with tension. A kerchiefed woman turned to me in indignation. Was it right that only the flats on the side streets were being given to people? What of those on the boulevard itself?

"You see, sir", she went on, "people with the right connections get the flats on the boulevard." Then she whispered that there was still some fine furniture inside – although the best had been sent to Germany – and that valuables of other kinds were there for the picking too. Finally, she asked: "And you, sir... what street are you from?"

"Fabryczna." I stepped away from her, and, when she was out of sight, distanced myself from the crowd.

I returned to the train station and stood in line at the ticket booth. In front of me was a man in peasant's clothing, clutching an empty basket; behind him stood a man wearing a hat and carrying a walking-stick, which he pounded impatiently on the floor. The line behind me grew longer. Beside the columns stood a group of German soldiers who, by their faces and behavior, appeared to be new recruits. The way they laughed and made passes at the girls walking by, showed they were imitating combat troops. The last traveller in the long line was a young, nice-looking girl with lovely almond-shaped eyes. Her round, fair-complexioned face was framed in black, heavy curls which brushed her delicate shoulders. The soldiers began to bait the girl. She tried to ignore them, gazing nonchalantly into the station's waiting room. The policeman at the platform gate approached the soldiers and, smiling like a big brother, joined the raucous performance at her expense. Suddenly a cynical smile flashed across his face. Quickly he stepped up to the girl and, with a gesture of the hand, demanded her papers. Her face, pallid to begin with, went totally white. She peered into her purse in search of something, finally withdrawing a document of some sort and handing it to the policeman. He turned the scrap this way and that, and suddenly grabbed her forcefully by the elbow and yanked her out of line. As he passed the soldiers, he smiled: "You want this one? Look, a Jewess." The soldiers erupted in laughter, as people in the waiting room remarked about how these Zhids still had the gall to take up space in line for train tickets. I observed the scene in dread.

With about two hours to kill, I left the station and considered how to spend the time. Across the street from the station was a cluster of cheap restaurants. It was better to wait there than at the station. As I entered one of them and found it empty, a bell attached to the upper part of the door awakened the dozing proprietor. Though I ordered only bread and cabbage, the food reached my table a few minutes later accompanied by a bottle of vodka. The proprietor picked up a glass, wiped it with the fringe of his dirty apron, and set it before me. I began eating, pondering uncertainly what to do with such a quantity of vodka. If I did not drink it, I knew, I would betray myself. No real Pole would fail to down any quantity of vodka placed before him.

I finished the meal, filled my glass with vodka, and looked at the owner. Noticing his curiosity, I raised the glass and emptied it in one gulp. The liquid burned my throat like gasoline; I could hardly get it down. The owner contemplated my amateur performance with contempt. I got up, paid and left.

I returned to the train station, wobbly this time, reeking of alcohol. I do not recall how I succeeded in opening all the doors and crossing all the passageways. But now I was no longer a suspect, for my behavior fingered me as a Pole through and through – a young drunkard who could hardly stand. I stumbled to the back of the ticket line. A women who noticed my bumbling movements offered to let me ahead of her; with everyone's consent I stepped up and bought a ticket to Opatow.

I crossed the waiting room calmly, reached the platform and handed my ticket to the inspector. Lurching about, stinking of booze, I passed the dreaded policeman as if a calling card reading "Clean" were plastered to my forehead. I boarded the train and, with no further ado, fell asleep. Thus I reached Opatow without mishap – and, from there, Treblinka. Candlelight flickered on the rickety table. The prisoners dispersed to their bunk-beds to pass another night in sleep.

A Sisters' Embrace

It rained all that night. At daybreak the wind scattered the clouds; sunbeams warmed the sorting yard and its mountains of clothes and bundles. At 6:00, after roll call, we reached the yard and contemplated the day's work ahead of us. We found shirts, underwear, vests, towels and tablecloths, all wrapped in sheets and arranged in towering multicolored pyramids, separated by aisles dozens of meters long. Everything was engulfed in blazing red fire and billowing white smoke. The sight paralyzed us. What, in fact, we were observing was vapor rising from the damp cloth, colored by the red gleam of the rising sun.

Now came the familiar sights and sounds of a Treblinka morning: the clatter of railroad cars being pushed to the platform, and, several seconds later, a procession of naked men clutching suitcases or various other possessions with trembling hands. As the guards pounded them they began to run, scattering unmatched socks, laced pairs of shoes, vests and other objects on their last journey. The Germans ordered them to throw everything into the small space between the pile of shoes, where the sorters were toiling, and the heap of multicolored clothing which had been brought in from the yard. There the naked arrivals laid the objects they had lugged from the transport yard. Kiwe (a nickname for Kurt Kuttner of the SS) called the *Vorarbeiter* and ordered him to sort the loot from the new transport at once. The garments were still warm from the bodies of the men and women who had just taken them off. The rain had made things damp, Kiwe noted, and the goods must not be allowed to spoil.

My job that day entailed collecting coats which had been sorted previously by the prisoners and rearranging them in another pile. I would run the full length of the yard, from Death Avenue to the *Lazarett*, along the hut bordering the platform. The yard was cluttered with thousands of open suitcases of various sizes and types: suitcases of dull or glossy leather, trunks with complicated locks, plastered with labels of hotels and international health resorts — evidence of the wealth of their former owners — or simple suitcases of fiber or cardboard, tattered at the corners. These bore only the owners' names, freshly painted on the lid. All the suitcases, of all sizes, had two things in common: the locks were broken, and their owners had been gassed to death. The suitcases were first strewn randomly and then arranged in the sand by size, after which they looked like stands in a small town market where itinerant peddlers offer their wares. Prisoners would take up positions amid the open suitcases beside the hut and sort their contents, day after day, arranging the last effects of perhaps a million Jews who had been transported from all over occupied Europe to this dead earth. The suitcases were filled with spoons, knives, eyeglasses, pocketknives, shaving brushes, fountain pens... all the little items packed by the people who had been brought here. Special prisoners were assigned the task of collecting the suitcases and, on the run, rearranging them in towering piles.

The yard thundered with the shouts of the *Vorarbeiters*, the veins of their necks tense from the effort: "*Arbeiten schnell*, sons of bitches!" As they howled, they brought their whips down on prisoners' heads to show the Germans that they considered the work urgent and that all the prisoners worked well under them. In fact, the *Vorarbeiters* always kept an ear cocked for the approach of SS men, making sure no prisoners were caught clutching some object too long instead of placing it in the proper suitcase. We did not work with excessive speed in any case. We had time; despite our tragic situation, we knew the Germans could not sort all these rags without us. Every day's work prolonged our lives.

I crossed this crazy piece of territory on the run hundreds of times a day. Some of the prisoners assigned to this task pushed empty baby strollers. The children who had previously ridden in them were delivered to the willing arms of their mothers, who were ordered to undress them and drop the clothing to the hut floor. After this the women, clutching their children, were ordered to run to a row of hairdressers. These, after shaving them bald, directed them to "Death Avenue" – and the gas chambers.

The newly available strollers were used for collecting bottles, thermoses, jars and aluminum containers. The prisoners who handled these items had the right to cross the transport yard to a storeroom reserved for them. It was situated behind the hut where the women undressed; there, behind the hut, bottles of odd and sundry shapes were piled. The prisoners in charge of bottles were nicknamed *Flaschensortierungkommando* – the Bottlesorting Detail.

As I passed the clothes and the bundles strewn about the yard after the morning transport, a *Vorarbeiter* named Neumark from Czestochowa called me over and told me to move a bundle of coats. The bundle was already sorted and tied with two belts. Stooping to lift it, I noticed a familiar color amid the pieces of clothing strewn on the ground. Bending again, I lifted a small brown coat which had belonged to my little sister Tamara. A skirt worn by my older sister Itta clung to it – as if in a sisters' embrace. I was holding a coat and a skirt which had belonged to my sisters. Mother had lengthened the sleeves of the coat with bits of green cloth.

Mother's efforts to free my sisters from the Czestochowa jail had been futile, I understood. I looked at the multicolored sorting yard, at the prisoners bent over at work, and at the naked men beside them who were carrying the clothing of their families who, at that very moment, were being exterminated in the gas chambers. From the platform I heard the familiar clatter once again: an approaching train, bursting with fresh victims. I was about to emit a scream, a shriek, a demand for retribution – at whom, I did not know. I raced to the mountains of clothes, towering over the transport yard, in which I was working. Stooping in the pile of coats, out of sight, I buried my face in my hands and sat motionless. When I lifted my hands, I saw they were dry. I touched my cheeks. They, too, were dry.

That evening I found a new prisoner in the hut, a man who had been taken out of the morning transport. He introduced himself as

Sodovicz, an agronomist and a lecturer at the Warsaw Agricultura Institute on Grochowska Street. Like everyone on his first day in Treblinka, he talked about himself at length. After that one day, he would shut up like everyone. We listened out of politeness only, and perhaps not even for that; since he had arranged his bedding next to ours, Alfred and I would have found it unpleasant to tell the newcomer to shut up and keep his damned stories, which concerned none of us, to himself.

So he went on: "I'm from Warsaw, but I was in Czestochowa with Aryan papers. The Polish police arrested me there with my wife and children. We sat in jail in Zawodzie, and it was from there that they took us, all the prisoners, about 200 Jews – men, women and children. All had been arrested in Czestochowa, on the Aryan side, at the train station. They put us into two freight cars and sent us to Radomsko, where they coupled the cars to a train with Jews rounded up from Radomsko. That's how we got here this morning."

I blew out the candle on the table and settled onto my bed. Alfred, next to me, whispered: "They came here today?" "Yes", I answered. Silence reigned. Suffering was more easily handled in the dark, and my mind's eye contemplated my two sisters at the health resort near Warsaw where we had lived before the war.

Loading Freight Cars

Nighttime, and the several hours of relative quiet which they allowed us for sleep, became a godsend for us. It enabled us to forget the harsh camp life, alleviated our suffering, and, at times, permitted us to venture into the world of the imagination. More often, however, we were afflicted with terrifying nightmares which were actually reenactments of things we had witnessed during the day. Our miserable physical condition, which verged on the unbearable because of constant starvation and grueling toil, produced strange and unrealistic thoughts which turned first into daydreams and then into surrealistic nightmares. The tranquility of the night would be disrupted by someone's sigh or scream of terror, the dry cough of a consumptive, or loud snoring. Any of these might waken someone who would blurt a crude epithet, rouse his neighbor with a blow of the fist, and return to slumber. All told, sleep was more a doze a few hours long than a normal night's rest. And then there were the wholly sleepless nights – nights of work, beatings and endless running. Once they roused us with shrieking whistles and murderous blows. Like madmen we raced about, as if the entire camp was ablaze, sure that our last hour had come. The brutes had something quite different in mind: twenty empty freight cars had arrived during the night, meant to accommodate all the packages we had sorted, the possessions of the murdered Jews.

The *Wachmanner* herded us, on the run, toward the giant piles of packages. Each of us had to run with a 60-kg package or suitcase and load it onto the train. Once done, we returned – at a faster clip – to do it again. SS men and Ukrainians lined up in two columns along our path, and we ran between them. As the prisoners ran, an occasional suitcase would open, its contents tumbling to the ground. As the unfortunate inmate tried to scoop everything up with a quick motion, SS men would come up and whip him as if it were his fault. The Ukrainians' commander, Sergeant Rogozin, stood in our way as we ran and, with a board he had procured from somewhere, whacked us murderously. When we balanced packages on our shoulders, we could use them for a little self-defense. If our loads consisted of two heavy suitcases, leaving our heads and chests exposed, we had no way of eluding Rogozin and his plank.

It was on such an occasion that Rogozin smashed me in the face with all his strength. I felt my teeth crack; a mass of blood welled up on my face. I spat out the blood and the teeth (six, it transpired), and continued to race toward the freight cars. When my strength failed utterly, I recalled that one of the suitcases contained thick candles. I opened it, and, amid screaming SS men and Ukrainians, handed candles to the prisoners who returned from the cars and ordered them to light the way for those who were coming. For this duty I tried to select older prisoners who had run out of steam, such as Professor Merring and Gershonowitz. They stood on wobbly legs, leaned on the bundles of clothing and clutched flaming candles. Krakowski called me over and ordered me to continue handing out the candles, thus allowing them to catch their breath. The SS men, thinking that we were organizing the work so as to bring it to a swifter end, raised no objections.

We managed to load sixty freight cars in several hours. As we toiled, I entertained the thought of hiding in one of the cars while no one was looking, burying myself in the bundles, and climbing through a window to freedom a few kilometers down the track. I began to design a maneuver by which I might lay a bundle in a car and not re-emerge. Luck, however, did not go my way. The *Wachmanner* had me well covered every time I climbed into one of the cars. Dawn finally broke. As the darkness dissipated, so did all dreams of escape.

Returning to the hut, we found that ten prisoners were missing. Our block *Kommandant*, a Jew from Lodz with the rank of *Baumeister* in the camp, noticed this immediately. During roll call, by his command, we swiftly orchestrated the countoff; the SS men did not discern anyone's absence.

The "Reds" pulled fifteen men out of the day's new transport, not only replenishing our forces but producing a surplus. Had our comrades truly succeeded in slipping away from the freight train? Had they achieved their longed-for freedom? I don't know. We in Treblinka, at any rate, had seen the last of them.

A Little Girl from Warsaw

The platform emptied – except for one little girl who stood beside the adjacent hut. Her age was hard to ascertain. The torn rags which covered her delicate, slender body had apparently been a dress at one time. On her head was a colorful kerchief; she gnawed at its fringes with her white teeth. Her large, doe-like black eyes flashed about in fright. Her skinny legs were red with frost and her feet were sheathed in gleaming shoes with very high heels, which stood in total contrast to the rest of her miserable attire. She had evidently acquired these from someone in the ghetto who had pity on her; perhaps, too, she had found them in a flat which was empty by the time she came upon it. She was clutching a partly consumed loaf of bread to her chest, as if afraid that someone might steal it from her. That chunk of bread – how had she obtained it in what we knew as the Starvation Ghetto? – was her total wealth. With her frightened eyes she gazed at the platform and the freight cars pulling away from it.

A figure appeared at the gate in the barbed-wire fence with its interwoven pine branches. It was Mitte of the SS, striding onto the scene in the high-cut shoes which shielded his crooked legs. We called him the Angel of Death. Creeping like a cat, a smile of satisfaction on his dull, fair, mustached face, he stealthily approached the new prey. Reaching her, he pushed her gently, almost imperceptibly, as if not wanting to dirty his murderer's hands. He pushed her as a child might push a large ball, prodded her with a stick so she might start rolling by herself. Thus the Angel of Death led her to the rear gate between the two huts abutting the platform. He propelled her toward the sorting yard and the innocent fence at its edge, with its pine branches. Behind it was the *Lazarett*.

The sorting yard overflowed with giant piles of multicolored clothing. As the Angel of Death nudged her along, the girl stepped into the yard with her red shoes, heels sinking into the sand. Like an apparition from another world, she approached the sorters one after another, glancing at the contents of the suitcases as if she were visiting a market or a sidewalk of street peddlers. She wandered among us, showing us a gentle smile and terrified eyes. Stopping at one of the suitcases, she withdrew kerchiefs of various colors and flung them into the air, as if dancing. Work came to a halt; everyone contemplated this strange specimen of colorful Warsaw misery. She roamed from one prisoner to the next, one bundle to the next, one suitcase to the next. In every suitcase she found something, tossed it into the air and went on. She stopped beside one suitcase and pulled out eyeglasses, part of the rich collection which had once belonged to the many who had been exterminated by gas.

Suddenly her skinny face froze with fear. Terror seized her from top to bottom, driving the madness from her. She seemed to have become a normal person. She clutched the eyeglasses of a small child, gazed at them with disgust and threw them into the sand. Her eyes radiated a terrible fright. She looked at us, at the prisoners, the whip-toting *Vorarbeiters* and the SS men strolling around the yard. She contemplated us with the fear of a person who, with the intuition of an animal, senses that her end is near.

She began to step back, to distance herself from the towering multicolored mountain. The terror in her eyes grew. Mitte of the SS approached her and pushed her toward the opening in the green fence with its flapping Red Cross flag. No one said a word. The *Vorarbeiters* stood with their heads down, their whips slack. The prisoners stopped working. Everyone watched the little girl from Warsaw as the Angel of Death, Mitte of the SS, pushed her toward the *Lazarett*. She vanished behind the fence. A few minutes later we heard a gunshot. Silence, utter silence everywhere. Then Mitte strode through the gate in the *Lazarett* fence with its green branches, slipped his pistol back into its black holster, and slapped invisible dust from his palms. At that very moment, as if by order, the *Kapos* and *Vorarbeiters* began howling, spurring the prisoners back to work. Their voices hit us from all sides — "*Arbeiten*, sons of bitches! *Schnell! Schnell!*" Whips sliced the air over our heads. The ruckus, we knew, was not meant for us. It was the only possible way to protest the spectacle we had just witnessed. Thus we paid the little girl from Warsaw our last respects.

13

Ruth Dorfmann

After a short hiatus in mid-January, new transports from the Warsaw Ghetto began reaching Treblinka every day, early in the morning. The people were unloaded and ordered to race through the wide-open gate into the transport yard. Once they had come this far, SS officers ordered the men to undress and the women to enter the hut. As this scene played itself out one day, Kiwe burst onto the sorting yard, where we were packing up the personal effects of murdered Jews, and ordered a few of us to race across the transport yard to the hut where the women were undressing.

We ran through the gate with its interwoven pine branches as far as the beginning of Death Avenue. We entered the hut and proceeded to a little room where a row of prisoners in white hairdressers' smocks stood, each beside a small stool, and attended to the new arrivals' coiffure. I donned a smock which was hanging on the wall, pulled a pair of scissors from a crack between two boards and stood, like the other "hairdressers", beside one of the available stools. Through a hole in the wall I saw the Germans order the women to undress. The women helped one another as small, skinny children clung to their legs. Despite the large number of women and children in the hut, the deathly silence was disrupted only by the Germans, who barked, "Strip faster!"

The chilly hut filled up with naked women. They stood motionless and terrified, their eyes reflecting nothing but a horrible fear. Suddenly a kind of mist began to rise from the ground; a mysterious halo began to envelop the naked women. The clothing they had just taken off, which still retained the warmth of their bodies, was emitting warm vapors.

The women moved toward us and sat on the stools. Some brought their children along. They looked at us in fright as we, the prisoners, began to cut their hair – black, light brown, or totally white. The touch of the scissors caused a glimmer of hope to flicker in their eyes. We knew they imagined that this haircut was a prelude to a disinfecting operation; if they were being disinfected they were to be left alive. They did not know that the Germans needed their hair for the manufacture of mattresses for submarine crews, since hair repels moisture. After the coiffure the SS man opened a door and ordered the women out – onto Death Avenue, the one-way promenade to the gas chambers.

Hundreds of women went through my station that day. Among them was a very lovely one about twenty years old; though our acquaintance lasted only a few short minutes, I would not forget her for many long years. Her name was Ruth Dorfmann, she said, and she had just finished matriculation. She was well aware of what awaited her, and kept it no secret from me. Her beautiful eyes displayed neither fear nor agony of any kind, only pain and boundless sadness. How long would she have to suffer? she asked. "Only a few moments", I answered. A heavy stone seemed to roll off her heart; tears welled up in our eyes. Suchomil (Franz Suchomil of the SS, the man in charge of sorting gold and dispatching transports to the gas chambers; sentenced to 6 years' imprisonment in 1965) passed by. We fell silent until he was gone; I continued cutting her long, silken hair. When I finished, Ruth stood up from the stool and gave me one long, last look, as if saying goodbye to me and to a cruel, merciless world, and set out slowly on her final walk. A few minutes later I heard the racket of the motor which produced the gas and imagined Ruth in the mass of naked bodies, her soul departed.

14

Kronenberg

The day was almost over; the prisoners, by order of the Germans, were *Sauber machen* – scouring their work area for stray bits of paper and cloth, and closing the suitcases containing the sorted objects. My job at the time brought me to the hut alongside the train platform. This hut and another across the way framed the walkway from the platform to the sorting yard. Now the day had ended; darkness took over. Mitte, crossed the platform, which was totally empty at the time, and continued to the second hut. He crept along like a cat in search of prey, as if every step were planned, as if he were about to rethink the profitability of every stride he took. He wore gleaming high-cut shoes over feet which, in length, were mismatched with his short body; he resembled a plantation owner filled with self-importance. Now he marched toward the hut known as the *Pferdestall* or "the stable". This was actually a pair of abutting huts without a dividing wall, and it served as a giant storeroom. The partitions which had once demarcated stalls still stood, as did a few of the posts to which the beasts had been tied. Now the double hut housed valuables left behind by victims of the gas chambers. All new and usable articles, together with especially valuable objects, were kept here – linen, clothing, fountain pens, watches. Here they were sorted and arranged in special suitcases. In the center of the vast hut stood a mountain of furs, all kinds of furs. Most had been brought here by Jews from Germany and Austria; some of the fur coats had been brought by Jews from farther east, from the territories conquered from the Russians in 1941. We knew the origin of the furs by their commercial labels. The Jews in Poland, by order of the Germans, had to hand over any furs in their possession while still in the ghetto; violation incurred the death penalty.

A typhus epidemic was raging in the camp at the time, and anyone who even looked sick was taken by Mitte to the *Lazarett* for instant death by gunfire – either by Mitte himself or by one of the servile Ukrainians. Three hundred prisoners were killed in this fashion. There was not a day when Mitte failed to order the "Reds" to take sick prisoners, previously anesthetized by the camp doctors, from the clinic to the *Lazarett*. He would often make the selection himself, yanking prisoners from the lineup as they tried to overcome the crisis on their feet. He would personally bring them to the *Lazarett* and shoot them.

One day *Kommandant* Galewski devised an excellent way of saving sick prisoners: as long as they were still able to stand, they would spend the day in warm places in the camp. The best place of this sort was the pile of furs. With the help of their comrades, sick prisoners were brought to the warehouse and assigned to various groups of *Vorarbeiters*. There, warm and concealed from the SS, they lay in the pile of furs and slept almost all day long. Their comrades, risking their lives, provided them with tea which they heated secretly in a corner of the hut. Some prisoners actually recovered this way. The site was more or less secure, because we knew the Germans would not go near the furs for fear of being infected with lice. The proliferation of lice in warm places was something everybody knew, and Galewski made sure to remind the Germans of it at regular intervals.

One of the prisoners who spent time in our pile of furs was Kronenberg, a journalist who had worked for *Chwila*, a Polish--language Zionist daily which was published in Lvov until the war. He was dark all over: complexion, hair, eyebrows and mustache. His face was full, his gaze wise. He floored us with his eloquence, ideas and inner calm. He was one of the first organizers of the camp underground, and Galewski trusted him completely. Some of us did not share his confidence; to let people in on the secret of the underground was to invite betrayal. Just the same, Kronenberg was told in general terms of the rebellion to come. The plans changed every day and night in accordance with the situation.

Now Mitte approached the hut with his cat steps. Kronenberg chose just that moment to climb down from the mountain of furs. Without seeing the German he took a shaky step toward the *Vorarbeiter*. The stunned *Vorarbeiter* knew it was too late to warn Kronenberg to return to his hiding place. The vast hut plunged into silence. Everyone went about their work very busily, eyes down. One of the *Vorarbeiters* raced over to Mitte, whipped off his cap, snapped to attention and informed the German that everything was just fine. Mitte shoved him aside with contempt and went up to Kronenberg. "Are you sick, by chance?" he sneered. The very sound of his own joke moved him to raucous laughter; pleased with himself, he began to propel Kronenberg in his customary way toward the exit from the hut and, from there, across the yard to the *Lazarett*. Kronenberg's face reflected terror, helplessness and deathly fear. His body seemed to have shrunk; every clod of earth had become an obstacle for him. He marched to the *Lazarett* on buckling, disease-weakened legs, his face dripping sweat. Despite his fever and exhaustion, he was fully conscious and aware of his destination.

At that moment Kommandant Galewski burst into the hut, sized up the situation, and shouted at me, "Katzap, follow him". I grabbed a sheetful of garbage, added a few bits of paper, hoisted it on my shoulders and raced toward the *Lazarett* by the "back" way, avoiding the corridor and the room to which the victims were brought. This route enabled me to reach the place by following the sand bank as far as the pyre and the heap of corpses. Approaching the heap, I threw in the paper I had brought so as to liven up the flame. Just then Mitte and Kronenberg came through the entrance to the *Lazarett*. Another prisoner, Kurland, undressed Kronenberg. Then the naked journalist was shoved to the area above the pit. A *Wachmann* emerged from the adjacent structure. There they stood: naked Kronenberg, Kurland and Mitte, with the *Wachmann* behind them. They pushed Kronenberg to the edge of the raised area. The Ukrainian loaded his rifle and took aim in the usual manner. One more victim today... Suddenly Kronenberg threw himself at Mitte's legs and began to scream in German: "I want to live! I'll help you. I'll tell you everything! There's an underground here – an underground of a hundred prisoners."

Mitte stopped. Despite his raised pistol, he did not shoot; he simply gazed at Kronenberg, who was clutching his legs with all his might. Realizing how serious the situation was, I began laughing and running about like a madman at the base of the pile of corpses. Kurland did the same, tracing a sign on Kronenberg's forehead – a clear hint that the newspaperman had gone mad and should not be taken seriously. The Ukrainian *Wachmann*, who did not understand German, shot Kronenberg in the head to free Mitte of his embrace. Kronenberg's body rolled into the pit, his blood staining the sand and human ash mixture which covered the ground, and came to a stop at the foot of the mountain of burning corpses.

A prisoner emerged from behind the fence which enclosed the *Lazarett* building. He was *Kapo* Kurland's aide. His face was unshaven, he was dirty and sooty, and he exuded the vile odor of the smoke of charred human bodies. Sliding down from the raised area, he shouted at me: "Katzap, wait". Having reached the base of the pyre, he called: "Katzap, take him by the legs."

I grasped Kronenberg's naked legs, and the other prisoner, his hands. Thus we lay his body among the others. Just then Mitte's voice, spitting out professional orders, reached us from the raised area. We were to lay the still-warm corpse atop the pyramid of human bodies. Tongues of fire immediately enveloped it and danced at its feet. I came down from the pile, stumbling to solid ground on a path of entangled, caked bodies.

As I took up the sheet in which I had brought the papers and climbed out of the *Lazarett*, a prisoner named Kott pursued me, shouting, "Katzap, wait! Step into the building". There he took out a small soot-stained pot of thick, recently-cooked soup. Might he share it with me? There was terrible famine in the camp at the time, and my guts were churning with hunger. Just the same, I could not swallow a thing. Not wishing to offend Kott, I thanked him politely and promised to take him up on his hospitality in the future.

I returned to the hut and continued sorting the clothes. A little later Kommandant Galewski appeared and gave me a sad look. Though we said nothing, I understood that Kurland had briefed him on the day's events.

15

An Attempted Breakout

In the morning, by the weak light of the candles, we began to dress. The *Wachmann* who guarded us outside the hut (one of many) opened the door, allowing the prisoners to go to the outhouse behind our hut. A few minutes later we heard shouting *Wachmanner* and the sound of gunfire. We were ordered back into the huts. Later we learned what had happened: before dawn, in total darkness, four prisoners had gone into the outhouse, knowing that the guards would not be able to see them. They cut the barbed-wire fence between the outhouse and the sorting yard, then successfully crossed the empty yard. Across the yard they cut the next fence of barbed wire. Now crossing into the free territory behind the camp, it took them only a few minutes to reach the nearby forest.

A few minutes after the rude awakening of the *Wachmanner*, Mitte of the SS opened the hut door and ordered us into the transport yard. We stood beside the hut in fives as the *Baumeister* counted us. So effective were his efforts to hide the absence of four prisoners that we noticed it only after we were ordered back into the hut. Two brothers from Czestochowa, it transpired, had not returned to their beds. They had apparently been the original architects of the breakout. Another two beds were empty; their occupants had evidently joined the brothers in their escape.

The SS immediately launched a pursuit. We were kept in formation outside the hut much longer than usual, surrounded by *Wachmanner*, their rifles trained on us. Though apprehensive over the consequences of the breakout, we bore the escapees no grudge; any of us, we knew, would have done the same if only he had a chance.

By order of the Germans, we crossed the yard and went to the mess hall for breakfast. After drinking the beverage called coffee in Treblinka, we lined up at the gate leading from the prisoners' quarters and working area to the area where the Germans had their huts which were arranged in an open rectangle. The two sections were separated by a double barbed-wire fence which was not interwoven with pine branches, as the Germans wanted to be able to observe our every motion. Mitte, carrying a light machine gun, emerged from the door of the German hut opposite the gate facing the railroad platform. He carried the weapon to the platform and returned to the hut for another, a procedure he repeated several times. The rifle-bearing Ukrainians had mounted the platform in the meantime.

I stood in the first group of five, with Dzialoszynski, Alfred, Professor Merring and the reverend. The reverend whispered: "They're preparing a bath for us". After we had waited half an hour, Mitte approached the closed gate with his cat-like steps and ordered the Ukrainians to open it. He pointed a finger at us and ordered: "Hut No. 1! Go!" We embraced one another, for we did not doubt for a moment that they would gun down the lot of us the minute we reached the yard.

We began to move. We were in the front rank, with the *Baumeister* at our head. We entered the platform area, confronting a large contingent of SS. Behind the fences, aiming their rifles at us, were the Ukrainians. A *Stabscharfuehrer* – an SS staff sergeant, a fat, stubby man with a bulldog face whom we called Fessele (Yiddish for "little barrel") – ordered us to stop. The *Baumeister* emitted his usual cry of *"Muetzen ab!"* In front of us were SS men; behind us, the railroad track. Past the track was a trench filled with cut pines, which concealed any incident which might take place at the Treblinka train station.

We stood at attention, caps in our hands. Fessele of the SS began to orate. With this, we knew we had been sentenced to life. Just as a dog which barks does not bite, an SS man who speaks does not shoot. Fessele would not have spoken to us had he intended to shoot us. Bulldog face stained with sweat, he informed us that we must not try to break out, and that violators faced very severe punishment indeed. As he shouted, I thought in envy of those who had fled. I regarded the SS men as they tried to convince us that there was no way out, that the long arms of the Germans would find the escapees wherever they might be, that many of us would be killed for each escapee. The whole effort was aimed at persuading us never to entertain a desire to resist the might of the Reich.

His oratory completed, Fessele ordered the next two huts of prisoners onto the platform; we took up our usual rollcall position alongside the hut. As always at morning lineup, the block *Kommandants* began to recite the number of prisoners under their charge to the SS. As on any other day, they handed the SS men little notes reporting the number of prisoners in each and every hut. One thing was exceedingly strange: the "Red" *Kommando* was not present. Now the gate leading from the working area to the platform burst open and the "Reds" poured through, carrying stretchers bearing twenty sick prisoners whom our doctors had drugged. They headed in the direction of the *Lazarett*. A few moments later we heard shooting from the *Lazarett* and understood that the Germans were avenging themselves on innocent sick prisoners.

After work, Alfred and I walked to supper and discussed the day's events, including the execution of the twenty sick prisoners. Aloud we pondered the function of the Jewish doctors in the camp. As we sat beside the kitchen hut, eating the thick soup the cooks had prepared for us, Alfred said:

"Look how we fell into this trap. So young, and already in the world's biggest murder site, in the death factory. And we are really here only by chance…"

"For us it may be chance", I broke in, "but the Germans know exactly what they're doing, what they're aiming at. They've set up an industry of a certain kind here, an industry which is highly profitable for them."

We stood up and headed for the metal workshop. This structure, together with two residential huts, formed an open rectangle. The Strawczyński brothers, who toiled here as metalworkers, made delicious coffee which they were always willing to share with us.

A large, old pine tree grew inside their little workshop, its crown protruding as a natural roof. The hut had been built around it.

On the way, we encountered the camp physician – a skinny brown-haired woman whose swift steps testified either to self-confidence or, perhaps, to nervousness. Her white smock marked her from afar as a doctor. Everyone in the camp tried to emphasize his role by outer appearance. Painters, for example, donned broad-rimmed hats and tied kerchiefs to their necks to be recognized for what they were. Each of us, knowing that the worst thing of all was to remain anonymous in the masses of prisoners, wanted it known from afar that he was useful.

Once the doctor had passed us by, I said to Alfred: "Look at our doctors, the sons of bitches. They are really criminals in what they do. With their poison injections they help the Germans exterminate us. Today they worked overtime: they wiped out twenty sick prisoners." The camp physician overheard my comments, looked back at me in terror and went on her way without a word of self-defense. We entered the metal workshop, greeted Zygmunt Strawczyński, and had coffee with him.

After evening rollcall and in reaction to the morning's breakout, the *Baumeister* ordered us to transfer our belongings from our hut beside the transport yard, to another hut which was already occupied by prisoners. The new quarters were equipped with two tiers of bedding. Shouldering our possessions and surrounded by a chain of armed Ukrainian guards, we made the move swiftly.

Alfred, three other comrades and I claimed places on the upper bunk, which was about eight meters long. We lay down in two parallel rows, head touching head. The men in the lower bunk organized their bedding in the same fashion.

Professor Merring had news for me: a Dr Riback from the Revierstube had been looking for me and asked me to visit him, for reasons Merring did not know. Alfred, who had already lain down in the upper bunk, tried to guess: "Katzap, it probably has something to do with what we were talking about. You raised your voice, as usual, and Riback probably overheard your accusations of the Jewish doctors."

The door to the Revierstube was across from a narrow section of our hut which was separated from the rest of the structure by two partitions. A three-tier bunk abutted the wall to the right. To the left of the entrance was a little cell; there, under a grated window, stood a table and beside it a dentist's chair apparently brought from Germany by a practitioner who had hoped to make a living somewhere in the East by virtue of his profession. His chair now stood beside a table made of boards, piled with various medicines which had also been brought here by victims from all over Europe.

This tabletop inventory offered a cure for any disease on earth, from simple headaches to rare diseases treatable only with expensive, hard-to-get medicaments. All drugs were brought to prisoner doctors for sorting. The stock included cyanide capsules. Most of the prisoners who brought them to the clinic did not know what they were handling. Alfred and I were more astute, however, and made sure to obtain some of these pills from the doctors. The knowledge that we owned the poison was a boon to our self-confidence: we could take our lives whenever we chose. The Germans would not kill us! If ever we reached the conclusion that we had no further chance of staying alive, we would commit suicide.

I entered the *Revierstube*. The clinic, of course, was empty following the execution of all the sick prisoners. Everyone knew that getting sick in the camp was something to be avoided at all costs. Each of us tried to conceal his infirmities as best he could. A prisoner too sick to go out to work could not stay in the hut; he had to check into the *Revierstube*. There the tragedy would begin. More precisely, it was a gamble. A sick prisoner might survive the day. Alternately, August Mitte of the SS (we called him the Angel of Death in Yiddish) would come in, demand the roster of the sick, and would order everyone on the list anesthetized. The doctors had no choice but to obey. Then the "Reds" would load the new victims on stretchers and haul them across the camp to the *Lazarett*, where the *Wachmanner* would shoot them.

In the otherwise empty *Revierstube* we found Drs. Riback, Reislik and Choronzitski together with the camp physician (whose name I do not recall). The latter two treated only Germans and Ukrainians.

Dr. Choronzitski, about fifty, had a very interesting face. Wise, clear blue eyes peered from under thick eyebrows. He had an athletic build and his slim legs were encased in brown boots, laced at the top and buckled at the knee.

I felt very ill at ease as the doctors regarded me with the stern glare of judges about to pass sentence. To defuse the tension, I turned to the group jokingly: "With all due respect to the esteemed company, may I perhaps know the actual reason for my invitation to this place?" I enhanced the impression by doffing my hat and bowing deeply – nearly dusting the floor. Dr. Riback stopped me short and said: "Katzap, don't be a fool. I asked you to come here after we heard you telling Alfred that we're murderers. Though I really don't think it necessary to justify my actions to anyone, I'll do it anyway. Every one of us, and you and your comrades as well, are in fact corpses whose lives have been prolonged a little. It's pure chance that we're still alive. Between ourselves and those who go to the gas there's only one difference: they'll be gassed to death and we'll be shot to death. Everyone knows it, yourself included. And now, try to understand what I'm telling you. What can we do when the Germans order us to throw all the patients into the *Lazarett*? Is it not better to drug them than to make them run hundreds of meters across the camp to the *Lazarett* in front of all the prisoners, screaming and crying? Don't you think it's much more humane to inject them with anesthetics? And believe me, it wasn't easy to arrange. We really had to fight to get Kiwe and Mitte to agree to it. We asked them if we could drug people whom they meant to wipe out in any case. It is no easy thing at all to inject our patients with a killing anesthetic. Do you think it doesn't trouble our conscience that we've become murderers instead of doctors? But given our situation, we think this is the most humane thing that we, the doctors, can still do here."

Dr. Choronzitski paused a moment and then approached me: "If you want to avoid a trip to the *Lazarett*, it's up to you. You should know that we have cyanide pills which were in the possession of self-confident, big-mouthed prisoners like you, Katzap. The fact that you can take the pill out of your pocket and use it whenever you want makes you more self-assured. It's easier to survive here when you feel you're in charge of your life. But you should know that people who had pills like these, and who intended using them at the critical moment, refused to believe what was awaiting them to the very end. As they ran stark naked down Death Avenue to the gas chambers, with SS men prodding them along, the pills stayed in their clothes in the yard. They didn't have the strength – or the courage – to use the poison."

"I, too, am unsure if we'll have the strength or the courage to use the poison at the right moment. When I think of myself, I'm afraid I'll crack and won't be able to do it. To swallow poison of your own free will takes extraordinary courage. You always hope that perhaps, everything notwithstanding, you'll survive this hell."

"Shalom, Katzap. Whenever you go past my *Revierstube* – you know, where I treat my Germans and Ukrainians – come in. I often see you on your way to the forest. You're building a new fence near us. When you come in, I'll always treat you to some good liquor. I know you like to drink."

I contemplated Dr Choronzitski's handsome face, regarding the wise blue eyes which radiated a humaneness so absent in the camp. He gazed at me, as if wishing to reach a final diagnosis in my case, as if wanting to ascertain the condition of my body and, above all, my soul.

16

Golddigging

The day after they moved us, the Germans ordered the "Reds" to dig up the ground in the hut where we had previously lived. They suspected us of having cached valuables in the earth. SS men supervised the prisoners as they worked. Indeed, gold and valuable jewelry were discovered – about 40 kilograms in all. We were terribly embarrassed.

The reaction came swiftly. During rollcall we were informed that each of us would undergo a personal body search, and that anyone who wanted to avoid trouble would immediately return all silver, gold, watches, rings and documents in his possession. Only *Vorarbeiters* and *Kapos*, for example, were allowed to possess watches. I was one of the few who had no valuables to return. As the announcement was made, Fessele of the SS stood behind us and monitored our reactions. Suddenly he spotted a few gold coins at the feet of one of the prisoners. He pounced on the offender, shoved him into the barbed wire and, his head against the wire, punched him. Then he ordered us to stand beside the hut. Now Fessele began to circulate among us, and ordered each rank of five to pass before him. Now and then he singled out specific prisoners for body search. Suddenly I recalled that I had a false "Aryan" birth certificate which I had kept in case of an escape from Treblinka. Such a document, at this time, could prove my undoing; it would be hard to rid myself of it while standing in line. So, without giving the matter great thought, I shredded it in my pocket and, carefully, stuffed it into my mouth, chewed it up with no perceptible motion, and swallowed. The reverend, standing beside me, thought I was eating. I laughed and passed him a bit of paper. He looked at me angrily, thinking I was unwilling to share my delicacies and that I was mocking him – and stopped talking with me. Only that evening could I explain what had really happened.

Though Fessele continued to search the prisoners in the meantime, he found nothing apart from some scattered coins whose owner would not confess. As we watched, Fessele grabbed the two prisoners closest to the gold coins and shot them, together with first man he had pulled out of line.

A prisoner of the "potato detail", too, was murdered that day. This group was in charge of dealing with mountains of potatoes and turnips. For having been caught cooking some potatoes, he was beaten viciously, made to stand for a whole day with his hands up, and then shot. This was not an isolated case in Treblinka; prisoners were frequently exterminated for taking potatoes while at work.

17

The Turnungskommando

Around this time *Kommandant* Galewski pulled me out of the clothes-sorting detail and reassigned me to the *Turnungskommando*, a group with the rather easy task of camouflaging the camp from the inside against outside observers. I had hungered for such an assignment and was grateful to Galewski, who had interceded with Sidow of the SS to get me the position. I was thankful because such work entailed going out into the forest. Even then, I was thinking about a breakout.

Our fifteen-man detail engaged in digging holes, slipping tree trunks into them, and stretching barbed wire between them. Once the wire was in place, we inserted pine branches which we procured in the nearby forest, tied into bundles, and lugged to the camp.

We lined up every day at 6:00 a.m. after rollcall, beside the hut, like the other work details. Sidow came up to us. Seeing me for the first time in the group, he sized me up from all angles, like a farmer with a new horse, and pronounced me fit for the job. Sidow was a squat fellow of about 1.5 m., and the high-cut boots he always wore made him look even shorter. He wore a cap with a skull emblem; his face was round, his nose red and creased, and one could immediately identify him as an alcoholic. He sported a little black Hitler moustache. His full lips were poised crookedly, and he worked very hard at looking cruel. He manipulated his whip like an orchestra conductor and pounded it against his boots. To look taller, he not only wore high heels, but also tried at all times to walk on tiptoe.

We stood beside the hut as *Vorarbeiter* Kleinbaum approached Sidow, reported the number of workers, and added a few compliments about his appearance. Sidow ached for compliments, and Kleinbaum did not spare any. Now six armed Ukrainians in black uniforms came over. They balanced on one leg, and, looking at us all the while, perched their rifle butts on their raised knees to load them bullet by bullet. Then they surrounded us and took aim. With a crack of the whip, Sidow ordered us forward. Off we went, toward the camp gate and into the forest. To the left we passed two SS huts, spanking clean and surrounded by flowerbeds. To the right was the *Revierstube*, an infirmary reserved for SS men and Ukrainians. Standing at its door was Dr. Choronzitski, who smiled at us. The SS officer on duty (his dogtag testified to his position) stopped us at the gate opening into the forest. After counting us, he ordered the Ukrainians on duty with him to open the gate, a country-style affair built by Wiernik of the *Todeslager*. Outside the entrance stood a sign in German: *"SS Sonderkommando Treblinka, District Warsaw"*.

We were outside Treblinka. The forest immediately took over, and there, with Ukrainians on all sides, we worked. Stepping away from the group was *verboten*. We worked next to one another and, by order of Sidow and the Ukrainians, sang aloud. When we had gone about a kilometer from the camp, Sidow decided he had found a good place to start chopping branches. A good place, to him, was an isolated one where the forest was not too dense, so his Ukrainians could watch over us. We climbed nearby trees, sometimes in pairs. The Ukrainians followed our every movement, rifles trained. We threw the cut branches to the ground; once enough had been accumulated, we jumped from the trees and tied the branches into bundles with some belts, the legacy of murdered Jews, which we had brought from the sorting yard for this purpose.

We tried to keep the piles as light as possible, of course; we did not have the strength for heavy hauling, and wanted another opportunity to leave the camp. Sidow examined the bundles with the opposite intention. When he felt the bundles were too light, he sometimes forced us to add to them. Only after rechecking and reweighing them did he let us sit down. From that moment we were not to stand up; we could only move about in a very small area beside the bundles, and only on our knees. This stricture applied also to our *Vorarbeiter* Kleinbaum. Then, without shame, Sidow unzipped his pants. He turned his back to us, took a few steps and, with his stumpy, taut body, strained to urinate.

The Ukrainians, rifles aimed, surrounded us throughout. Now one of them flipped us a skull-emblem cap and said in Russian, "So, comrades: give money!" Each of us gave what he had. Dollars, gold coins and gold rubles imprinted with the Czar's visage spilled out. Kleinbaum asked the *Wachmann* what kind of package we would get in return. If its contents sufficed only for an immediate lunch, Kleinbaum would pay $300-$400. Hearing the offer, the *Wachmann*, like a typical beggar, took the dollars which Kleinbaum pulled out of his cap and walked toward the railroad. The package proved to contain a 4-kg loaf of dark village bread, a liter of vodka, three kg of bacon, a few cans of sardines and some chocolate. The amount of money involved was a Rockefeller fortune in Poland at the time. We divided the victuals equally, irrespective of each prisoner's contribution, if any (not everyone had foreign currency), and downed the food on the spot. Now it was time for personal business. For $100 – or $20 in gold – the *Wachmann* provided us with parcels which we might take back to the camp. Such a package usually contained half a liter of vodka, a kilo of bacon and a loaf of bread. We concealed the treasure in the bundles of pine branches and under our shirts, where our sunken bellies left ample room. I was particularly qualified for this, because I had become so skinny that a loaf of bread hardly showed.

Just as we had hidden our booty and prepared to return to the camp, Sidow materialized with a half-liter of vodka which the *Wachmanner* had given him in one hand, and a slab of bacon in the other. He approached several prisoners and stuck the bottle under their noses. We sucked the vodka into our throats without letting our lips touch it. We sat and drank, the bottle going from hand to hand. Suddenly Sidow turned to me. "Katzap, come here. Crawl!" I obeyed. As I reached him, he sat down on my back and, like a disturbed child, brought his whip down on me and shouted "Faster, Faster!" He imagined a famous master horseman astride a wild stallion. The steed, to my distress, was me. I circled the seated group of prisoners with my rider, to the applause of the Ukrainians and the *Vorarbeiter*. Suddenly I slipped and crashed to the ground; my intrepid equestrian tumbled through the air and landed flat beside me, arms outstretched and stubby legs splayed. I burst into laughter, as did Sidow. We rested on a moist, green patch of earth with dense pines overhead. For a moment we forgot our situation. Then came a shout: "Up! Back to the camp". We gathered the bundles of branches, loaded them onto our backs and marched toward the camp, watchful Ukrainians all around. Sidow tottered drunkenly, issuing confused orders. The Ukrainians, rifles trained, were sober despite the booze they had imbibed; they led us to the camp. Their spirits were good, for they had earned great quantities of gold and dollars from our dealings. Now they could afford to cavort with whores in the neighboring villages – sluts whom the peasants had brought from Warsaw especially for them.

The Ukrainian on duty at the camp gate admitted us. As we headed toward the guardroom, we beheld Lalka of the SS standing on its porch. He hopped down the stairs and, slowly, approached Sidow. Hands on chest Napoleon-style, he looked us over smirkingly. From a distance we saw Sidow gesturing in our direction and muttering something in his alcoholic daze. Whatever it was, Lalka reacted by giving him a ringing smack in the face. Then he shouted at us: "*Raus zur Arbeit!* – Out to work!"

Buckling under the pine branches, we marched unchecked into the camp. Once we had passed through the gate, the Ukrainian *Wachmanner* returned to their huts and we went to the fence to insert the branches. Our comrades came up to us as we worked and unloaded the food we had procured. Alfred approached me with his ever-present baby stroller. Meant in fact as a tool in his position as garbage collector, it allowed him free movement throughout the camp. When he asked if I had brought anything for him and his friends, I reached into his pile of rags, as if bending to insert branches into the bottom section of the fence, and slipped in the package I had concealed under the pine branches and the bread hidden in the cavity of my stomach.

In general, we ventured outside the camp several times per month. The determining factors were the need for wood in the camp, or new fences which required camouflage. Though we always returned with food, they never searched us. Even Mitte, who substituted for Sidow during the latter's vacation in Germany, tolerated our speculation. Other prisoners, sent into the forest by chance or for a one-time job, were scrupulously searched, and anyone caught with food or vodka was hauled to the *Lazarett* for a bullet in the head. We wondered why the *Turnungskommando* merited such exceptional treatment, and concluded that it was meant to dissuade us from trying to escape. Truth to tell, we had ample opportunity to massacre our guards, because our work often required the use of axes. None of us, however, dared to take so extreme a step, and for good reason.

One day at dusk, after work, Kleinbaum joined me for a stroll along the hut betwen the barbed-wire fences. He initiated the conversation: "Katzap, don't dream about escaping into the forest. I see how you study the trees and the railroad around us, as if you want to photograph the whole area with your eye. It won't work! You'll never get out of here alone. I won't let you, because I don't want them to butcher us after you go. When one prisoner escapes, the entire group and every tenth prisoner in the whole camp is murdered."

"I wasn't thinking of doing it alone", I replied. "My plan was that all of us would jump on the SS officer and the *Wachmanner* in the forest. Then we'd be armed, and we'd escape into the forest."

Kleinbaum reminded me that everyone remaining in the camp would suffer, that every tenth prisoner would be shot. If this were not enough, he added, I should recall the fate which awaited successful escapees:

"Look at everyone who's working with you, at their Semitic faces. They all look like typical Jews. Some of them can't speak good Polish. I myself am from Gdansk; my own Polish is not good. Where can I go? Who'll take me in? Any Pole I run into on the way will see I'm Jewish. Most of the peasants will rob us first and then either murder us or turn us in to the Germans. Katzap, you are more likely than the others to get along after the breakout. What's more, you have people to turn to. You told me your parents are in Warsaw, hiding there with Aryan documents. But you've got to understand that you won't succeed in getting out, because I'm watching you more carefully than Sidow and the Ukrainians."

A few days later we were taken to the forest again. As we marched along the railroad a passenger train passed, a crowd of faces in its windows. They observed us with curiosity, looked at the forest and at the pillar of smoke rising from the burning corpses, and pointed at us as they gestured to one another. Some of the faces looked fearful, others pitying. A few smiled with satisfaction.

The sight of the languid, smiling Poles aboard that train reminded us that we could not hope for much help from the outside. The awareness of what awaited us on the Aryan side depressed us and drained our will to live.

We marched along the track with *Wachmanner* on every side. Sidow of the SS cracked his whip in the air, as usual. *Vorarbeiter* Kleinbaum came up to me, as if straightening our ranks, and said: "Nu, Katzap, see? Whom do you want to escape to? Who'll help you as you go? Did you see the looks and those faces satisfied at the fact that the Germans are wiping us out?"

Back in the hut, Galewski pulled me to his corner behind the partition: "Have you gone crazy?" he whispered in reproach. "Whom are you confessing to? Whom are you talking to? Why do you tell him what you're planning? There's something else you ought to know. You won't get out of here alone, you son of a bitch, because you'll be sentencing everyone else here to death. Ask Alfred."

Alfred explained to me in a whisper that no one must try to break out alone. "We'll burn this death factory down, and if there's no choice, along with ourselves. It doesn't matter whether we live or not. Just let's wait for the right moment."

"Underground" was an unfamiliar word in the camp, for each and every prisoner was a great underground unto himself. An asset such as a slice of bologna was "underground" property in a way, for its discovery spelled an SS bullet in the head. The hunger which had dominated the camp for the past half-year, and the awareness that one would not survive the next day in any event, caused prisoners to live for the moment alone, without thinking of the morrow. Risking our lives, we would slip out at night and buy packages of food from the

Wachmanner, paying for them in dollars and gold. All this commerce went on through two open windows in the outhouse between the two halls of the first hut. The idea was that if by chance the Germans discovered the dealing, they would not punish the prisoners in the halls and would not suspect that the traders were the prisoners who slept on either side of the window. In order to buy a package, the prisoner would stick his hand through the outhouse window and pass his money to the *Wachmann* standing outside.

The SS men tried to discover the nocturnal smuggling. They stood outside the window and murmured, imitating the Ukrainians, *pachka* – Polish for "package". When a hand clutching the money appeared through the window, the SS man would slice it with a knife. At morning roll call they would inspect us for casualties and thus identify the delinquent, who would meet his end in the *Lazarett*.

The paradox of all this was that the Ukrainians who guarded us were not allowed to shoot or beat us without an order from the Germans (unless someone tried to approach the fence), lest they try to extort money from prisoners by beating them. The Germans knew we found money and valuables while sorting the clothing of dead Jews, and did not want the Ukrainians to lay hands on the treasure – because the destination of all of it was Germany. The Ukrainian who guarded us knew that as long as we lived he had someone from whom to extort money for his carousing and boozing in the neighboring villages. Though the Ukrainians who were caught at this commerce did not face death by shooting as we did, they, too, were punished severely for their offense. They did not hesitate to run the risk anyway, because they received tremendous sums of money in return for a few parcels of food. Supplies of this kind therefore reached the camp each night. During the typhus epidemic, we even "ordered" oranges and lemons for our patients. Enough money could procure anything. Thus, though it claimed many victims, trade with the *Wachmanner* persisted.

18

Typhus Strikes

One evening, as we sat on our beds with candlelight all about, Alfred told us that several prisoners had come down with a high fever. A dreadful thought crossed my mind that these might be symptoms of typhus, but I did not want to believe it and, of course, was apprehensive about sharing my fears with my comrades. The thought that we would have to face this, on top of everything else, was unbearable. The next day left no doubt: several cases of typhus had indeed surfaced in the camp. Talking with Dr Resnik, I learned that our physicians had known about the epidemic for more than a week, but tried to keep the SS in the dark about it. They knew how the Germans controlled disease: by gunning down the patients.

The reason for this was not only the Germans' desire to wipe out the victims, but also their own fear of contracting this terrible disease. The epidemic broke out because we did not have even the most elementary means of hygiene, such as water and soap. Because the transports had come to a temporary halt at the time, our inventory of sanitary supplies and clothing was running out. With no fresh clothes or laundry soap, we began to find lice in the clothes, and the lice were carriers of typhus. We tried to fight the plague of lice by holding the seams, where the lice bred, over burning candles. This primitive extermination technique, as one might expect, was futile.

The prisoner population stood at about 1,000 at the time, and many had already fallen ill. The high fever defeated even those in relatively good health. We tried as best we could to drag the sick to the roll call yard, so they would be considered workers. To leave them in the hut, we knew, would mean their death. We tried to hold them up in our rows by main force. In the fives in which we stood at roll call, we would prop up the patient as the fourth man, concealed by the three prisoners in front of him and supported by the fifth man behind. The last man would stand beside the barbed-wire fence, so that the Germans would not see the sufferers even when giving the order "*Muetzen ab!* – Caps off!". The fifth prisoner in the row would whip both caps off in a flash. Thus we might get the victims through roll call, since their sickly appearance did not attract the Germans' attention. Once we were at work, we concealed the sufferers in the piles of clothing we were sorting. Though the Germans often paid us surprise visits, they never suspected the presence of sick prisoners in the heaps of clothing and rags. We repeated the whole performance during evening roll call.

Thus some of the prisoners passed the crisis and managed to overcome the disease. Others, despite their strong bodies and good health, gave up and keeled over unconscious. These could not be saved. Thus, every day, the "Reds" would carry dozens of anesthetized victims on stretchers from the huts and the *Revierstube*.

As we sorted the clothes, we observed the convoys of drugged prisoners on the stretchers being carried by the "Reds" to the *Lazarett*. They did not enter the *Lazarett* by the main door, where a Red Cross flag fluttered against a white background. That entrance was usually reserved for sick, elderly and exhausted Jews who had arrived in transports. The drugged prisoners were brought straight to the pit at the foot of the pile of burning corpses. As they went down by the sand bank, the *Wachmann*, seated in a chair on the raised area over the pile of burning bodies, got up lazily, shuffled down the hill, loaded his rifle placidly, warmed his hands over the corpses and ordered the prisoner to be laid on the ground. Gently he raised the rifle and aimed it at the victim's head, at a distance of several centimeters. As the shot echoed, the anesthetized body often failed to issue even the slightest tremor. Without delay, the "Reds" would take up the empty stretcher and the sheet in which the patient had been wrapped, and would climb back to the transport yard. Kott, Kapo Kurland's aide, would approach the naked corpse (it had been stripped before leaving the hut) and dragged it to the pyre. Sometimes he would stand the body up and push it against the pile vertically. As he added sulphur to the mass, the fire would burst out anew, licking at the murdered bodies and sending smoke sky high. All the victims were nude because clothing could not be burned. The clothing of the murdered Jews was the cheapest raw material available for the German war machine. Thus, day after day, they dealt with Jews who had contracted typhus.

One evening Alfred raised his head, fixed wondering eyes on me and said, "Katzap, I think I've got a high fever."

Horrified, I lay Alfred on his bedding, covered him with a blanket and gave him two aspirin tablets from the private medicine inventory we had collected in the sorting yard.

He slept well that night. At daybreak, I dragged him out of bed by force and, struggling, dressed him and laced his boots. Hesitantly, supported by me, he made it to the roll call yard. I stood behind him, as the fifth man in the row, supporting him from time to time and holding his body erect. After roll call, instead of heading out to work in the sorting yard, I took Alfred back to the hut and placed him under a bed which had already been made. No one could see that a man was concealed there. I covered him carefully with blankets and left only a very small hole to admit some air. I gathered a few folding chairs and arranged them in a straight row on the blankets. The bed looked tidy; no one would sense the presence of a man under the covers. Alfred lay there until work was over. Then, for evening roll call, I rushed back to the hut, dragged him out and – with the help of our friend the reverend – brought him to the roll call yard as his legs buckled. As Mitte of the SS strode into the roll call yard, we feared he might notice Alfred's deathly appearance. The reverend and I immediately staged a fight. I grabbed Alfred's head, as if beating him, and supported him with my shoulder. The reverend held Alfred from the back and struck him in the posterior. As this went on, we laughed loudly. Smirking in satisfaction, Mitte added a crack of his whip – a joking, lighthearted one – and walked away. We sighed with relief, kept Alfred erect again and lined up for evening roll call.

We kept this up for five days, always deeply concerned for Alfred. His typhus attack peaked on the fourth night. Though drenched in

sweat, Alfred trembled with cold. I wiped his perspiring face and fed
him the oranges I had bought in the forest from a *Wachmann* in
exchange for quite a few dollars. The peasants all around had long
known that a typhus epidemic was raging through the camp, and
supplied us oranges and lemons at extortionate prices. It was business
as usual with the *Wachmanner* who made a fortune from their
brokerage. I force-fed Alfred the dearly-obtained fruit in the hope of
seeing him recover. He could not swallow a thing. I requested, begged,
forced him to eat, reminding him that he was not at home but at
Treblinka, and that his good friend Katzap was at his side. But his
thoughts were at home. Over and over, half-conscious, he called for
his mother and little sister. The next morning we dragged him to the
roll call yard once again. This time, however, we were not able to
drag him to the hut after roll call. Our block kommandant, fearing
for his skin, would not allow us to repeat the operation. For lack of
choice we hid him among the rags in the sorting yard, covering him
painstakingly against onlooking Germans and positioning the reverend
beside him at work. I headed for the forest with the camouflage detail.
On two occasions our day's work brought us back to the camp through
the transport yard; as I passed the reverend each time, I understood
that everything was all right. On the fifth day, we hauled Alfred to
the roll call yard as before. It is hard to imagine how and from where
he derived the strength to hold on through these days of illness, but
slowly he began to recover. I ran to the mess hall, procured some
hot water and made tea in the hut. Then I volunteered for potato-
-peeling duty in the kitchen, accepting a slice of bread in exchange
for each pail of potatoes. I had lost contact with the outside world
at this time, because I no longer went to work in the forest. Confined
now to the camp, we depended on the scanty rations we received
there. Even as stretcherloads of drugged prisoners were taken out
day after day from the *Revierstube* to the *Lazarett* for their ultimate
cure, Alfred's recovery accelerated.

More than half the prisoners were murdered in this fashion during
the winter. When I had been taken to Treblinka, our camp population
stood at about 1,000; by the end of the summer, after the typhus
epidemic, only some 400 remained – although transports from Warsaw

and Grodno had been arriving all the time to replenish the quota. In the *Todeslager* ("Death Camp"), separated from us by a bank of sand, things were much the same.

One day naked figures began to climb over the sand bank from the *Todeslager*. They were people, marching in a row, straight down to the *Lazarett*. As the sand spilled from under their naked, faltering legs, they were led into our camp and thence straight to the *Lazarett*, where they were gunned down without anesthetic. It was strange: when prisoners in the Death Camp fell ill, they were brought to us for extermination by gunfire.

It was my job at the time to collect documents from the clothing of the people who had been gassed. As I worked, observing the group of sick prisoners, I suddenly saw a childhood friend of mind – Kubek (Jacob) Wilhelm. Groggy with typhus, he gazed ahead in confusion, seeing nothing, recognizing no one. From the pit I saw a *Wachmann* shoot one of my best friends. Atop the sand bank stood an SS man who prodded the miserable naked men, stumbling on their weakened legs, on their last walk.

Near our railroad station, was a labor camp for Poles, Treblinka 1. This facility was reserved for Poles who had committed administrative offenses – failure to meet or submit their quotas of farm produce, speculation in foodstuffs, etc. The Germans would detain these people for a few months and then release them.

The Germans would occasionally take several dozen Jewish men from the transports and send them by train, or on foot under Ukrainian guard, to Treblinka 1. There Poles and Jews were segregated and sent to work. A train would pick up the Jewish laborers at "our" Treblinka in the morning, transport them to a quarry five kilometers from our train station, and return at nightfall. The rolling-stock comprised low-riding freight cars which were crammed with workers to the last centimeter; the workers sat on the floor, and the Ukrainians sat opposite them on raised surfaces, rifles pointed. They were not fed, and were tortured by the Ukrainians as they worked. Dressed in rags, they looked like living skeletons. When their last strength was spent, the train would return them to "our" Treblinka and, by order of the SS men, disgorge them. The Ukrainians were arrayed beside the gate to the tracks as for any transport reaching the camp. SS men and Ukrainians who did not belong to our camp's staff were not allowed to enter Treblinka territory. The prisoners were lined up in fives and driven from the platform through the open gate to the transport yard, where their *Kapo* reported their number to Kiwe. Kiwe would accept the report and yell, "*Achtung! Alles runter!* – Attention! Everything off!" The prisoners undressed. When they were totally naked, they were sent running down Death Avenue. A moment later we heard the racket of the motor which produced the death gas. This was followed immediately by a whistle, whereupon the sorting detail, led by the *Vorarbeiter*, raced into the transport yard. At the command "*Sauber machen!* – Clean up!", they would instantaneously sweep the yard clean, leaving no trace of what had occurred there a minute earlier.

The Germans brought in another crane one day. The railroad car bearing this machine was pushed to the far end of the track. There an SS man unloaded the machine onto the sand bank alongside the track. To bring the crane from our camp to the *Todeslager*, the death camp of Treblinka, we assembled under heavy SS and *Wachmann* guard and cut the barbed-wire fence. After the machine had been taken through, we repaired the fence and camouflaged it with pine branches. There was a conspicuous difference between the repaired section and the rest of the fence: the new stretch had the living green color of the fresh branches we had inserted into it, in contrast to the dry branches elsewhere.

As we worked, we heard shouting from the other side of the tracks, behind the sand bank and the fence: "Jews, help! We're starving!" I raced to the sorting yard, took up some loaves of bread, and slipped gold coins into each. Returning to the platform, I made sure there were no SS men around – ignoring our *Wachmann* – and threw the loaves discus-style over the high fence. This way, we hoped, at least a few of the prisoners might hang on. Perhaps one would escape, and the gold coins and his awareness of the money in his possession would provide him with the encouragement and the help he would need to survive.

19

The Visitation

One day in March 1943, upon returning from our work for the afternoon break, the SS men locked the gate to the area in which our two huts were located. The Germans, *Kommandant* Galewski announced, had ordered the work details to stay in the huts for the time being; we were to make our beds military fashion.

It was shortly after the typhus epidemic. We were greatly surprised by the order; each of us tried to interpret it in his own way. After we put the bunks in order, we washed up, shaved, and visited the "barber". We were all spit-and-polish; even the weather, a beautiful and invigorating combination of frost and sun, was auspicious. Suddenly *Kommandant* Galewski's whistle sent us flying from our beds. We ran out of the huts into the narrow passageway between them. The *Kommandant* then ordered us into the yard beside the first hut, where we were to line up according to our rooms.

A total of three rooms in the two huts served as prisoners' quarters; a fourth room in the rear section of the second hut was reserved for women. The first hut, adjacent to the lineup yard, had two rooms with a latrine and washroom in between. Each room housed several hundred prisoners. Abutting the first hut from its outer side was a storeroom which contained each detail's work tools. Anything could be found there: scissors, wirecutters, cement, nails, barbed wire, everything we needed for our work. The mess hall was located at the front of the second hut; behind it was a food storeroom. The third room was reserved for the camp *Kommandant*, the *Kapo*, the "Reds" and the *Hofjuden*. The fourth room was a very small place equipped with a three-tiered bunk. This was the prisoners' *Revierstube* or infirmary. The *Hofjuden* – shoemakers, tailors, metalworkers and butchers – worked in three other rooms. The metalshop stood between the two huts and, together with them, formed an open rectangle. We were already into our third month of residence in these huts, having been moved here after the four prisoners had escaped from our previous accommodations alongside the transport yard. Our original quarters, though surrounded with Ukrainians, were hard to guard – especially before dawn, when the prisoners visited the latrine under cover of darkness.

Our new huts were wrapped in double barbed wire with no camouflage. Along the interior side of the fence was a narrow path, patrolled by armed Ukrainians. Prisoners were allowed to come no closer to the fence than two meters; violation was punishable by death. The lineup yard, about thirty meters wide, was located between the first hut and the fence.

By order of the Germans we sang "Mountain man, aren't you sad?" Though all of us hated this song by now, we sang with all our might. We were always ordered to sing it that way, because the Germans wanted to give people in the vicinity the idea that our establishment was an ordinary labor camp whose inmates loved their work.

A lone pine grew in our yard, a last remnant of the forest which had covered the entire area. Our group gathered regularly beside the tree. A bird often sat in the treetop and greeted us with song. I loved the bird: it symbolized freedom. Each time I approached the tree, I wondered whether its lyrical greeting would await us this time, too?

Suddenly *Kommandant* Galewski roared, "*Achtung!*" We snapped to attention. A group of SS officers emerged from behind the hut. At their lead marched Franz Paul Stangl (an SS captain appointed *Kommandant* of Treblinka 2 in August 1943; sentenced in Germany to life imprisonment in 1970, he died in prison of a heart attack in 1971); behind him were three very high-ranking SS officers whom I did not recognize. Our SS men surrounded them, though at a distance, as if wishing to do them an honor. Kiwe positioned himself in the middle of the yard, stood stiffly and barked, "*Achtung, Muetzen ab, Augen links!* – Attention, caps off, look leftwards!" He strode nimbly to one of the guests, who stood at the entrance to the hut without entering the yard. We whipped off our caps and slapped them in unison against our thighs. Kiwe stood at attention before the visitor, raised his hand, exclaimed "*Heil Hitler*" and reported that the whole camp was in the lineup yard. He culminated all this by adding "*SS Sonderkommando Treblinka*" and "*Obermajdan*". The officer who received the report, too, raised his hand and snapped "*Heil Hitler*". The dead skull emblems on the SS caps gleamed from afar.

The SS officer who received Kiwe's report took a few steps forward and began to orate. Though he faced us, we were nonexistent, transparent as far as he was concerned. We were zeroes, nonentities – perhaps corpses, if premature ones. I kicked Alfred's leg gently (it was our way of opening communication during lineup) and whispered, "Look how the sons of bitches parade us for their amusement."

The visiting SS officer, launching into his speech, said we had been very fortunate to have been selected for work, for once all the Jews were gathered into camps, they would organize a new Jewish state where we would be free. Our stay in the camps would cost us nothing, because all the valuables taken from the Jews were sent to other camps and put to exclusively Jewish purposes. Work, he urged us; if we learned to carry out our functions faithfully, we would be attached to the *Wehrmacht* as *Ordnungsdienst* – order services personnel.

The reverend, standing beside me, kicked my leg and whispered: "He's feeding us shameless lies, Katzap."

Franz Stangl, *Kommandant* of Treblinka, now stepped forward and started his own speech. A new code of regulations for the prisoners was about to go into effect, he said. Then he recited the new rules from a scrap of paper in his hand: what we could or could no longer do, what would cost us fifty lashes and what would entail only twenty-five. Possession of money, jewelry or gold? Death by gunfire. Possession of food originating outside the camp? Death by gunfire. Damaging belongings of the murdered which had been prepared for transport? Death by gunfire. Misexecution of the camp *Kommandant*'s orders? Fifty lashes. Any violation involving *Vorarbeiters*? Fifty lashes. Failure to obey block *Kommandant*'s command? Twenty-five lashes.

A list of prisoners would be drawn up, and each prisoner would have a card on which every transgression would be recorded.

These speeches were followed by an ordinary evening roll call. After having sung, the camp anthem, "Mountain Man", the SS men left us and we entered our huts. The block *Kommandants*, ordering us to sit on our bunks, approached each man and asked for his first and last name. This was for the master list of prisoners of which Stangl had spoken – the first such roster in Treblinka.

We pondered which names to report. Unencumbered with documents of any kind, we could choose freely. The question was what was best. I favored the use of real names. Even if we perished here, the list might survive us and enable posterity at least to know who we had been. I won the day; each of us reported his full name. Several days later we were given triangular bits of leather about eight centimeters across, each with a mounted piece of colored cloth bearing a number. We were divided into three groups according to huts: prisoners in the first hut got blue and green triangles, those in the second hut, red triangles. Kiwe would henceforth find it child's play to find us, record our numbers and summon us to the yard for lashings. One abrupt decision, then, turned a chaotic den of murder into an organized death camp. From that day we were official prisoners in the camp – *Obermajdan Treblinka*.

An order was given that evening to shave us bare, heads included. We were told to repeat the process every twenty days. Though the official rationale was hygiene, we didn't believe it. We suspected that this was one more method of confining us to the camp; if we ever tried to break out, we would have yet another obstacle to overcome.

Newly baldheaded, we sat on our bunks: Merring, the reverend, Alfred, Dzialoszynski and I. We examined each other's naked pates. The shave had altered our appearance radically. We tried to guess why the SS had paid us an unexpected visit and why the new instructions had been issued. Rumors circulated among the prisoners that the visitor had been Himmler. Professor Merring wondered if we were such fools as to believe such utter nonsense. No one was thinking about us at all, I said; we were only bits of matter called *Obermajdan* which took part in the great exhibition put on for them in the camp; they also wanted to step up their control of us.

Another prisoner approached us as we talked. He was a professional painter from Warsaw, a man of medium height with a hawk nose and a very black moustache on his fair-skinned face. He was wearing a wide-brimmed black hat, and a narrow black bow-tie around his neck. He and I had started up a warm friendship, because our talks took me back to my childhood. Venturing into his little booth in the *Hofjuden* section reminded me of my father; the smell of the paints kindled a fierce yearning for that early stage of my life. His distinctive figure stood out from afar, and his professional status (his skills were in great demand in the camp) was evident. He was certainly no one's nonentity. He often talked with me at length about his work: "I do color paintings, portraits, for the Germans. They bring me photos of their relatives, wives, mothers and children. Everyone wants to have pictures of their closest kin. The SS describe their families to me with emotion and love – the color of their eyes, their hair. I produce family portraits from amateurish, blurry black-and-white photos. Believe me, I would rather paint black-and-white pictures of the children in the piles of corpses in the *Lazarett* than the Germans' families. Give 'em pictures of the people they murdered; let 'em take them home and hang them on the wall, the sons of bitches."

The artist was especially distraught on this occasion. He had been ordered to paint a sign reading "To Bialystok and Wolkowysk" in black letters against a white background, with a guiding arrow. He had also been told to prepare signs three meters long and 80 centimeters high, with the message *Obermajdan*, again in black letters. Then they had him produce an array of little white signs: First Class, Second Class, Third Class, Waiting Room, Cashier. The last order: a model of a large, round wall clock. We tried to fathom the meaning of these instructions and the purpose for which the inscriptions were necessary; lengthy arguments led to no conclusions of substance. Exhausted and extremely tense after our harsh day's work, we settled into tormented sleep.

Several days later, the Germans ordered us to hang the *Obermajdan* sign over the gate to the transport yard; the *Nach Bialystok und Wolkowysk* sign on the pillar at the gate with the arrow pointing toward the entrance; and the clock on the wall of the hut alongside the platform. Now we understood: the platform was being dressed up as an ordinary train station.

Now the SS men procured a tankful of crude oil and lugged it into the *Todeslager*. A few days later we saw black smoke billowing from the area behind the towering earth bank between the sorting yard and the death camp. The smoke rose hundreds of meters into the air. Germans raced without end to the *Todeslager*, and a larger number of Ukrainians than the usual guarded us.

We had no idea what was happening behind the high earth bank, even as the black smoke relentlessly soared skyward day after day. But Galewski knew: "The Germans, the sons of bitches, are opening the graves, pouring crude oil on the corpses and burning them. That's how they want to cover up the the crimes they've committed here. But it's not working. The way the bodies were stacked up in gigantic piles in the deep pits, only the upper layers burn. They're trying anything they can think of to get rid of those thousands of corpses, but they found out right away that pouring crude oil on them isn't going to do it."

A few days later a train of open freight cars with a cargo of iron rails pulled up. Mitte, screeching, ordered all the prisoners to begin unloading. With Mitte alongside, I shouldered the end of one of the rails and set out. Suddenly I noticed that the rail was becoming heavier. I turned my head and saw that the number of prisoners carrying the rail was dwindling. Those who remained approached the death camp, legs buckling. Mitte ordered us to throw the rail to the ground beside the fence of interspersed pine branches, which separated the death camp from our complex. So it went for several hours; as they beat and shoved us, we carried dozens of iron rails – on the run – from two freight cars to the gate of the death camp.

Several days later, peering over the five-meter sand bank, we saw the tip of a crane which had previously been used to dig pits and erect the sand bank between ourselves and the death camp. Now it was digging up corpses and scattering them. As its scoop rose in the air, we saw corpses fall between its serrated edges. We did not see where they landed, because the sand bank blocked our view. Then a tongue of fire shot out, accompanied by a plume of smoke tens of meters high.

Workers in Wiernik's group, constructing a country-style wooden gate at the main entrance, informed us that the rails we had hauled were assembled into a massive grill, onto which the crane scattered the corpses it had extracted from the graves. A terrible stench of burning, disintegrating bodies spread throughout the camp as the crane worked without letup. We saw pieces of human bodies flying in the air. Little strings dangled from the teeth of the scoop; they were the human intestines. Again and again the crane's maw opened anew for fresh prey; every few minutes we saw it rise inch by inch, again filled with corpses – hands, feet, other parts of the anatomy. The crane toiled thus, dumping bodies into the blazing furnace, for days on end.

One evening after work, Merring noted that the Germans' determination to conceal their crimes in Treblinka might be a good omen for us. They were evidently taking a beating on the fronts, and had apparently stopped believing that they would vanquish and dominate all of Europe. If it were otherwise, what would it matter to them that the graves of millions of people were situated here in the wilderness, near some Polish villages? They were burning the corpses because they were losing the war. If the soldiers on the front did not know what was really going on, the SS and the Gestapo knew it only too well and were covering their tracks accordingly.

I interjected that I did not understand how the Polish villagers around the camp remained passive. They certainly smelled the rotting bodies being exhumed and incinerated; they must have seen the smoke as it spread tens of kilometers around the camp. How could the Poles, aware of what was happening here, fail to alert the entire world? Where was the Polish underground? I had always toyed with the thought that the Polish partisans would attack the camp to get a hold of the treasures which had accumulated here. Just to liberate us, I knew, no one would make an effort. If the underground would only stage an armed robbery, however, we might find it convenient or at least easier to escape. While on the Aryan side, I had seen underground newspapers which described the Germans' crimes. But none of them referred to crimes against the Jews.

When they wrote about the underground, camps, abductions and imprisonments, they wrote only about Poles; Jews did not exist for them. My friends nodded in agreement. The knowledge that the world was passive to everything happening in the camp left us hopeless and despairing.

20

A Lashing

We returned from a session of work in the forest doubled over by an especially heavy load. In groups of four we had to carry the freshly cut-down pines, each about 6 meters long. The waterlogged bark of the trees increased their weight. The point of all this was to raise the height of the fence at the southwest side of the camp. Having dug holes in the ground, we inserted the trunks against the existing fence of barbed wire and pine branches. The old branches were so closely packed that no one could look in even at very close range. We stood on ladders as we worked, and, for the first time, I saw the lifeless sandy earth outside the camp. Apart from a few lowly bushes, nothing at all grew in it. The southwest section of the camp was positioned between the railroad and the line where the forest began. The railroad led to a work camp several kilometers past Treblinka. This was the line on which the transports of people designated for extermination were brought to our camp. Whenever a transport arrived, they closed the entrance to the work camp, shifted the train onto a siding to the left, and pushed the cars to the platform of the death camp.

We now added more than three meters to the height of the fence. From this side, the Germans apparently knew, one could see the top of the pile of clothes and the crane which scattered the bodies. We were producing a barrier of such height, however, that the camouflage method used on other fences was impractical here. The Germans reached the decision that the little bush which grew nearby, a dry and therefore lightweight plant, would serve the purpose well. They ordered us to tie these shrubs to the fence with wires which were strung between the fenceposts. The porous shrubbery enabled air to pass through freely, eliminating any risk that a gust of wind might knock the fence down. Once we inserted the branches, we could no longer see anything going on in the camp. Sidow, moving the posts, moved away from us and left us guarded by the *Vorarbeiters* alone. We exploited these moments to sit down on the logs and recover from the grueling toil. Once we reentered the camp, the Ukrainians left us alone. Their job was to guard us outside the camp only; inside, we were surrounded with guard towers, with the armed Ukrainians stationed at all times along the fences.

Just then, Kiwe of the SS materialized from behind a mountain of rags. His sly, suspicious fox's face smelled an underground everywhere, and he often suspected us of trying to shirk our labors. Now he charged toward our group and, whip in hand, lashed at *Vorarbeiter* Kleinbaum. After demanding to know what we were up to, he took down our numbers.

After work we took our positions in the lineup yard. The block kommandants accounted for the prisoners: how many had been shot to death during the day, how many were sick (i.e., to be shot to death tomorrow) and how many had worked. Kiwe hardly listened; he merely muttered, "*Tzetele, Tzetele*" and waited for notes with the numbers of prisoners, duplicating the details previously reported to him aloud. The notes were presented to Kiwe. Then came the Polish folksong which the Germans loved to hear us chant: "Aren't you sad, mountain-man?" Whenever they thought we had not put feeling into the rendition, they had us repeat it several times. I have no idea why they loved this song so much as to force us to sing it day by day, sometimes several times in succession. Perhaps they wanted the villagers in the vicinity to hear the heart-gladdening little thing; perhaps, too, it was another way of camouflaging the atrocities of Treblinka.

Having finished the song in the usual manner, the Germans called the warehouseman – a prisoner from Warsaw called Malpa (Polish for "monkey") because he was so ugly, and ordered him to bring a stool from his storeroom. Then, without delay, Kiwe called the numbers of the prisoners who were to be punished that day. Mine was among them. We stood in a row beside the hut and were summoned one by one. When my number was called I approached the stool, where I was ordered to take off my pants. It was general practice to beat prisoners with their pants on, but Kiwe did not like something about the shape of the posterior of one of the cooks, who had earned 25 blows for some offense. Though the delinquent chef was already tied to the stool, Kiwe walked up to him, felt him and found a little lump in his pants. Everyone in the camp – SS, Ukrainians, even the prisoners – burst into laughter. It was the identity of the victim that made the situation so amusing; all of us had many complaints about him, some well grounded and others imaginary.

It was my turn. As Malpa tied my legs to the stool, I pressed my stomach into its concave seat and bent my head over. The warehouse-man tied my back to the stool with two belts and pulled my hands forward. As the Ukrainian lashed me with his whip, I had to count off in German; each blow turned my innards upside down. In dread and terror I anticipated each additional stroke, and after each I thought I would no longer survive. Though the Ukrainian aimed at my posterior, the lashes often landed on my back. After number twenty--five (I had been sounding off throughout) the belts were released and, half dead, I pulled my pants on. Despite terrible pain, I stood up and, as one must after being punished, said, *"Ich danke* – I thank you"*. Then I trotted back to the ranks of prisoners, for I could not show the Germans that the beating had weakened me. Any such indication led to extermination by gunfire at the *Lazarett*.

The wounds in my back were the most painful and dangerous of all, because they aggravated an old wound caused by a ricocheting tank shell during the battle for the town of Chelmno in 1939. I lay in sleepless torment that night, the pain in my back growing with each passing moment. Toward morning I found myself with a fever of 40°C (104°F). I had reached the end of the road, I told Alfred, for the pain was so fierce that I could not get out to the lineup yard. Staying in the hut, of course, meant certain death. Alfred could not let me give up. He forced me into my clothes and, supporting me, pushed me to the lineup yard. With a high fever, in terrible pain and with a swollen backside I worked several days. My friends, who saw me in agony, helped as best they could.

On the fourth day I felt the swelling along my spine increasing. Infection had set in. My swollen welts transfixed me with pain. Realizing I was in very bad shape, I recalled that the man in the next bunk had a penknife (an instrument forbidden to prisoners). I took it to the carpenters' shop, sharpened it on a rock, put it into my mouth and sucked at length. This was the only way I had of "sterilizing" the instrument. Then I lay on my stomach and asked Alfred to make a straight incision down the spine. Alfred did not have the guts to do it. "Cut or they'll shoot me!" I yelled. He knew I was right. Hand trembling, he seized the dagger and sliced deep into my flesh. An unbelievable quantity of putrid black pus burst from the bleeding incision. I asked Alfred to dress the wound; he complied obediently. Without further ado, exhausted by everything I had undergone that evening, I fell asleep. The pain abated; so, did the fever, the very next day.

The next day I dug holes for the wooden poles which we were placing in the ground. Every movement brought on terrible pain. As I moved about, the bandage worked its way into the wound and sent me into agony. Mishke of the SS, sensing that my behavior was different from the usual, stood beside me and observed my work. The next day after roll call, as the entire *Tarnungskommando* lined up at the hut, Mitte approached me. Motioning with his finger in a gesture which usually spelled a verdict of execution, the Angel of Death asked me, "Aren't you feeling well?". In reply, I stiffened, stood at attention and barked a negative. He accepted the answer without a word; to this day I do not know why. He turned around and walked away, and I rejoined the group at work. I tried to labor with redoubled vigor that day. As I toiled, I asked my friend Cohen what he thought. Had the danger passed, and would I go on living... or would the Germans exterminate me? No one could answer; no one could calm me. I continued to go out to my daily work; the fever went down and my wound healed.

The Greeks

Early in the spring of 1943 the whistle of a train heralded the arrival
of a new shipment. A slightly strange crowd spilled out – people
with dark faces, curly, raven-black hair, and a foreign tongue on
their lips. The suitcases taken out of the cars bore labels reading
"Saloniki". Word that Jews from Greece had arrived spread through
the camp like lightning. Among them was an especially large
number of rich people, intelligentsia, professors and instructors.
Though they had made their way here in freight cars, they had not
been packed together in the usual manner. Strangest of all to us was
the fact that the cars were neither closed, locked nor sealed. It was
a well dressed group of people, who had brought copious amounts
of luggage. We looked in amazement at the magnificent Oriental
carpets, wonderful rugs, and, in the main, the gargantuan quantities
of food. In addition, we noticed extensive wardrobes, various pieces
of furniture and possessions of all kinds. Every last one of them
exited the cars in a state of total calm. Grandly dressed women,
beautiful children, and elegant men fussing over the creases in their
attire all filed placidly from the platform to the transport yard. Mitte
found three Greeks with a command of German and drafted them as
interpreters. None of them understood the place they had reached or
the fate that awaited them. The sad, tragic reality dawned on them
only when they marched, stark naked, to the "shower" and when
they absorbed unexpected beatings as the Germans shouted *"Schnell,
schnell!"*

In the meantime, the camp warehouses were replenished and enriched with mutton, large quantities of oil, preserved meat and fish, sardines, wine, top-grade cigarettes and many other rare commodities of extremely high quality. Mitte and the other SS men walked about in glee, faces aglow. They were so uplifted that they pounded us on the shoulder. The bad times in the camp had finally come to an end, they said; henceforth we would know no more hunger. Best of all, there were many such transports still to come.

All this proved to be true: another fifteen transports of Greek Jews reached Treblinka in short order. The Germans fed them the old refrain about the necessity of being strict about washing and disinfecting, working, and surviving in war; the storerooms bulged, the gas chambers worked overtime, and pillars of fire continued to consume the tortured bodies.

We worked vigorously, and everything, according to the SS men, was *"Alles in Ordnung* – O.K." They began to compensate us for our grueling labor with cigarettes, three per day for every prisoner. These, of course, had arrived in the transports from Greece. We were given low-grade cigarettes; the quality brand was reserved for the German staffers. The SS men considered themselves an elite, ordained by the Fuhrer for hard, responsible duties. This was a favorite topic for conversation between them and Galewski, who kept us informed on the intimacies of SS thinking.

They spoke about the supremacy of the German race and people, their advanced culture and their important role in organizing and introducing the new order in Europe. Though they believed they were doing something natural and necessary, they were not carrying out others' will automatically. They actually took pleasure in cruelty, torture, the infliction of suffering. Their occasionally wild extremes in behavior presented their nature as an utterly incomprehensible riddle – human beings on the outside, and, as manifested by their actions, monstrous predatory beasts on the inside. How could one explain phenomena such as instructing prisoners who were condemned to death to organize choirs and orchestras, to dance, to play football, to box? Several SS men cultivated a special hobby: raping girls who had come in the transports. After spending themselves, Treblinka's dispensers of life and death would lead their victims in a coldblooded promenade down Death Avenue to the gas chambers. It was hard to picture these monsters as husbands and fathers who cared diligently for their families. Their bosses, though, cared for them well, appreciated their difficult positions and rewarded them with frequent furloughs in Germany. Every morning they did calisthenics to maintain their health, and tried to keep the huts in handsome shape with flowerbeds and well-tended gardens, sparing no effort to improve their living conditions.

22

Artur Gold

A new transport from Warsaw provided us with the fifty men needed to round off the prisoner contingent in the camp, which had dwindled greatly as a result of the many on-site executions carried out by the guards. Among the new men was the famous Warsaw musician Artur Gold. The moment Kiwe ordered fifty young men taken out of the transport, the "reds", who had known Gold back in Warsaw, made sure to include him. There he stood, clutching a violin to his chest.

That day after roll call, Lalka shouted *"Kapellmeister raus! –* The conductor: out!" At the sound of this, Gold and two other prisoners stepped out of line and faced us. Even before this we had thought it strange that they had not ordered us to sing "Mountain Man", which we chanted every day after roll call, and the camp anthem, *"Fester Schritt"*. Artur Gold and the other two prisoners formed a violin trio grotesquely-dressed in the standard prisoner uniform of rags and high-cut boots procured in the sorting yard. Now they mounted a small wooden platform which was hardly big enough for them. Behind them was a hut with little grated windows. Beside them, on the ground, stood the whipping stool where the Germans punished prisoners for imagined transgressions.

The trio of musicians began to play popular prewar tunes which, reminding us of years gone by, left us depressed and sore of heart. The Germans were pleased with themselves: they had succeeded in organizing an orchestra in the death camp.

As we stood at roll call, Artur Gold entranced us with the old melodies he produced with his violin – amidst the sweet, nauseating stench of decomposing bodies which clung to us as if never wanting to part. The odor had become part of our very being; it was all that remained of our families and loved ones, a last remembrance of the Jewish people, exterminated in the gas chambers. Once done with us, it filtered through the wire fences covered with intertwined pine branches, wafted for tens of kilometers all around, and attested to the camp's existence and what transpired there.

After one of these concerts the Germans decided that the maestros did not look good. Their clothes were too big, held up by all kinds of belts, and their boots were high and heavy. They ordered our tailors to sew jackets of shiny, loud blue cloth, and to attach giant bow ties to the collars. Dressed not as prisoners any longer but as clowns, they provided entertainment after roll call, day in, day out. However spent we might have been after a twelve-hour work day, we had to stand in ranks and take in a concert.

The music was usually accompanied by the tenor of the crane engine. The diligent machine kept on exhuming and relocating corpses in the death camp even after 6:00 p.m., for the Germans had decided to expedite the matter of covering all traces and burning the bodies. The moment the concert ended, the SS men ordered us to march toward the entrance to the hut, even as we remained in roll-call formation. Our groups were organized by blocks, and each block *Kommandant* marched at the head of his group. Lalka of the SS stood at the fence, arms folded across his chest, regarding us with a smirk. He felt like a lord with powers of life and death over us. The block *Kommandants* screamed, "*Muetzen ab* – hats off, left face!" Their hats came off and so did ours; pressing them to our thighs, we marched in place vigorously. We were very careful to take no chances with this monster named Lalka, whose cruelty was all too well-known to us. His career in brutality had begun even before the Treblinka camp was established; as early as 1939 he had participated in exterminating chronically ill or insane Germans. In this fashion, then, we returned to our huts each day, after finishing our work to the strains of music.

23

A Latrine

The lack of sanitary facilities, toilets in particular, was a serious problem. After great efforts on *Kommandant* Galewski's part, Kiwe agreed to let the *Baukommando* build two latrines. Until then we had only one in the sorting yard and another between the two rooms of the hut, from which a horrible stench spread throughout our living quarters. To minimize the use of this toilet, another latrine was now erected in the line-up yard, out of pine logs supporting a crisscross pattern of boards. We would stand on two of these logs and see to our needs.

Just as the two previous latrines were enclosed in a structure of poles and barbed wire, so were the back side and roof of the new outhouse wrapped in barbed wire. Where the wire fencing was erected, we, the *Tarnungskommando*, inserted pine branches until the whole thing looked like a verdant hunter's blind. Once the branches dried up and turned brown, of course, the new fencing was indistinguishable from all the other camouflaged fences in Treblinka. While the work was in progress, we used a latrine next to the *Lazarett*.

When the Germans noticed that the prisoners were going to the latrine too often and spending too much time there, Lalka ordered the *Vorarbeiters* to go to the storeroom and procure two rabbinical black suits and a couple of black hats with pompoms on them. Two prisoners were equipped with whips and ordered to don this getup. It was their job to make sure no more than five prisoners entered the outhouse at any one time, and that they spent no longer than one minute inside. Alarm clocks dangled from their necks on strings. They were called the *Scheisskommando* – the "Shit Detail". The Germans enjoyed their joke raucously; from that day, when they summoned the various groups to work, the last one was the *Scheisskommando*.

Thus the two prisoners, in their grotesque garb, set to their task of guarding the latrines. As for their job of limiting the amount of time we could spend there, they took a contrary attitude to it: thanks to them, the latrines became rendezvous points between ourselves and prisoners from different groups. Here we exchanged news and information, each describing developments in his surroundings, with the *Scheisskommando* hovering protectively outside. Whenever a real guard approached, the *Scheisskommando* began to make a racket which indicated that it was time to hurry out.

24

Langer

One day we were working energetically in the sorting yard as usual; the *Vorarbeiters* and the *Kapo* shouted and cracked their whips over our heads as we ploughed through open suitcases strewn on the ground in every direction. Our job was to extract various articles of clothing from the piles and to empty the pockets. Then one of our party stopped working momentarily to converse with two friends. The *Vorarbeiter*, oblivious to this, went on shouting as usual: "*Arbeiten schnell!*" Just then Mitte, the Angel of Death, emerged from the hut across the way. This hut, situated next to the fake railroad station, was used for the storage of the best and newest objects, which were put there just after sorting to spare them damage from the elements. The Angel of Death, seeing three prisoners at conversation, raced over to them. Now the *Vorarbeiter* realized what was transpiring, and began to shout and strike the threesome with his whip. Two of the offenders fled immediately, leaping over the strewn suitcases and clothing and vanishing behind the pile of rags. The third prisoner had no time to follow suit. He remained where he was and returned to work without delay, sorting the clothes like all the prisoners beside him. It was Langer, a friend of mine from school days in Czestochowa. Mitte bounded over to Langer and ordered him to turn his pockets inside out. As Langer obeyed, a few gold coins fell to the sand. At the sight of them, Mitte began beating Langer murderously and demanding the names of the two men who fled. Without as much as a tremble, Langer held his peace. Mitte ordered him to strip, continuing to whip him. Langer's face turned blue; blood gushed from his mouth. Mitte's assault continued with inhuman brutality as he repeated his demand. Langer heroically maintained his silence. Seeing that his onslaught was getting him nowhere, Mitte ordered all the *Vorarbeiters* to stop the work, gather all the prisoners and bring them to the edge of the hut where the best and newest booty was stored. Mitte ordered the prisoners to nail a wooden board to the hut, parallel to the ground. Mitte seized a pair of belts, tied Langer's legs to the board and suspended him upside-down. Aiming his pistol at Langer, he again demanded that Langer denounce his two conversation partners. Now Langer broke his silence: "Men!" he shouted. "Get back at 'em. Start a revolution and kill them. You've got to burn down this hell. They're murderers!" Mitte recognized this for the incitement it was, and, seeing that he was getting no real information from the battered prisoner, shot him in the head.

Night, and the few hours of relative quiet which the authorities allocated to us for rest, were a godsend. Sleep detached us from the cruel reality of harsh camp life, blunted our suffering, and sometimes carried us into a world of enchanted imagination. More often, though, we were afflicted with nightmares in which the terrible scenes we had witnessed by day were reenacted.

A scream of terror or a groan occasionally split the silence of the night. At times, someone's coughing or snoring awakened a fellow prisoner. The latter would rouse his noisy neighbor with a blow of a fist and a rude curse, returning afterwards to his sleep, or, to be more precise, his lengthy nap.

The harsh living conditions, starvation, overexertion and constant fear which pervaded our surroundings occasionally drove someone insane. It hurt to witness someone go over the brink, and it hurt even more to see how the Germans mocked and abused him until they finally exterminated him in the *Lazarett*. I remember one night in particular. Most of the prisoners were sleeping, and a small group, wrapped in the traditional shawls, was praying by candlelight. Suddenly the tranquility of the night was pierced by insane laughter which sent chills down everyone's spines. The sound had something of the threatening caw of an owl, the sad crying of a jackal, and the crazy wail of the irrevocably condemned. The laughter would stop intermittently, and the miserable soul uttered one and only one word – *Mentsh*, Yiddish for "man". Then, without another moment's letup, the insane laughter resumed. I had the feeling that I would be the next to perform thus, that I would scream until my skull burst open and sent my brain spilling from it together with my torn, aching nerves. I buried my head in a blanket and plugged fingers into my ears to block out that deranged laughter. The doctors anesthetized the man the next day, and the "Reds" hauled him on a stretcher to the *Lazarett*, where he was shot to death. Fortunately for him, he never knew what had befallen him.

When we got our number badges, the Germans ordered us to pin them to the left side of the chest. Mitte added an order of his own: every prisoner who sorted clothes of the Jews, who had been murdered in the gas chambers, had to slip a note with his number into every bundle he had sorted, enabling the Germans to know who had done the work. The sorters were not to content themselves with emptying the pockets and searching for hidden treasures; they also had to remove all identifying marks from the clothes, including white ribbons with Stars of David or yellow badges. Bundles of good clothing peregrinated in directions unknown, and any indication of their origin meant death for the sorter. Even so, we tried to leave some sign of the origin of every bundle. Though we did not know whom they would reach, we entertained ourselves with the hope that our action would hint at what was happening here.

As Mitte entered the sorting yard, the *Vorarbeiters* began their usual frantic performance, racing about and screaming *"Schnell arbeiten!"*. Mitte approached the pile of sorted bundles, ordered the warehouse-man to take one apart, and, slowly, began to feel it. After a moment he pulled from a coat pocket a yellow badge and the note bearing the number of the prisoner who had processed that bundle. He ordered us to stop working and stand at attention amid the open suitcases and strewn rags. Mitte bounded past the suitcases with his cat-steps, pulling up to various prisoners and reading their personal numbers. Then he stopped beside one of them, called the *Vorarbeiter*, and displayed the note and the yellow badge he had found in the bundle.

Mitte ordered the prisoner to step out from behind the suitcases and rags, and commanded *Kapo* Rakowski to get all the other prisoners out of the yard. We lined up behind Mitte. Now the SS officer ordered the offending prisoner to undress, and had him face the rest of us. He quaked in fear and cold, despair in his eyes. Mitte spied a Ukrainian at the bottom of the sand bank between the sorting yard and the death camp, and called him over. The Ukrainian ran over to Mitte and stood beside him. Shoot him, Mitte ordered. The Ukrainian fired into the prisoner's abdomen. The victim crumpled, gushing blood and writhing in death agony. Mitte approached the dying prisoner, smirking, unholstered his pistol and finished him off with a bullet in the head. Then he lectured us on how we must not commit the slightest infraction of the rules, and how there should be no recurrence of today's misdeed. Two prisoners carried the corpse to the *Lazarett*. Mitte strode off, ordering us to sing something with gusto.

25

Kapo Rakowski

To conclude our daily labors, we assembled in the lineup yard to be counted and have our attendance checked. This done, the SS duty officer recited the names of the prisoners to be punished that day and the number of lashes each would receive. Once the evening's brutality was done, the artistic part of the affair came: a concert of well-known tunes with Artur Gold and his orchestra. At the end, the musicians led us in "Aren't You Sad, Mountain Man?" Before turning in, we all marched around the yard in fives. This parade was no punishment; it was clearly meant to provide physical exercise. The man who instigated it was our own *Kommandant* Rakowski, a young, intelligent fellow who owned a farm before the war. Rakowski had been appointed camp *Kommandant* during the typhus epidemic, when Galewski, had fallen ill. His selection had much to do with his impressive appearance – tall, well-built and strong. The Germans were sure no prisoner could survive his beatings. In fact, Rakowski was very humane; he understood us and, though he concealed it, obviously pitied us. In certain situations, of course, he could not help us, and he had no choice but to be brutal with the prisoners under his command when the Germans were around.

Rakowski dreamed of staging a great rebellion in which the camp would be overrun and destroyed, the Germans and Ukrainians slaughtered, and all the prisoners would take to the forests as partisans. Hence the evening exercise. Wanting to accustom us to long marches, he had us perform various exercises meant to toughen our bodies and prepare us for harsh partisan life.

To our sorrow, our *Kommandant* never saw his dream come true; he was not destined to participate in the rebellion which broke out later in the camp. Rakowski, like many others, had many enemies and had to be ever wary of informers and tattletales. One such misfit told the camp authorities that Rakowski was concealing a canteen filled with gold. The investigation which immediately ensued ended with his execution. Everyone who had been in on his plans took his death bitterly. In profound grief we parted from this hero, who never put anything higher than the general welfare. To the end he believed he would succeed in extricating us from this hell, taking us into the forests and attaching our fate to that of the partisans. We never knew who had informed on him, though we suspected Kuba or Moniek, the Warsaw-born *Kapo* of the *Hofjuden*.

The Germans were glad to be rid of Rakowski; they reinstated Galewski, who had recovered from his bout with typhus. Galewski, too, was in constant jeopardy of informers and schemers of various kinds. One of his most dangerous enemies was a *Kapo* named Blau. A very fat man with an imbecile face and crooked legs, Blau reminded us of the Hunchback of Notre Dame. This creature, not worthy of being called a "man", must have had many people on his conscience. He and his wife had reached Treblinka from their place of residence, Kielce, where he had collaborated with the Gestapo. After the ghetto was liquidated and they were sent to Treblinka, both of them were taken out of the transport and worked together for a long time. Blau enjoyed certain privileges: he was first appointed *Oberkapo* and then kitchen *Kommandant*. He surrounded himself with a gang of criminals of the worst kind, who kept him informed of everything in the huts – prisoners' discussions, plans, and so on. Blau handed out double portions of the best kinds of food to his cronies, at the expense of the rest of us, of course. His hatred of Galewski stemmed from his ambition to be camp *Kommandant*; he refused to accept Galewski's authority.

The new *Kommandant* was reinstated in an official ceremony held in the regular lineup yard, before all the prisoners. At the end, after a rendition of the camp anthem, Galewski stood in the middle of the yard and thanked the SS for the trust they had placed in him. He promised to obey all orders and instructions faithfully, to ensure order, and to adjudicate all disputes among the prisoners honestly and justly. As the Germans walked away, our new boss dispersed us with a wink.

26

Tiergarten

One night it was so dark that the electric lights hardly dispelled the gloom in the hut. The reverend, sitting on the blankets beside us, turned to us and exclaimed in his fractured Polish: "These Germans totally gone crazy! Unbelievable: they tell us to build cages for a zoo."

Unbelievable indeed. "A zoo? Here?! Who needs it? I think you didn't hear correctly, or perhaps you didn't understand what you heard..."

The reverend cut me off: "Katzap, I understand what I hear very well. Yes, they want to build a zoo here. They brought two peacocks, a doe and some foxes, I do not know from where."

"If what you're saying is true", I said, "the sons of bitches want to create an illusion of a little gem of a spot on earth. Now I understand why Sidow of the SS ordered us to hoe the ground around the huts and to plant some flowers. The next thing they'll do is set up a merry-go--round and turn this death factory of theirs into an amusement park."

Professor Merring's towering figure emerged from behind our bunks. He approached us, stooping slightly so as not to bump his head on the supporting beams of the hut's roof, and sat down on a folding chair which I pushed in his direction. Overhearing our conversation, he peered at us over his glasses in the manner he had once used before his pupils:

"I want to tell you about the mentality of the German people..."

I burst into laughter: "You're going to tell us about the Germans and their mentality?! Sorry, we know them well enough!"

"Very well. Nothing is as simple as you think, Katzap. It will certainly sound strange to you, but the Germans are by nature a sentimental people. This does not contradict their cruelty; it only conceals and disguises it. Even the most brutal sadists among them love the warmth of home. Their customary home furnishings include ornate embroidery with sayings of love, loyalty and brotherhood, which their wives produce in calligraphic script. Their homes burst with sayings and adages of the noblest kinds. Over their beds, on which they rest after a day of murder and hatred, they hang brightly designed inscriptions about love of one's fellow-man. They try to camouflage their true nature. Even their children's stories, however, express atrocity and cruelty now and then."

The reverend broke in: "I know the Germans better than you do. I spent many years with them, and I find it hard to believe that the Germans whom I knew are capable of doing everything that's being done here. I try to explain this to myself by thinking that we're surrounded with the dregs of this people and not its nobility..."

"That's only partly true. Yes, the people who are doing this disgusting, dirty work here are petty murderers. But they weren't the ones who created and designed this mighty death machine. Neither subhumans like Sidow, with his alcohol-eaten brain, nor even maniacs like Lalka, could have designed this mechanism. Look how efficiently it works, from the trains which put in just on time to the sophisticated gas chambers. People with academic degrees, noted scientists, were the ones who established this hell. They also receive detailed reports about everything done here and make sure their plan is carried out flawlessly. These are the true murderers, and, to me, they are far worse than the ones around us. They planned everything that's happening here in cold blood, and their hands didn't tremble when they drew up the plan for annihilating the Jewish people!"

We fell silent.

The next day we went out to work in the forest as usual, surrounded by seven sentries under Sidow. Once we reached the forest, Sidow ordered us to look for wild animals. Then a little squirrel caught Sidow's eye, and he ordered us to chase and capture it. We pursued the frantic creature which, in its flight, scampered to the top of a tall tree. Sidow ordered me to climb after it. I did his bidding, reluctant and disgusted. From below, eyes dancing with joy, Sidow followed my movements. The Ukrainians and my fellow prisoners, too, looked on – one group happily, the other sadly. The little animal, already within my grasp, looked at me with fear-filled glistening eyes. I could not trap it. It symbolized freedom...

I slid down the tree emptyhanded, whereupon Sidow, boiling with anger and disappointment, meted out twenty lashes on my posterior then and there. My old wounds, which had only just healed, reopened and filled with pus.

Soon after this a little zoo was set up in the service area of the camp. Its pretentious name: the *Tiergarten,* or the Zoological Garden.

Symbolic cemetry and monument to the victims of Treblinka,
erected 1959-64. Each of the stones represents a particular
Jewish community whose members perished in Treblinka

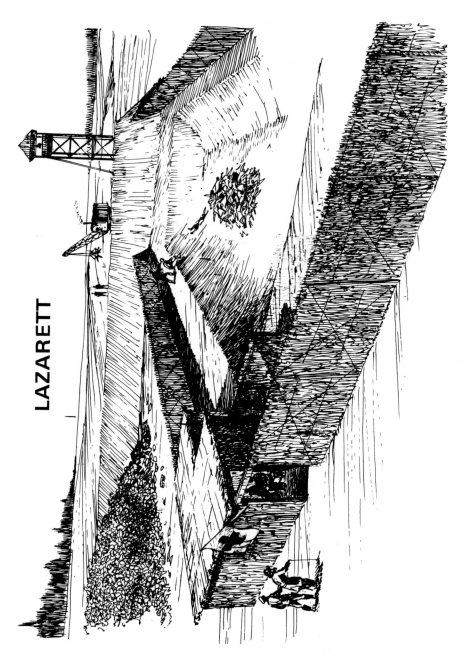

LAZARETT

The execution site (*Lazarett*), drawn by the author

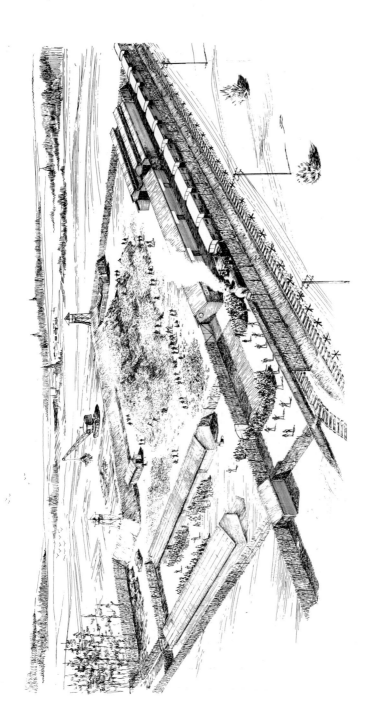

Treblinka – general view of assembly and undressing area, sorting area and railway ramp. In the centre of the sorting area a heap of clothes and other belongings of the gassed victims. (Drawing by the author)

Professor Mering   Engineer Alfred Galewski

Counterfeit German identity card issued to the author by
the clandestine "Polish People's Army"

The author at the underground telephone cable
pit in which he stayed at night

The author and his mother in
Warsaw on the "Aryan" side

The author after his escape
from Treblinka, photographed
to obtain a counterfeit
German identity card

Professor Willenberg
author's father

Celling – Synagogue in Częstochowa painted by Prof. P. Willenberg

Head of Jesus painted by the author's father above the cellar stairs at the house Marszałkowska 60 in Warsaw. The painting and the painter's false signature were discovered by the author during a visit to attend the 40th anniversary of the Warsaw Ghetto Uprising

Old Jew painted by Prof. P. Willenberg

Author's father's card printed on the "Aryan" side. It says:

I RECEIVE ORDERS FOR PORTRAITS
HAND PAINTED OIL COLOURS
FROM PHOTOGRAPHS AND NATURE
VERY REASONABLE PRICES
THE ARTIST IST MUTE
When spoken to in loud voice
he hear and understand

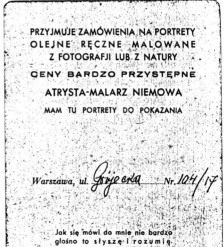

Stained glass – Professor Willenberg work

27

"The Last Sunday"

The hut was half-dark, despite the lights hanging between the two-tiered bunks. The motor which generated electricity for these lights was the same one which provided the burning gas for the gas chambers where tens of thousands of humans were poisoned day by day. To dispel the gloom which the weak lights left in the hut, every prisoner tried to bring candles from the sorting yard. Every evening we positioned these candles on the stools which we had brought from our previous quarters and lit them. It was not only the added light we wanted; the candles also enabled us to restore the former atmosphere. It was our way of trying, at least in the evening, to tear ourselves away from the horror around us and forget everything we had endured that day.

Each of us had a bunk about forty centimeters wide. Tonight we had a new guest, a Jew from Czechoslovakia who had arrived in a transport from Theresienstadt. He had a treasure from which he never parted – a little metal harmonica, with which, in a whisper, he played sad old prewar songs. I had spent the day working in the forest with the *Tarnungskommando* in the forest. In the pine branches I had hauled to the camp for camouflaging the barbed-wire fence, I had concealed a bottle of vodka and some bacon. Also, the hollow of my sunken abdomen had left ample room for hiding a loaf of bread. We sat down that evening – Merring, Gershonowitz, the reverend, Alfred and I – around a folding chair which served us as a table. We hung a red blanket to protect us from the wind, which penetrated through the open door and window. The blanket had the further effect of creating an intimacy in our corner which seemed to set it apart from the rest of the hut and its many inmates. The evening began, as usual, with a surreptitious distribution of the spoils; Alfred divided the bacon and bread equitably. In view of the terrible starvation which had engulfed the camp that winter, I tried to eat my fill in the forest, leaving anything I might succeed in smuggling into the camp for distribution among my comrades. I did reserve an honest share of vodka for myself; Alfred and I were the only drinkers there in any case.

The Czech was an intermittent guest at our feasts. He approached our corner, stepping around prisoners who had already gone to sleep. Following him like a shadow sneaked a prisoner from a little town in Poland. Between his fingers he clutched two spoons which he manipulated dexterously against each other and his thigh to produce pleasant melodies. One of his favorite tunes was "The Last Sunday", a popular ditty from before the war. Its sad melody and evocative lyrics – "I'll make you a bed and wait for you patiently for this last Sunday" – transported us to another world; for a few moments we forgot where we were. Each of us allowed his memories to return to distant prewar years. I saw myself in a summer resort near Warsaw, playing some afternoon music and dancing on the porch. There was an ambience of lovely fragrant forests, innocent flirting, and the consenting gazes of pretty teenage girls none of whom, it appeared, were alive now. Each of us in his own mind's eye beheld his personal "last Sunday" of freedom. We had absolutely nothing to look forward to, we were sure. No one was waiting for us; everything we had left behind was utterly gone.

Someone in a neighboring bunk flung a shoe. It whizzed past our musician just missing him, and struck the chair, causing the candle to fall and go out. A shout came from the same direction as the shoe: "Hey, son of a bitch, stop playing and singing!" No one in our group reacted; no one said a word, and silence overtook the hut. We scattered, each man to his multicolored bunk, together with his personal "last Sunday" memories no one could steal.

The volume of clothes-sorting work diminished greatly as spring began. The detail under *Kapo* Salo Bloch, a captain in the Czech army before the war, actually finished the whole job. Everything was now arranged in the hut, waiting for an empty train. Every bundle had ten items: ten pairs of boots, ten jackets or ten coats. Every *Kapo* had to record all the objects in his hut, noting the quantity and type of each and every bundle. With this, the Germans knew the number of objects in every storeroom. As we loaded an empty train which had pulled up, the SS men consulted their records and decided that many bundles were missing. *Kapo* Salo denied the allegations, explaining that the bundles must have come apart in the storeroom, had been retied, and were mistakenly recorded as new bundles. The Germans were not about to accept this; they insisted that the objects had to turn up, and they did not care how.

Kiwe interrupted the work and ordered all the prisoners to gather in the lineup yard. We lined up in fives, as usual. Kiwe shouted at us that the operation was in chaos. *Kommandant* Galewski, cap in hand, raced up and down the yard angrily, not knowing what to do. Now Kiwe fell silent, called Galewski over and whispered something into his ear. Galewski nodded his head and turned to us. He ordered us to remove our trousers, jackets and coats, bring additional clothes from the huts, and gather it all in the yard. Once we had scoured our hut of personal effects, Kiwe said that anyone found with concealed garments would be shot to death. We packed our belongings into bundles and loaded them onto the train. Thus they stole our clothing, absolute necessities for our existence, and left us with nothing but a shirt and pants.

Kapo Salo and *Vorarbeiter* Wolff were called out of the line. Kiwe ordered them to pull the prisoners under their command out of line as well. The group of fifteen was ordered to line up beside the hut, with Salo and Wolff at their head. A moment later a group of Ukrainians, rifles cocked, came through the gate into the lineup yard. They surrounded the group of prisoners and led them out of the yard with their weapons trained. The look in our eyes bade them a last farewell. We were sure they were being taken to the *Lazarett* – and to death. Then we saw the group turning right, toward the death camp. That evening in the hut, Galewski told us that they had been taken to the *Todeslager* as replacements for prisoners who had been shot to death there. Since shooting prisoners to death was standard *Todeslager* procedure, workers were always scarce.

Several days later I and my group were repairing the fence near the main entrance. Beside us was a group of working prisoners from the *Todeslager*, led by an elderly Jew, a carpenter by trade, named Wiernik. They were building a stylized wooden gate. As he toiled, Wiernik updated us on events on that side of Treblinka. We asked him in a whisper about the fate of our men who had been sent there. They were all alive, he said. Then, bursting into what sounded to the world like a Yiddish song, he continued: "You have no idea what hell our side of the camp is. We have thirteen gas chambers in operation. The gas is produced by the motor of an old Russian tank. They built the gas chambers with sloping floors, making it easier to take the bodies out. We take corpses out of the graves and burn them on a giant grill made of iron rails, 2,500 bodies on each incinerator." An SS man approached, and Wiernik abruptly halted his song-story. When the day's work ended, we returned to the lineup yard for a concert under the baton of Artur Gold who, together with the "Warsaw Warbler" – a cellist named Schutzer – entertained us with prewar ditties.

28

The Transport from the Warsaw Ghetto

A very strange-looking transport reached Treblinka one fine day in April. The freight cars were in terrible condition, their boards knocked out of place all over. Ukrainians lay on the roofs, armed with a variety of weapons, all cocked and ready. They fired the moment anyone even peeped out of one of the cars. Apparently the Jews had engaged their guards in a pitched battle en route.

The Germans chose this occasion to inaugurate a new method of stripping new arrivals designated for extermination. In addition to the "Reds", who made their usual appearance in the yard and handed out bits of string for tying shoes together, the Germans brought in other prisoners who usually sorted clothes in the yard. These men were lined up in threes in the transport yard, together with the "Reds". As the new arrivals were herded from the freight cars to the transport yard, they were ordered to remove certain items of clothing as they filed past the prisoners and hand them over. The first trio received the coats, the second the jackets, the third the pants, and the others underwear and shoes. The Germans considered this bucket-brigade tactic a sure way to streamline the work. As the process went on, we heard a sudden explosion. Someone in the transport had apparently concealed a hand grenade in his jacket pocket, pulled the pin and hurled jacket and grenade at the receiving prisoners. The grenade went off, injuring three prisoners in the yard and several of the new victims.

Commotion broke out in the yard. The most frightened were the Germans themselves; all the SS men immediately fled the scene. Those

German monsters, the SS officers, so terrifying and mighty-looking all the time, appeared cowardly and ridiculous now as they scurried from the yard like sniveling, frightened dogs under pursuit. The Ukrainian guards, too, hurried away. But nothing really happened; a few minutes passed, and the Germans recovered. Kiwe of the SS raced into the yard and ordered an evacuation of the wounded prisoners to the *Lazarett*. We did his bidding, but only in part. Though we took them out of the yard, we brought them not to the *Lazarett* but, in violation of orders, to the hut beside the platform where we lay them on a pile of sorted clothing. This was the product of some inner impulse, of course. The explosion had given us the courage and the fortitude to disobey the SS; we feared that our wounded comrades would be shot to death as lost causes. To our amazement, the Germans took it in their stride, pretending to be unaware that their order had been ignored. They did not even react to the fact that we had taken the casualties to the *Revierstube*, where our doctors cared for them painstakingly. This nearly unimaginable event opened our eyes. The Germans had looked scared, and we, suddenly, discovered that perhaps we were strong.

That same day, people in the last transport informed us of the rebellion which had broken out in the Warsaw Ghetto. The news struck our ears like thunder. We were aware, to be sure, that a faction of Jews in the Polish capital was ready for life-and-death war with the Germans. We knew that an underground had come into being there and had geared up for an insurrection. People taken out of the transports from Warsaw in January described the terrible conditions of ghetto life in that city. We had devoted entire nights to discussion and debate of the situation in Warsaw. Lying on our bunks, isolated and locked up in the camp, we took great interest in anything going on outside. Warsaw was the center of our quiet hopes and dreams. And now, with no preliminaries we were told that the embers of rebellion had burst into flame in the half-deserted streets of the Warsaw Ghetto, and that the staccato of machine gun fire intermingled with the thunder of hand grenades. We imagined the most stubborn and terrible battles. Our hearts were with the rebels, and we worried for their fate. The Jewish uprising warmed our hearts, infused us with new strength and led to new decisions. Our spines stiffened; we wanted to act; we would not let them claim our lives easily. The hut buzzed like a beehive that evening as the prisoners, sitting in groups, exchanged whispered reports and rumors. Agitated to the last man, we distanced ourselves from the miserable greyness of the camp by entertaining imaginative hypotheses and sundry theories. An overwhelming desire to act at any price seized us. As time passed, the plan began to develop form and substance. We would conquer and destroy Treblinka in a general mass uprising, weapons in hand, against the German and Ukrainian murderers.

People in subsequent transports from the Warsaw Ghetto updated us: the Ghetto uprising had continued, Jews were heroically fighting the Germans and inflicting heavy casualties on them. We learned that the Germans had begun to torch the Ghetto house by house, and heard about people leaping from the upper stories of burning houses, and heroic battles in which women and children joined.

Lalka of the SS went away for a few days at this time. When he returned, he approached Artur Gold and told him that he had brought some of his prewar phonograph records. To us, this was proof that he had been in the Warsaw Ghetto. To the artist it was something else. Gold momentarily forgot where he was; his voice choking with joy, he told me of the recordings of his orchestra which had shown up in Treblinka. Unwilling to jar him back to tragic reality, I let him float in the clouds a little longer.

29

The Policemen's Caps

One evening after work, we unfolded our chairs and sat down on our bunks (during the day we kept the chairs folded and flat on the blankets, with one blanket covering them. This arrangement gave our bunks a straight edge, as the Germans demanded). It was our regular group of Prof. Merring, Gershonowitz, the reverend, Alfred and myself. Whenever we had guests, Alfred and I tried to treat them to food of some kind, if we had any. As we smoked cigarettes, various and occasionally unrealistic arguments went on. In every case, however, we returned at some point to the day's events.

The reverend, in his halting, funny Polish, marveled at the fact that the transports which had come in January from the Warsaw Ghetto had left a trail of Jewish militia caps along the entire route from the train station to the camp. The Ukrainians gathered the caps, which had been thrown out of the train windows, and brought them to the camp.

Prof. Merring explained in his quiet voice: "They had good reason for doing that: feared that the people they'd meet here would take revenge on them. When the Germans established the ghettos in the cities and towns, and brought the Jewish population to them, they cut them off from all their institutions apart from the *Judenrat*. The *Judenraten*, of course, had been organized earlier by the Germans and had assumed all the functions previously handled by municipalities and other administrative bodies. By organizing the *Judenraten*, the Germans created an 'address' to which all their demands might be brought. They forced the *Judenrat* to shoulder a tax of gold or of cash, *objets d'art*, expensive furniture and the like. The *Judenrat* usually knew where and how to meet the Germans' demands. *Judenrat* members were mostly Jews who had been rich men or public figures before the war. At the beginning of the war they meant to relieve the suffering of the Jewish population by paying off the German robbers; they thought this would make them act more moderately in carrying out their superiors' orders. The *Judenraten* established welfare institutions and offices which helped the masses of Jewish poor. To impose order in the ghetto, a Jewish police force came together, mostly made up of young Jews 'of good family', as they say. Most people who enlisted in the so-called 'police' were youngsters who were impressed by the uniforms and high-cut boots. They had to pay for these items themselves, but this was no problem since they came from rich families."

I interrupted the lecture to venture an opinion that these people believed that joining the "police" would improve their chances of survival. Prof. Merring, agreeing, resumed: "At first their job was to keep order in the ghetto. They supervised the distribution of soup in welfare kitchens for the poor. Afterwards, when the Germans needed people for the labor camps, the Jewish policemen grabbed the children of the poorest Jews and turned them over to the German gendarmes. Starvation in the ghetto intensified as time passed; then some of the policemen tried to see to their families' needs by seizing little Jewish children and sending them over or under the ghetto wall to the Aryan side. The children risked their lives in order to trade belongings they brought from home for some bread or potatoes – which the Jewish 'policemen' appropriated in any case. When the *Judenrat* was ordered to provide the Germans with valuables, they sent the policemen to whatever addresses they thought appropriate for confiscating property for the Germans."

"The duties entrusted to the 'policemen' caused some of them to become crude and greedy. When the Germans began resettling the Jewish population, the 'police' participated actively in catching the people and bringing them to the *Umschlagplatz*, the 'loading place', as the Nazis called the square where they gathered people for transport.

From there they were sent to Treblinka. To fool the Jews, the Germans demanded that they organize workshops in the Warsaw Ghetto to serve the *Wehrmacht*. It was believed for a little while that anyone employed there would stay alive in Warsaw. Thus the population was divided into two groups. One comprised people who either pulled the right strings or bribed the workshop owners generously enough to get work and obtain work permits. The second group comprised the unfortunates who could not acquire these documents. The first to reach Treblinka were the poorest Jews of the Warsaw Ghetto."

"The *Kommando* which we call the 'Reds' consists mostly of people who could not buy their freedom from the Germans. They reached Treblinka in the first transports. Whenever they find Jewish policemen in the transports, they grab them and lead them right to the gas chambers. Even if there's a need for workers at the time, they choose other people. That's why these well-mannered kids from good homes throw their policemen's caps out of the train before they reach the camp."

The reverend asked Prof. Merring about the origin of the people in the "Blue" *Kommando*. These were far more modest in dress and behavior than the "Reds" or the *Goldjuden*. I explained that this detail usually consisted of Hasidic Jews. When the Germans ordered us to sing, they chanted Hasidic songs and Psalms because they did not know even a single Polish song. One could see by their demeanor that most of them had been yeshiva students before the war, and had dressed until very recently in traditional attire. Their *Kapo*, Meir, a plump, hump-backed redhead, was also an Orthodox Jew. This modest group, with a broom as its emblem, was in charge of cleaning the railroad cars and scattering disinfectant (mainly chlorine). The "Blue" *Kommando* was one of the pleasantest groups in the camp.

The reverend interrupted me with a comment: "The Germans knew very well how to wipe out a people. All the instructions and restrictions they imposed on the Jews created an atmosphere of threat. Not everyone knew how to stay human to the end under inhuman conditions." He asked me if *Judenrat* members and Jewish "policemen" had also come with me from Opatow. I told him that the wealthy Jews, together with the *Judenrat* members with their families, left

Opatow for Sandomierz, where the Germans had organized a labor camp, before the transports began. Something of this nature had happened in most of the small towns. The rich Jews apparently shelled out a fortune for the few places available, and only they, together with *Judenrat* members, could do this. The vast majority of the Jews were turned over to the Germans for annihilation, fully aware of where they were heading. In the end, however, those who thought they had bought an escape from certain execution found themselves in the death camps too.

30

The Death of Professor Merring

A mountain of various and sundry bottles and vials had piled up behind the hut where the women undressed before being led to the gas chambers. Early that winter, *Kommandant* Galewski suggested to Kiwe of the SS that he organize a group of *Flaschensortierer*, whose job it would be to sort and clean the bottles. He suggested a location for the necessary workshop: an unused hut beside the transport yard. When Kiwe gave his consent, Galewski selected some of the older and more intelligent prisoners for the task. Professor Merring was one of them. The news about the new workplace pleased us, especially in view of the easier and better working conditions it would afford. Not only was indoor work warmer; one could also heat up some tea or food.

Conversation about the *Flaschensortierer* went this way and that along the bunks in our hut. The reverend opined that the reason the Germans had ordered them to collect all bottles, including broken and small ones, which had once held medicaments, was not for their value but to enable the Germans to cover up what had happened in Treblinka. Once the war ended in their defeat – by which time we would no longer be here – how could they explain the presence of so many medicine bottles on this little piece of territory? This was the only reason for the Germans' decision to gather them up and ship them to a destination unknown to us; it was like their efforts to obliterate the remains of the murdered Jews by incinerating the bodies.

Silence.

One spring day during afternoon break, Professor Merring burst into the hut, his eyes radiating terror. That morning, he said, Kiwe had entered the hut where he was arranging bottles and took down the numbers of all the prisoners there. We were frightened at the news, too. After evening roll call we sang our anthem to a melody composed by Walter Hirsch, a Czech Jew who was fated to die in the Treblinka rebellion. It went roughly thus:

The Treblinka Anthem

Let us strengthen our steps and strides
And direct our gaze ahead.
With steadfast spirit ever loyal,
Eyes aiming at the wide world
The brigades march to work.

So we are now in Treblinka
And our fate – tarara...
So we are now in Treblinka,
And our time is short.

We listen to the kommandant's tone of voice
And heed even the look in his eye.
Our every pulse and step is harnessed as one
To the demands of the burden and the duty.

Work here is the meaning of everything
Just like obedience and duty
We shall continue, continue to bear the load
Until the moment a bit of luck winks at us,
Ho-ha...

When we had finished our rendition, Kiwe recited the numbers of the prisoners due for lashing on their naked posteriors that day. Each such prisoner would be tied to the stool and given twenty-five lashes with a whip as he counted the blows aloud. Only three of us merited this treatment today. When the session was finished, the stool was removed.

Then Kiwe began to read off some more numbers – more than twenty, in fact. He ordered the prisoners in question to line up beside the hut. The three who had already been beaten returned to the ranks and, by *Kommandant* Galewski's order, marched with all the prisoners to the huts. Now only the last twenty men whose numbers had been called remained standing beside the hut. One of them was Professor Merring.

The moment we reached the hut we ran to the grated window which looked out onto the lineup yard. We saw the prisoners being lined up in fives. Most of the men were relatively old (45–50). SS personnel scattered them around the yard; one of them, Zepp, who clutched a giant whip, ordered them to begin running. At first they stayed together while circling the yard. When they reached Zepp, he shouted "Down on the ground!" and the entire group plunged earthward. As they lay there, Zepp and other SS men whipped them. Then the prisoners were ordered to stand up, at which point they were beaten murderously on all parts of the body, heads in particular.

The running resumed, at a faster pace now. The group of prisoners began to stagger; the stronger prisoners pulled ahead. The ritual of "Down!" and "Up!" was repeated many times. The ranks crumbled; instead of running in a group, the prisoners now ran in single file. The Germans assaulted the stragglers murderously with their whips.

Professor Merring had just recovered from typhus. Still weak from the severe illness and the camp conditions in general, he could not keep up. In terror we observed the group of prisoners pulling away from him. He tried to quicken his steps with his last reserve of strength; with superhuman effort, he tried to propel his skinny, buckling legs. We could see the terrible fear on his tense face. As he ran, his hands reached out for his friends – a typical motion of tortured men who feel their strength slipping away. SS men along the route continued to pound the runners mercilessly, saving a special fury for stragglers. Then Zepp raced up to Professor Merring and began to whip him. A choking madness rose in my throat. I could not stand to see old Merring, always willing to help others and serve humanity, subjected to such inhuman suffering.

Half an hour into the death run, the SS men ordered the entire group to undress. Then, naked as on the day they were born, they had to run... to the *Lazarett*. A few minutes later we heard gunfire from that direction. Having decided that a certain workplace was no longer needed, the Germans exterminated its workers...

The reverend and I went to the *Lazarett* the next morning, bearing a load of garbage for the pyre – a pretext to get us in, of course. So as not to be noticed, we stopped beside *Kapo* Kurland. Advancing gingerly, we looked at the pile of burning corpses at our feet, and could not utter a word. Mutely we parted from the man who had been my professor in youth, and my moral support in the camp.

31

Dr. Choronzhitzki

One day we were working beside the *Revierstube*, erecting a low fence concealing the Germans' living quarters from the camp entrance. There, in the *Revierstube*, Dr. Choronzhitzki would treat under-the--weather Germans and Ukrainians. We were engrossed in our work when Alfred arrived with his baby stroller, which he usually used to gather bits of trash. He was quite addicted to it.

Approaching our group, Alfred parked the stroller at the foot of a tree. Indicating with a gesture that I was to approach him, he told me to lift a dirty pail covered with a rag from the stroller, and to bring it to Dr. Choronzhitzki in the *Revierstube*. What's in the pail? I asked. Alfred said nothing. After looking this way and that to make sure no Germans were around, I strode confidently to the *Revierstube* and opened the door as if it were home. In fact, I visited the *Revierstube* quite often – whenever we worked in the area. Dr. Choronzhitzki would greet me each time with a full glass of booze.

Now, too, the physician gave me a warm welcome. The pail was from Alfred, I said; he told me to place it under a table beside the grated window. The table, covered with a sheet which draped to the floor, was his "medicine chest". He offered me a glassful of clear alcohol. It was so sharp, and I downed it so fast, that I thought my throat was on fire. After a moment's recovery, I thanked him and walked out, back to work.

A little later, Lalka of the SS materialized in holiday uniform, a satanic smile on his face. With his dancer's steps he pranced to the *Revierstube*, opened the door and disappeared within. A few minutes later we heard the sounds of shattering dishes and shouting from the clinic. The *Revierstube* door suddenly burst open, and Lalka tumbled through it to the ground. Dr. Choronzhitzki had thrown him out. As his bulky body rolled in the sand, the doctor slammed the door shut from the inside. Lalka stood up and, making no effort to brush off the sand, tried to push the door down with all his ample strength. When this failed, he retreated and, rammed the door with all the force he could muster. This time it burst inward, followed by Lalka.

We overheard the wrestling match which ensued. As it proceeded, the two men rolled out. Although Dr. Choronzhitzki was almost twice as old as Lalka, they fought as equals. The physician pounded Lalka with his fists, and Lalka returned blow for blow. Suddenly the doctor's body went slack. His hands dropped, his head sagged, his legs buckled – and he collapsed at Lalka's feet. Lalka began to kick him with sadistic cruelty. But he no longer had an opponent, for the doctor had lost consciousness and lay on the ground, dead to the world.

Infuriated, Lalka whipped out his pistol and fired into the air. As SS and Ukrainians rushed onto the scene, Lalka ordered them to bring water at once. The Ukrainians, returning with pails of water, forced Dr. Choronzhitzki's mouth open. Lalka poured water down the victim's throat, as one of the Ukrainians trod on his stomach. The physician had obviously taken poison; Lalka was trying to force him back to consciousness by flushing out his stomach. I knew that Dr. Choronzhitzki – like myself, Alfred and many other prisoners – always carried cyanide capsules.

It was no use. Kiwe, who had appeared upon hearing Lalka's shouts, summoned camp kommandant Galewski and ordered him to gather all the prisoners into fives in the yard. Standing there in silence, we watched a Ukrainian drag Dr. Choronzhitzki into the yard and lay him at a corner of the hut. Again they poured water down his throat; again the Ukrainian stepped on his stomach. Again, it was to no avail. Now the SS men called for the special low stool on which prisoners were beaten as punishment. They had Dr. Choronzhitzki's body tied to the stool – and dealt fifty blows. At the end of this macabre punishment, Kiwe began to shout furiously at us. Dr. Choronzhitzki had wanted to escape, he howled. The physician had foreign currency – 750,000 zlotys! Roaring, Kiwe demanded to know where Choronzhitzki had obtained this fortune. Enraged to the point of madness, Kiwe cracked his whip and shouted that Choronzhitzki had been a traitor who had intended to flee by himself and leave us behind.

The prisoners observed these developments sadly. After a while the drama came to an end: we were ordered back to work; the Reds loaded Dr. Choronzhitzki's corpse onto a stretcher and hauled it off to the *Lazarett*, where that beautiful, tortured figure was flung onto the pile of burning corpses.

From Kiwe's yelling I deduced that the money had been in the pail which Alfred had asked me to pass on to the physician. Alfred confirmed it that evening: "Of course you know what happened here, but please don't reveal a bit of it to anyone". This was my first chance encounter with the camp underground. It had only a few members; only a few of these knew of the plan, and no one knew it in its entirety. Alfred told me they wanted to buy handguns from a *Wachmann* who had been under Dr. Choronzhitzki's care. To everyone's distress, the attempt fell through – for reasons we do not know to this day. Perhaps it was this *Wachmann*, who had won Dr. Choronzhitzki's trust, who betrayed him.

One more plan, then, bit the dust. Had it worked, we might have taken over the camp, destroyed it and escaped. However, the image of the magnificent Dr. Choronzhitzki would live on in our memories forever as a constant source of inspiration. As Kiwe howled and roared, trying to demonstrate that the physician had wanted to betray us and escape alone, we stood there in anguish. We knew otherwise. We saw the body of the beloved Warsaw physician splayed on the ground, filthy, wet hair plastered to his head, as if mocking the Germans' hobnailed boots by having taken his secret with him.

I recalled that once, in the *Revierstube*, Dr. Choronzhitzki had told me: "Katzap, don't think you're strong just because you have poison. Cyanide in your pocket isn't enough. Even then one needs lots of courage to swallow it at the right moment. The people we inherited it from hadn't had the strength to use it, and they went to the gas chambers."

Late that night I pondered his words. Yes, to his good fortune and ours, our beloved doctor from Warsaw had had that courage.

32

The Rebellion

As the spring of 1943 approached, the Germans began developing and
expanding the camp. They brought in a truck, driven by an SS man, and
ordered construction materials, cement, iron building elements and
bricks. All these were dumped in a heap between the pair of matching
wooden huts where the Germans lived. These structures had been
covered with straw for the winter; now the insulation was stripped and
we could assess the design of the buildings. Down the center of each hut
ran a corridor, with SS living quarters branching off in either direction.
By order of Mitte, the *Vorarbeiters* scoured the mountain of Jews'
possessions for multicolored pieces of cloth suitable for use as "carpets".
The SS men, ultra-sensitive to any noise, wanted to silence even the
sound of footsteps in the corridor. The kitchen and dining room – the
latter furnished with little tables covered with snow-white tablecloths
– were located in the front. The two huts, like the other structures in
Treblinka's functional section, were situated in the forested area, the
camp's natural camouflage. The two huts were separated by a clearing
five meters wide, and here the Germans ordered us to erect a structure
consisting of a corridor and a single room. A small prisoner *Kommando*
began to build. A few weeks later, when the walls were already standing,
the Germans issued a strange command. Instead of having us clap
a tar-covered wooden roof on the new building, like those of the other
buildings in the camp, the Germans ordered one of cast concrete.

The Germans had designated several young prisoners as personal
servants, who would keep the Germans' shoes polished, their beds

made and their rooms clean. The boys did their work with painstaking diligence. In addition to these regular duties, they would bring the Germans any valuables or "interesting" objects found in the sorting yard, such as fountain pens studded with gems. The SS had set aside a special warehouse for these articles. Every three months, when they went home on furlough, they would gather the fruit of their hard, grueling labor and haul it home.

The young servants had free run of the Germans' huts. Since everyone knew their function, they did not need to fear that an SS man or an Ukrainian would stop them and inquire into their doings. The youngsters knew the exact composition of every SS man's family and the ages of his children; on the basis of this information they would prepare packages which the Germans took home on furlough.

A special iron door with sixteenth-century ornamentation and metalwork, obviously "requisitioned" from outside, was brought in. Our metalworkers installed it at the doorway between the room and the corridor, and were instructed to fit it with a stout lock. Now the *Baumeister* told the metalworkers to make two keys for the lock; they gave one to the Germans and hid the other. The *Baumeister*'s conjecture was that the room would serve as an arsenal. When the time came to organize an insurrection, its contents, and our copy of the key, would be invaluable to us. The *Baumeister* had guessed correctly, as everyone in the *Kommando* knew within a few days. The awareness of our access to the Germans' weapons depot spurred us to action and fanned our will to live and endure.

Alfred had been Galewski's aide until four prisoners escaped from our hut. He would to see to Galewski's needs and food, and was responsible for keeping our hut clean. In effect, he was a *de facto* block kommandant. He was rarely seen outside the hut; he seldom wandered about the yard. His work, and his close relationship with the kommandant, catalyzed an especially close friendship between the two. In the wake of the prisoners' breakout, we were transferred to new housing in the functional part of the camp. Now Galewski's quarters were across from our hut, and Alfred worked at sorting rags.

One spring night, as we lay on our bench/beds, Alfred told me that the kommandant had given him a new assignment: responsibility for cleanliness in the entire functional section of the camp, including the Germans' and the Ukrainians' residential huts and staff head-quarters. This section of the camp was in the forested area; it also had a telephone, enabling communication between the camp and the railroad station and thence the outside world. Alfred's job was to roam the camp picking up trash and rags, and he was issued a children's stroller to this end. The Germans had placed whitewashed barrels along the paths in various corners of the camp. After emptying them, Alfred would clean, sweep and level the area. He would then take the garbage to the "eternal flame" in the *Lazarett*, where it would be incinerated together with the corpses. Galewski's intent in putting his personal aide to this task was to augment the number of men at work in the functional area of the camp, apart from the Germans' servants. These workers had free run of the heart of Treblinka while neither arousing suspicion nor incurring danger.

To execute his plans under appropriate cover, Galewski took Alfred (who spoke fluent German because he was German-born) to Kiwe of the SS. The two doffed their caps and stood at attention before the officer. In his humble opinion, Galewski said, someone had to be given responsibility for cleanliness and order in the camp, since the Ukrainians were dirtying the area to no end. The idea appealed to Kiwe; he nodded his approval. Galewski then suggested Alfred as the man to entrust with the functional part of the camp.

From that very day, Alfred roamed the camp day in, day out with his garbage stroller. The kommandant's plan was to use the servant boys to reconnoitre the Germans' huts, while Alfred would serve as liaison between them and the camp.

This marked the birth of a well-organized underground and the first step in planning the Treblinka rebellion. All previous schemes, such as Dr. Choronzhitzki's unsuccessful attempt to buy weapons – had fallen through. Now the plan was simple: on a day when a maximum number of Germans were on furlough and a minimum number of Ukrainians were in the camp, the servant boys would unlock and empty the arsenal. They would move the weapons to predetermined locations in the camp, the first being the potato kommando area opposite the Germans' huts and the functional structures. It would be rather easy to hide them there. Then the boys would move the weapons out and distribute them to prisoners throughout the area.

A prisoner nicknamed Malpa had access to various wirecutting tools in the storage area. The prisoners, each singly, so as not to arouse suspicion, would walk to the storeroom during the afternoon break and obtain tools – pliers, axes, hammers, even kitchen knives previously buried in the ground – with which they could not only cut the wire but kill our butchers as well. Each of us would have a sum of money or gold – which we would need if we succeeded in escaping the camp.

According to the plan, the boys, immediately after moving the weapons to all the predetermined points, would hurl grenades into the Germans' living quarters as our drivers and mechanics set the Germans' cars ablaze. The *Baukommando* prisoners would have to cross the fence along the Germans' huts to an armored vehicle which was permanently stationed at the main gate. They would seize the car and open the gate. Most of the prisoners would not receive rifles; they would set fires wherever they happened to be when the insurrection broke out.

It was August 2 1943, a date I shall never forget. The trees in the functional section of the camp stood motionless. A cloud of smoke and a nauseating stench hovered overhead, both wafting from the charred and rotting bodies of the gas chamber victims. It was a singular and unique day, one which we anticipated and hoped for. Our hearts pounded with the hope that maybe, just maybe our long-nurtured dream would come true. We harbored no thoughts of ourselves and our lives. Our only desire was to obliterate the death factory which had become our home.

We rose from our bench/beds, excited, tense, anticipating. Thousands of thoughts raced and collided in our heads. Far beyond the fences, a glowing world displayed itself to us in its wonderful colors as the sun crept into the blue, innocent sky. The first light of day revealed the full horror of our humiliation and misery in the depths of the abyss named Treblinka.

By the time that day was out, that accursed hell, hidden deep within the wilderness, would present a different face. As we gulped down our last meal, we may not have reflected on this. Neither did we imagine that we were perhaps standing at our last prisoners' roll call and that we were about to face our last day of toil and enslavement.

Utter silence reigned in the camp. The familiar sentries were positioned on the watch towers, as usual, fixing languid eyes on us. SS men hurried about the area just as they did every day. Nothing at all hinted at the future about to unfold here.

The silence was meant to fool our enemy. Down to the last man we thirsted for revenge, harboring rage and murderous hate in our hearts. With great difficulty we plastered polite smiles on our faces as we greeted the murderers.

Smoke rose from the *Todeslager*, as usual. Routine conversation went on all around, and the woodmen's axes produced their dull whacking sound to the accompaniment of the workers' normal cheers of encouragement. The Germans, ordinarily so suspicious, were off their guard this time. They did not imagine that a prisoners' insurrection was about to break out this day.

Zero hour was set for 4:30 p.m. At 3:30, Alfred appeared beside the structures, pushing his ubiquitous stroller and its load of garbage. Now and then he stopped to gather some more. He approached our woodcutting squad (no work in the forest that day), motioned to me with his head. I turned, noticing a large pile of cut logs. I joined Alfred behind it, placing ourselves out of the view of a *Wachmann* on duty beside the gate leading to the vegetable patch. Alfred whispered that he was heading for his predetermined position, adding that the rebellion would begin in another half hour. Pushing his stroller again, he continued toward the potato *Kommando*. A few minutes later I approached *Vorarbeiter* Kleinbaum and asked him what time it was (prisoners were not allowed to carry watches; this privilege was reserved for *Vorarbeiters* alone). Twenty to four, he said: in another twenty minutes I would race to the Ukrainians' hut for the weapon which the boys in the potato squad were to bring me. Impatiently I waited, tense from head to foot.

Then, without notice, Suchomil of the SS appeared, riding a bicycle down the path along the fence. Suchomil, a German from Sudetenland, was in charge of the *Goldjuden*, the group which handled the plundered precious metals. He inspected the Ukrainians' positions along the fence, passed the *Wachmann* at the gate to the vegetable garden, and disappeared in the direction of the death camp. Shaken by this unexpected visit, we recovered slowly. A few minutes later the potato men appeared, bearing two rifles which had been excellently concealed in a pile of work tools and rags. Two men began to struggle for possession of one rifle. Then we heard an explosion from the direction of the Germans' huts. The Ukrainian at the gate to the vegetable patch let loose a burst of gunfire. One of our men returned fire; the Ukrainian fell lifeless at the fence. I seized the second rifle and ran to the Germans' compound. I could see rifles protruding from the windows of the Ukrainians' huts, firing into the southern part of the forested area. The reverend stood behind one of the trees, firing at the Ukrainians. A group of prisoners, including many *Hofjuden*, ran toward the open gate opening into the vegetable patch. Men of the potato kommando joined us a momemt later. As the hail of gunfire gained in intensity; other prisoners followed us toward the gate.

We heard thunderous explosions from the garage; tongues of fire soared over the trees, mounting with each passing moment. These originated in the gasoline drums positioned between the railroad platform and the Germans' huts. They had been ignited, according to the plan, by two Jewish mechanics. A pillar of fire burst from the garage and towered overhead. The Germans' huts burned in a devil's dance. The dry pine branches we had inserted in the fence burned as well, giving the fence the appearance of a giant dragon with tails of fire. Treblinka had become one massive blaze.

Beside the men of the potato squad I saw a little children's stroller, overturned. Recognizing it as Alfred's, I looked for my friend. There he was, prostrate beside the fence as if in firing position. Reaching him on the run, I found his head slumped to the left and oozing great quantities of blood.

The reverend grabbed me and pulled me through the gate. We ran from tree to tree, firing, until we reached the pile of logs we had downed previously. While firing, the reverend crumpled to the ground beside the pile of logs, struck in the leg. I leaped on him, and our eyes met. He showed no fear — only a last will and request. His pale lips trembling, he begged: "Katzap, finish me off – in the name of He in whom you do not believe."

I gestured at the death camp. "Look over there", I said. "There are your wife and children."

As he squinted at the gate between ourselves and the death camp, I pushed my rifle to his head and squeezed the trigger.

Now I ran with the others toward the vegetable garden gate. Reaching the fence, a horrifying sight greeted me: masses of human corpses strewn between the tank obstacles. Dead prisoners stood erect like tombstones; thick masses of human bodies leaned against the obstacles and the barbed-wire fences.

Machine gun fire continued to rain relentlessly from the guard towers. As I skipped across the bodies of my dead comrades, I suddenly felt a jolt of pain in my leg and a sharp blow. My shoe filled with blood. I had been hit in the leg. Limping, I reached the railroad track, crossed into the forest and resumed running. We encountered a girl from a nearby village. She looked at us as if at apparitions from another world. I began to shout madly: "Hell is burnt to the ground! Hell is burnt to the ground!"

Leaving the tracks and crossing the road, we entered the marsh area. Concealed by treetops, we ran as a disciplined group of several dozen men. As we approached a village, the group split – one party to the right and the other to the left. Only I, acting thoughtlessly, went through the village. Once past it, I plunged again into the depths of the forest.

I was alone, terribly thirsty, and dressed only in a shirt and pants. One of my shoes was filled with blood; my leg throbbed horribly. I removed the cap from my shaven head.

33

The Escape

How long had I run after the breakout from Treblinka? What distance did I cover that day? Where did I summon the strength for the long, grueling trek after having been wounded? I hardly know, and cannot explain. I only remember crossing a railroad track in one place and a road in another, wandering in the forests and stumbling through swamps and waterlogged earth.

In the end I emerged from the forest. I broke off a large branch, held it on my shoulder and strode through open territory. Though I was wounded, the injury was no great impediment. Even if I stumbled now and then, my will to live ordered me to distance myself quickly from the danger zone. Night had fallen by the time I reached the marshy bank of the River Bug. With difficulty I dragged myself to the village of Wolka Nadbuzna. I heard cows mooing in their barns, the sound of water being pumped from a well, a group of children wandering about the village streets. Weak light illuminated house windows.

I knocked at the first house I saw and asked for a clean piece of cloth and some iodine. The cloth was available; no iodine. They dressed my wound, and the relief was immediate. The peasant asked from where I had wandered in. I told him I had just been released from a Polish labor camp to which I had been sent as punishment. This provoked a torrent of questions and names. One woman inquired about one of her relatives; someone else asked if, by chance, I had met a man named Jakobowsky. A third man was concerned about his brother. Quite a few men had been released, I explained; they'd certainly come home tomorrow, if not today.

One of the men apparently had sympathy for me. He led me along a narrow lane to the riverbank, where a wooden plank served as a bridge. I crossed over to a small island, which was completely enveloped in reeds, bushes and water foliage. I lay down and immediately fell asleep – only to wake up in terrible discomfort. Mosquitoes had attacked every exposed spot on my body and produced stinging wounds.

Across the river I heard the voices of men talking. One spoke Russian or Ukrainian. I heard a few shots. Then the men went away and left me again in silence. Despite the aggressive mosquitoes, I slept until daybreak.

That morning a peasant appeared on the island and was very surprised to see me. Approaching me, he asked how I had slept. I answered reluctantly and looked at him with distrust. The peasant, however, had nothing malicious in mind. Apparently aware of who I was and how I had reached the island, he told me that the Germans were scouring the whole area and that they had mobilized the entire garrison force in the Malkinia, Sokolow Podlaski and Siedlce areas. They were checking the identity of everyone on the roads and were searching villagers' homes; they had broken into his that night. Now they were proceeding to the upper stretch of the river. I lay on the island several hours longer, until my hunger and thirst became truly irksome. I drank from the river, bathed, and slowly began to move on.

I had no clear plan of action. Relying on intuition alone, I went in the same direction as the search parties, and advanced in their wake. At the first village I reached, I again told of my liberation from a labor camp, mentioning some names I had heard in Wolka and thus earned the peasants' trust. Though I was well received, they clearly wanted to be rid of me as quickly as possible. I accepted some food and went on.

Reaching another village toward evening, I approached a group of peasants who were arguing about something in the street and asked for a place to spend the night. Startled, they refused categorically and, to make sure I could not repeat my request, dispersed to their homes.

I struggled on. I encountered someone else, issued my plea again, and received another absolute refusal. I wandered about the village until dark, and settled down in a silo for the night. While making myself a "bed", I suddenly felt I was lying on someone. By moonlight I recognized one of my comrades from the Treblinka escape, a Jew from Grodno, who was disguised in a large hat which concealed his face.

At daybreak I discovered that at least four men had slept in the silo. No one said a word. Each of us terrified of the others, we headed in our respective directions without farewells of any kind.

I spent the day meandering like a fox in a hunt – dragging myself across fields, skirting marshes, stopping at the edge of villages or farms – smelling danger and the possibility of betrayal each time. My wounded leg bothered me, but I doggedly kept going. I wanted to put the greatest distance possible between myself and the incinerated death camp; I would give society a try later. I had concealed a $100 bill in one of my shoes. That would suffice for proper clothing and provisions for quite some time.

At sundown I reached a village once again. Approaching a group of young men congregated around a silo, I asked them what the village was called. "Radosc", someone replied, and the group broke into wild laughter. Radosc means "mirth" in Polish, and I understood I was being mocked.

I turned to the spokesman in impudent rage: "And you, you son of a bitch: what regiment did you serve in? I was in the 66th Infantry."

He lowered his eyes in shame; the others, too, were discomfited. One of them showed me the way, advising me to follow the path because it was safer. I went in the direction he suggested and followed the path several kilometers into the forest.

There, at the edge of a clearing, stood a little country house surrounded by an old black wooden fence. Weak light came through its window. I knocked gently, and, hearing no answer, opened the door and entered a large room. On its wooden floor sat a young woman with a little boy. She stared at me in fright. When I asked for something to drink, she gathered herself up slowly, went to a cupboard and took out a loaf of dark bread, some cheese, and a hunk of butter wrapped in green leaves. She placed these on a wooden table and, gesturing, invited me to eat. Starving, I pounced on the feast – the best I have ever had.

The women took the little boy behind a partition; returning alone a moment later, she seated herself at the table facing me and observed my wild dining with pleasure. Now satiated, I said I did not know how to thank her.

"You must be from..." she said in a country accent, pointing in an uncertain direction.

I understood that she suspected me of having escaped from Treblinka. I nodded in confirmation.

She approached me. I stood up, and our bodies drew close. I felt the touch of her firm breasts and I embraced her gratefully. Our mouths met in a passionate kiss. She put out the kerosene lamp; darkness closed in.

The next morning she sent me on my way. Walking through a dense and very beautiful forest, I reached the road leading from Treblinka to Siedlce around noon. The sight of soldiers in armored vehicles, stopping and checking all travelers, greeted my eyes.

I approached the next village from behind and planned to cross the road at a run. As I sized up the scene carefully, someone grabbed me by the shoulder and asked: "Who are you?"

"I'm returning from a work camp", I answered without thinking.

My assailant was a tall peasant. Maintaining his hold on my shoulder, he studied me up and down. With a sudden and sharp motion I wriggled out of his grasp and, with lightning speed, whipped out a kitchen knife and slashed his hand. He leaped aside and I leaped across the road, plunging into a side alley. Only then did I slow down.

I spotted a sign on one of the houses: "Doctor". Without giving the matter much thought, I went in. A young woman was waiting inside. I told her I had to see the doctor. When she explained that he was not in, I asked her for a bandage and some iodine. As we talked, the door opened and an elderly man appeared. The physician admitted me to a little clinic, seated himself at a table laden with papers, put on his glasses and peered at me suspiciously.

"What is your problem, sir?" he asked.

"I've got a very little problem", I replied, "a leg injury. Can you bandage it?"

It was no easy matter to remove the shoe from my massively swollen leg. Congealed blood caked the rags around the wound; these, too,

I struggled to remove. He examined the wound carefully, and did not seem surprised. He could only wash the area and wrap it in a temporary bandage, he explained. I agreed to all of this. Before he began to apply the bandage, he opened his record book:

"Name?"

"Not important", I answered.

Without a word or a comment, he carefully washed the wound, bandaged it and helped me squeeze the shoe back into position. Though plainly suspicious, he wanted to know nothing. His greatest wish was that I should disappear from his house as fast as possible. Before I left, he gave me directions to the railroad. Back on the street, I saw a peasant wagon creaking under a company of Polish police. Beside them were several of my partners in the escape, bound in barbed wire. Once again I was warned of the need to behave with caution and act in cold blood.

On the fourth day, progressing with great difficulty, I reached Skibniew, a large village which had a grocery store and a church. I approached the latter. A woman caretaker dressed in black opened the door and looked at me suspiciously. I greeted her politely and asked to see the priest. He appeared at the door, obviously on his way out. Instead of inviting me in, he turned with me toward the exit, via the garden. I asked for a few zlotys for a train ticket. In reply, he stammered (it was the first time in my life I saw a priest stammer; it was plainly a consequence of my appearance) that all he could give me was a blessing for a safe voyage.

I decided to try my luck at the little grocery. Fearful and anxious of what awaited me inside, I entered. It was strange, after a year in the death camp, to find myself all at once in a shop filled with the aroma of foodstuffs. I had no small change on me whatsoever, did not dare uncover my dollars, and was ashamed to ask for a handout. Behind the counter stood a lovely young girl. I stood bashfully at the door and waited for all the customers to leave.

"And what for you, sir?" she finally asked.

"A glass of water."

She disappeared for a moment, returning with a full glass of water which she handed me without a word.

"Is the train station far from here?" I asked, returning the glass.

"At Kostki – no more than half a kilometer."

The shop was empty. The girl looked at me with interest and a shadow of pity.

"Are you a fugitive, sir?" she asked.

"Yes."

"They've already searched here. And how", she said. "A whole gang of them came here. They looked for Jews in our home; they wanted to arrest my brother just because he had shaved his head. The village head had to testify that he'd done it not because he was a fugitive but because he was just crazy."

I listened to her story, thanked her for the water, and looked for an opportunity to slip out of the shop. But the girl stopped me, approached and slipped twenty zlotys into my palm.

"How can I ever repay you?" I whispered. "If you'd be so kind, please sell me a few cigarettes with the money you just gave me."

Laughing merrily, she wrapped fifteen cigarettes and a packet of matches into a little package which she handed me. Then she pointed in the direction of the station. The train to Siedlce set out at 5:00 a.m., she added; I should sleep in the field to the right of the road leading to the train station, where they had harvested the rye and left a pile of fresh straw. I thanked her again and went to the place she had described. I looked around. No one had pursued me. I walked into the field, uprooted a few shoots of straw, burrowed into the great heap, wriggled in and closed the opening with the straw. When night fell, I emerged and enjoyed the silence of an enchanting August night.

Suddenly a shadow approached from the direction of the village. I dropped to the ground and studied the intruder. It was a woman. As she came closer, I realized it was the young girl who had directed me to this place. I stood up to let her see me. She joined me at the base of the heap, and, shyly, said she had brought me some food. She pulled some salami, bread and white cheese in a newspaper from a basket. I thanked her, touched by her concern. Our hands met, and, amid the mingled scents of cut rye and wild foliage, I sensed the odor of her young body. Innumerable twinkling stars lit up the sky.

The next morning I was awakened by the voices of women hurrying to the train station. Some of them were carrying large packages.

Joining them, I volunteered to help one of the older ones. Would she speak to me in the informal second person and let me call her "Aunt"? I asked. She was amenable to this, and even bought me the train ticket I needed. Though I trembled violently as I boarded the train, luck went my way this time and I reached Siedlce with no special problems. The place I feared most was the station building, which I would have to cross. To my good fortune, however, the train stopped on the outskirts of town and I seized the opportunity to jump off.

My appearance – a dirty white shirt, trousers and boots, shaven head – was inauspicious. Pulling my cap down carefully, I set about the next task: finding someone with whom I might reasonably exchange my dollars – my entire capital. I truly hoped to meet my father in Siedlce, where he had gravitated from Opatow. Despite everything I had gone through, I remembered his assumed name: Karol Baltazar Penkoslawsky. Making inquiries at City Hall, I was sorry to find that his name did not appear in the local population registry.

Sticking to narrow side streets in an effort to avoid any encounter with German troops, I saw a doctor's sign. The pain in my injured leg so afflicted me that I was willing to risk another visit to a physician. The lengthy wait allowed me to concoct a new cover story by the time I entered: I had escaped from a POW camp in eastern Prussia, and had been shot and wounded while crossing the border at the River Bug. The doctor asked in what regiment I had served and where I had been taken prisoner. The 66th Infantry, I answered; I had been captured near the town of Kutno. In a flash I recalled that the bloodiest combat during the battles of 1939 had taken place exactly there. As we talked, the doctor examined my wound, nodded his head, and stated that I had been very lucky that gangrene had not set in. The bullet had lodged in a muscle, and should be removed as fast as possible. He could not do the operation, however, because its aftermath would require several days' bed rest for which he had no room. In other words: out of the question.

"But I have some good medicine for you."

He called his wife and asked her to make me breakfast. He led me into the kitchen, where the three of us ate heartily. Thanking him for his hospitality, I went to the marketplace to exchange my peasant's boots for simple soldier's shoes, cheaper footwear which would leave me a balance in cash. Indeed, after making this deal I came away with 120 zlotys. Feeling much better with the money in my pocket, I headed for the train station.

At the waiting room I immediately noticed a poster informing the public of the escape of three hundred Jewish bandits. After warning the public not to help the fugitives, the poster noted that the company included infected victims and bearers of typhus. One could immediately recognize the escapees, it added, by their shaven heads. I fled.

Dangerous as the train station was, I realized it was more dangerous still to stay in this little town, where everyone knew one another. I returned to the station cautiously, mingling with the crowd which pushed its way to the cashier's booth, and bought a ticket for Warsaw. With two hours to kill, and to avoid the risk of encounters with local people, I lay down on the grass behind the station. Joined there by other vagrants, I relaxed a little.

When the train put in, the crowd stormed the cars as if launching an attack. Most of the passengers were speculators bearing heavy loads of *rombanka* – chunks of pork – and were obviously regular travelers on this line. They knew each other, and as the trip proceeded they gorged themselves and swilled *samogon* – home-made vodka. These were the suppliers of food for the Polish capital. As the train slowed before every station, they looked around fearfully, lest German gendarmes or Polish police appear and confiscate their goods.

A woman seated in a corner of the car stood up, forced her way through the mass of people and stopped in the middle of the central aisle as the speculators cried "Let the countess through!" She was an older woman, a tall specimen with dyed fair hair and heavy makeup. A massive harmonica dangled from her neck and covered her entire chest. She gave her companions a haughty glare, as if contemptuous of the scene, like a great actress who had chosen for the moment to go "slumming". After riffing a few chords she began to sing a tune of some kind, accompanying herself on the harmonica. Though her voice was hoarse and alcoholic, it and her accompaniment were perfectly in tune. When she finished her concert, the passengers burst into enthusiastic applause, showered her with generous tips, and, as she moved away, shouted "Attagirl, Countess. See you next time!"

At one point a woman in fastidious dress boarded the train with her blonde-haired, blue-eyed daughter. As the girl stood beside me and I studied her slender face, my eyes fogged over: I saw my little sister. Memories flooded me; the passengers vanished in a haze. Tears began to pour down my sunken cheeks. The women around me noticed my agitation and asked what me what had happened. Where was I from? Where was I heading? I repeated the German POW camp story, and everyone in the car shared my anguish. When I said I was heading for Warsaw, people began advising me to change my plans. One woman offered to put me up in Wlochy, near Warsaw; another invited me to her home in Rembertow. I chose the latter.

34

Rembertow

I followed my new benefactor to her flat, two rooms and a kitchen in a miserable wooden house on the main street of Rembertow. The landlady looked old and sick, her son, about fourteen, looked like an adolescent hooligan, and her daughter, a sixteen-year-old in lipstick, rolled her blue eyes around as if she had already mastered the world's oldest profession.

As we sat down for lunch, the mother informed me that, to her great sorrow, her oldest son was not at home but would surely arrive soon. In the meantime, she offered me the single bed in one of the rooms; the rest of the family would make do in the second room and the kitchen.

During the night I heard the sound of a door opening, followed by whispering voices. I hurriedly put my pants on and walked into the kitchen. There I saw my benefactor warmly greeting a younger man who had just then arrived – the oldest son. When they saw me, the mother said to her son: "You see, Antosh? That's our fighter who escaped from the P.O.W. camp."

He was a man of about twenty, with fair hair and blue eyes. A long scar ran down his face from ear to mouth, lending him a strange appearance. He put out a hand and clasped mine firmly; I returned the pressure. Studying me intently with little, cunning eyes, he asked where I was from. We appraised one another like two dogs. I knew whom I was facing. His behavior and posture gave him away as a *bandzior* – a street criminal. Addressing him in the Powisle dialect used in a certain part of Warsaw, I replied that I had escaped from a *Stalag* (luckily he did not ask me which, and where) and fled across all of eastern Prussia as far as the river Bug, where I had taken a bullet in the leg while slipping across the border. He asked me if I had papers. I answered in the negative.

"If you had money", he said, "I could arrange a false *Kennkarte* for you."

That meant an ID card. I asked him how much this would cost, and he answered: about two thousand zlotys. Wordlessly I pulled out my $100 bill. Astonished and suspicious, he asked me where I had come upon the money. While crossing the Bug, I explained, I'd caught a Jewboy, searched him and appropriated the money in the process. When he asked me what I had done to the Jewboy, my imagination was spent; I replied that the Germans had begun to shoot at us just then, and I had fled, taking a bullet in my leg as I went. He took my worldly fortune and we headed for bed.

I lay awake all night, wondering about that "nice" boy and what might become of my capital. After breakfast, Antosh extended his hand and said: "Friend, everything'll be all right! I'm going to Warsaw and I'll take care of the papers for you. Just tell me what last name you want." He handed me a pencil and paper. "Ignacy Popow", I scribbled. I knew my mother had papers under this surname and I hoped I would meet her, and that this precaution would enable us to stay together more easily.

Antosh headed for Warsaw, and I spent three tense days waiting for him. He proved a man of his word: he came home and handed me not only a *Kennkarte* but an *Arbeitskarte* – a work permit – and a membership card in Organization Todt. Then he pulled out a black felt pen and smeared some ink on a chip of glass. With this, I fingerprinted my new ID card. All I lacked was a photograph. We went to a photographer. I kept my cap over my shaven head, even facing his primitive camera with the cap still in place. After lengthy preparations, the photographer informed me that he did not make *Kennkarte* photos for people whose heads were covered. After a moment's hesitation I took off my cap, and the photographer studied my bald scalp with a false smile and genuine curiosity. At this point my *bandzior*-escort intervened, telling him to get to work.

I took the photo while it was still wet and we went home. There Antosh pulled out a plier and, with professional skill, attached the photo to my ID with a bit of steel wire. Then he picked up a rubber stamp he had acquired with the *Kennkarte*, moistened it with ink from a red felt pen and, carefully, stamped the photo front and back. Finally he withdrew 4,000 zlotys from his pocket – the change from my $100, he explained.

Now equipped with papers and money, I wanted to go to Czestochowa. Antosh objected: my clothes would arouse suspicion. He offered me a few jackets, one of which fit me. They had apparently belonged to uniforms which had been dyed black.

"You're like a shop", I smiled. "You've got everything."

"What do you think? When the Germans murder the Jewboys, there's pretty good money to be made."

"How?" I asked, trying to force the terror out of my voice.

"I walk around Warsaw and look to every side. Suddenly I see this sad sack, and I can't help but notice that he's scared and insecure. I sneak up to him and whisper: 'Hey, Mr. Jew, are we walking around just for nothing this fine day?' Now he's scared all over – his eyes, his face. He begins to stammer, roll his eyes around and say: 'Sir, I'm Polish'. Then I tell him, 'If so, let's find a cop'. Then he's really scared and he says 'Mister, leave me alone'. I say: 'O.K., but let's go into this doorway together'. He goes in. He doesn't believe me and he's scared stiff. What do you think, that he's a big hero? Of course he goes in. There I give him a little shakedown and take everything. Jewboys usually have lots of goodies on them. If he's wearing a jacket, that's good for me. They almost always have green hats. They're good, too."

He pulled a green hat from a hanger and set it on my head. Turning around, I saw his mother looking on. With a smile, she assured me that it fit. She offered me a broken mirror so I could see for myself, and I turned the hat this way and that so my terror would not show.

I asked Antosh if he had any other sources of livelihood. In response, he whipped a pistol out of his pocket and gestured at it: "This is the best livelihood of all. Don't forget that we're living in Rembertow, where the Germans rehabilitate all the Ukrainians, White Russians,

Lithuanians, Latvians, and even Russian P.O.W.s. When these monsters recover – they're just skin and bones when they're brought from
the camps – they're sent to the Russian front a few weeks later. When
these bastards realize they're about to be shipped out, they sell
everything for money to buy vodka. They know they won't come
back from the Russian front alive. You grab one of these and buy
everything off him – uniforms, blankets, handguns, even rifles. But
transporting rifles is a problem, so we usually saw off the barrels.
When I have a chance to buy a submachine gun, it's worth doing
because you get a few thousand for the barrel, depending on whom
you sell it to. That's how you live under occupation! If you want,
you can make some money with us. If you get a customer you'll make
more. But remember, don't start up with the underground. Those
characters want everything free, see? And the most important thing
– don't say a word to anyone about having a source of weapons. If
you come alone, I'll always give you merchandise even without money,
because I trust you. Just don't bring strangers here."

The next day I made my farewells and took my first trip to Warsaw.
Avoiding the city itself, I crossed to a place where I could board
a train for Czestochowa. When the conductor entered the car for an
inspection, I gave him fifty zlotys and asked him if that was enough.
He took the money and warned me that gendarmes boarded the train
at Zyrardow to examine passengers' travel permits. Since I had no
such document, he suggested that I climb onto the roof of the car at
that point. That would be just fine, I answered.

Almost everyone on the train, and everyone in my car, got off at
Zyrardow. On the platform I saw two pairs of gendarmes boarding
the train, one at each end. As the train began to move, I opened the
door leading to the next car and climbed a ladder to the roof. Before
the next station, as the train decelerated, I came down, peeped into
the car and, finding it empty, crossed it to the toilet and locked myself
in. Through a crack in the white-painted window, I saw the four
gendarmes leading two passengers away.

On we went. Quite a few passengers boarded at the next station,
mostly without tickets. They paid the conductor, who apparently split
the proceeds with his colleagues and the engineer. Now, as the train

slowed down for its approach to Czestochowa (a trick employed by willing railroad workers during the war), people with packages and bundles jumped. At the station itself, they knew, gendarmes would confiscate any food in their possession. I, too, jumped from the car and walked downtown.

I turned onto Kosciuszko Street and stopped at No. 26, where my mother's friend Ella lived. As I recalled the tragedy that had befallen us here, eleven months ago, a frightened old woman opened the door. When I asked if Ella was at home, she pointed at one of the doors. I knocked, and, after a long wait, it creaked open a bit. There stood Ella. She looked at me in terror, admitted me to her room, and, making sure no one was listening, asked: "Samek, where have you come from?"

"From another world", I replied. "From Treblinka".

Something moved beside the bed under the window. There, from a niche, emerged Ella's husband Grossman, an apostate Jew. He struggled to pull himself erect. Agitated, he put out a hand and asked me how I had survived. Without replying, I asked what had become of my parents. They were alive in Warsaw, Ella told me. I sat down, my entire body quaking with excitement.

"Samek, aren't you going to ask about your sisters?"

"No, because I know where they were murdered."

"But you don't know that after they arrested your sisters they arrested me, too. They even put us together. I could not admit that I knew them, because they would have shot me." Ella burst into tears.

Grossman then told how he had hidden in the niche under the window when they came for Ella. At this point I took my leave and wandered about in the yards of abandoned factories. I found people there who fed me but made it clear they did not want me to spend the night with them. Toward evening I went downtown with Ella, to the mansion which had once belonged to the Grossmans. I spent the night there.

Early the next morning I reached the train station and, by nightfall, had returned to Rembertow. As cover, I told my hosts that gendarmes had sought me out at home, making it impossible for me to circulate there. They accepted this story unquestioningly.

Antosh and I walked to Warsaw the next day, each carrying
a handgun. We hiked through forests and groves as far as Wawer,
then took a local train as far as Kierbedzia Bridge. We crossed the
Vistula River and reached Kercelak Square. Antosh felt safer on foot,
explaining that arrests and assignments to work details had become
rife in Warsaw recently. Now he looked around in search of prey,
evidently wishing to impress me with his prowess in robbing Jews.
To my good fortune, he was out of luck. We reached Kercelak Square
and approached a friend of his who traded in guns. Though he praised
his goods to the sky, he did not have even a single "pipe" in stock.

A young man came up to Antosh and asked, in a whisper, if he
had any merchandise, and led us to a sealed-off hut which doubled
as a restaurant. We entered a room filled with people and smoke. It
was hard to see anything; it took a while to notice a bar. Its proprietress,
a Mrs. Jadwiga, served vodka, and the two men settled down to
business. Antosh questioned the customer as to the sort of "pipe" he
wanted. The selection was not generous. He had a Parabellum handgun
of German manufacture, a 6 mm. Belgian handgun known as
"Belgique" and a prewar Polish model called Vis; the latter was the
most expensive of all. The customer finally made his decision. Antosh
vanished, and, returning, handed the buyer his weapon. The deal was
washed down with another large dose of booze. Seeing that the binge
was dragging on and that Antosh had no desire to part from his
friends, I begged their pardon and bid them a warm goodbye. I wanted
to hurry to City Hall to try and discover the whereabouts of my parents.

City Hall was across from the Great Theater on Senatorska Street.
Pushing my way into the crowded population registry wing, I obtained
two blank forms; on one I wrote my mother's maiden name, Maniefa
Popow, and on the other, my father's assumed name, Karol Baltazar
Penkoslawski. After a few minutes' wait, a polite clerk returned
shaking her head; the name Maniefa Popow did not appear in her
registry, though there were two Maria Popows – one in Praga and
the other in a suburb named Wola. A Baltazar Penkoslawski lived at
104 Grojecka Street.

I went first to Praga. A strange woman opened the door, and
insisted on proving to me that she, and no other, was Maria Popow.

She could not understand why I disagreed. The scene repeated itself at the second address. One of the "false" Popows referred me to the White Russians' organization for information. But there, too, no one knew anything about my mother. One of the workers, though, did suggest that I join the White Russian Army and fight the Soviets alongside the Germans. "I'll come back tomorrow", I said, and hurried out of the office.

I still had a slip of paper with my father's name and address. It was late; the police curfew was about to begin. The streetcars emptied; only a few travelers rode them across the deserted streets. Gendarmes patrolled this way and that, checking passersby. The penalty for not possessing the proper documents or a permit to be out of doors at this hour was immediate arrest. I, of course, had no such permit, and Antosh's false papers were highly dubious. My shaven scalp and sunken cheeks only magnified the danger.

I reached 104 Grojecka Street on the last streetcar. No one was about. People scurried into their homes or into hiding places where they felt secure. I had nowhere to hurry, nowhere to hide. I moved along uncertainly, fearful of another disappointment.

I located the massive building, went inside and, in the stairwell, encountered the landlady – a woman of about forty who peered through a grille. "Who are you looking for, sir?" she asked.

"Mr. Baltazar Penkoslawski."

"Front apartment, second entrance."

Studying the courtyard, I saw that it was surrounded on three sides by wings of the building and separated from the garden only by a low fence. Examining the territory quickly, I decided to camp out in one of the gardens if my father was not here. The knowledge that I had found a place to spend the night left me feeling better and more at ease.

I climbed the stairs to the middle floor and moved to the right-hand door. The nameplate read "Berkan". Too tired and depressed to imagine that my father might be a subtenant, I headed for the stairs without knocking on the door. On my way out I again encountered the caretaker, who asked, astonished, "What, you didn't find him at home? Mr. Baltazar is usually at home at this time of night!" I reported what I had found. "Of course. He sublets with the Berkans. Perhaps you should try again."

I returned and knocked on the door. It was pulled open cautiously, and there, in a mantle of white hair, was the top of my father's head. Then I saw his deep blue eyes studying me through his glasses. We faced each other in utter silence, in disbelief. We stood thus for some time, without a word. Finally Father recovered, opened the door wide and admitted me.

He led me to his room and, with a motion of his hand, indicated that I was to be silent. Again we contemplated each other without emitting a sound. Suddenly I felt tears dripping from my eyes. Father stood at the corner window, which was covered with blackout paper. He, too, was crying.

In the corner stood an easel bearing a portrait of Jesus in a silken robe. From his chest dangled two straps, one white, one red. At his feet was an inscription: "Jesus, I Believe in You." Beside the easel, on the floor, was an unfinished picture of the Holy Mother of Czestochowa – her face dark, a gold crown on her head, and the two traditional cuts on her right cheek (made with a Swedish sword). She was clutching the infant Jesus. Other unfinished paintings and sketches were all around. The air reeked of oil paint. I knew that smell from childhood; it provoked memories of the days in our happy family home. A few sketches shared a small desk with a loaf of brown bread, a bit of butter, some cheese, and a dirty cup which had been used for tea.

Father, gesturing with eyes and hands that we must maintain our silence, pulled a sharpened fine-point pencil from a desk drawer. This, too, reminded me of childhood. He would always sharpen the pencil with a little knife; he despised sharpeners and those who used them. He pulled out some paper and, in his beautiful penmanship, began to communicate: "Samek, where were you?" "Treblinka", I whispered, and asked "Where's Mother?" Hastily he wrote that Mother was alive and that he was posing as a mute because of his halting Polish, which, when thugs had attacked him, had revealed him as a Jew. He explained to me, again in writing, that his accent was in fact Russian, acquired during his years of study in St. Petersburg. These days, however, anything which sounded foreign was considered Jewish. It was best, he realized, to go mute. He had printed up a "business card" of sorts which testified to this; the disability was even recorded on his false *Kennkarte*. From the chaos on his desk he extracted a scrap of cardboard which read: "Accepts commissions for hand-produced oil portraits, from models or photographs. Equal prices for all. Mute professional artist. Sample on display. If you speak to me not too loudly, I hear and understand." The message appeared in Polish on one side of the card and in German on the other.

Taking out a second piece of paper, he explained that he would add his precise address to the card by hand, as he had to move frequently. The last sentence, he added, was necessary because people would shout into his ears so violently that he was afraid of truly going deaf.

Father had become a painter of holy pictures. At times he halted his story and asked about mine, also enquiring whether I had met my sisters anywhere. I shook my head and summed up my story in a few whispered words. First of all, I wanted to know what had happened to him. He resumed his account. He would sell his holy pictures to stores which handled such goods. As for Mother, she was living in a small town named Glowno, near Lodz, where she worked as a laborer in the Norblin arms factory. Though they could not live together because she was under surveillance, she was able to visit him every two weeks. She had already been there that week, but he would telegraph her tomorrow and ask her to come at once.

As his hand raced across the white paper, he gestured to indicate that people were listening behind the door. I understood his apprehension and began to speak loudly: "Mr. Penkoslawski, I am very happy to have found you. My parents send you their warmest blessings! Several days ago we decided to have you do portraits of the whole family. We all miss you. It's good that you're in Warsaw."

Thousands of thoughts flashed through my mind as I delivered this insipid monologue. We were looking at one another, our eyes pouring tears. A few moments later Father left the room and returned with two cups of tea. He continued writing: "I spoke with the landlady and her daughter, an old maid. I told them I was having company, the son of an acquaintance of mine and a pupil as well, a painter who studied with me before the war broke out."

"Me and my great talents", I said, and we exchanged smiles despite the tragedy of it all. Father continued: "To explain your shaven head, I said you'd escaped from a P.O.W. camp. They're dying to see you. We have to visit them."

We went into the big kitchen at the end of the hall, where mother and daughter were waiting for us. The older woman had a large, flat face and no eyelashes. She studied me with curiosity and sympathy. Her skinny daughter, twitching nervously, fixed penetrating, clearly suspicious eyes on me. They invited us to sit down. How had I fared as a P.O.W.? one of them asked. Placidly, in fluent Polish, I answered their questions as my imagination raced.

"I live with my parents in a distant province. Before the war, Professor Penkoslawski would join us at a summer resort and go hunting with my father. My mother wants to order a few portraits of my godfather, a major in the Polish army who was killed at the front."

An experienced storyteller by now, I proceeded to "kill" my uncle on the battlefield, too, assigning him the rank of colonel. This particular version seemed to make a good impression; questions followed one another, and the initial tension slowly dissipated. We spent a pleasurable evening and did not notice that midnight had passed; then we bid farewell and returned to Father's room. We slept in one bed. Thus, alongside Father, I fell asleep securely for the first time.

I woke up to find a gloom permeating the room. Father sat beside me on the bed, his hand on my head. I shut my eyes. It was so good, and so reminiscent of years past. When I was a little boy, Father would lay a hand on my head when he wanted to wake me up. A hunk of cake, I knew, awaited me at the edge of my white wooden bed, a gift which Father had brought from the cafe where he had been the night before. I looked at the edge of my bed now and whispered with a smile: "Father, all we're missing is the cake." With tears in his eyes, he said: "All we're missing are my two daughters."

He went to the kitchen, returned with tea, and indicated that the landladies were about to leave. He took the black paper down from the window and looked into the street. Once he saw the landladies there, he could speak without fear.

Now he asked me to describe everything I had endured in Treblinka, down to the last detail.

"Do you see, Samek", Father said, "how strange man's life is? I, who devoted all my life to the creation of a Jewish painting style, who designed Hebrew letters, who painted synagogues and decorated them with designs I had created and produced typical Jewish characters in paint – now I'm painting pictures of Jesus and the Holy Mother."

"Daddy", I smiled, "you're still painting Jews." The two of us broke into laughter, and he continued:

"I have enough orders. Everyone in this building knows me as a nice old artist – and a mute, too. I've had to pose as a mute since I moved to the Aryan side so my faulty Polish accent does not give me away. Samek, my son, it isn't as easy as you might think. It's hard to be silent for a day, a week or a month. But to survive for a full year this way, as I have, takes tremendous willpower. I've slipped up a few times and had to clear out fast. I've changed apartments four times. When they realize it's a ruse, they realize immediately that I'm Jewish. I haven't always succeeded at being silent. Once, while I was in the middle of a painting and emotionally agitated, the landlady came into the room and asked me to shut the window. I forgot myself for a split-second and said: 'Just a moment.' The landlady was stunned to hear my voice and shouted 'But you speak, sir!' The next moment, she demanded that I get out of the flat. All I had time to take with me was my easel and the wooden chest with the oil paints. I stood helpless in the street, not knowing where to go. I spent the night in an institution for the homeless. Every time my disguise was broken, I paid a heavy price. Often I fell victim to extortion and thievery. I have been in this world for seventy years now, and only at the end of my life have I encountered filth, sub-humanity and cruelty of this sort. As a teacher and an artist in constant contact with beauty, I feel the bitterness of life under occupation more acutely than others."

"One day a Warsaw thug stopped me on the street, dragged me through a doorway and took everything I had, not leaving me with even a miserable kerchief. It was hard to defend myself or call for help, for if the Polish police or the German gendarmes interfered, they would have identified me – and I would have been in mortal peril. Helpless me, with no one to turn to in Poland. All this sent me into a terrible depression, and I contemplated suicide at times."

"When the Warsaw Ghetto burned in April 1943, I could not keep going at home and could not work. I sneaked out of my room and walked the streets of the noisy city toward the Jewish quarter, which was at war. I walked the streets next to the ghetto and absorbed the sounds of combat. I lived the tragedy of the entire Jewish people, prayed silently, heard how the crowd reacted to the sight of the burning ghetto, the adults and children leaping from the upper stories of the burning houses. They expressed sorrow for the burning houses and their contents, but harbored no sadness at all for the people. Samek, it's hard to describe what a hell we're living in. Most of the Polish population hates us. Only a few individuals help, and by doing so they are putting themselves and their families in mortal danger."

Father walked into town, leaving me in his room. He hurried to the post office to send Mother a wire: "Come immediately". Three days later the doorbell rang. Alone, I put on a hat to cover my shaved head and opened the door. There was Mother. She looked at me in disbelief and, as if waking from a dream, rubbed her eyes and whispered: "Is it you, Samek?"

I felt she was about to collapse. I supported her and helped her into the room. She clutched me, and we cried in each other's arms. As we sat in motionless embrace, Mother asked: "How did you get out of there?"

Stunned, I asked: "How do you know where I was?"

"Weissblum told me. He was head of the Judenrat in Sandomierz. When I returned from Czestochowa to Opatow after your sisters were arrested, I found out that most of the Jews in the town were hauled off to Treblinka. Only a few were not – Judenrat members with their families, and a few wealthy families. These were taken to a new camp built especially for them in Sandomierz; they were kept alive there. I went to Sandomierz thinking I would meet you there. When I asked Weissblum where my son was, he told me in shame that you were in Treblinka. He found out about you from one of the young men, Kudlik, who was transported together with you and all the Jews to Treblinka. He'd been pulled out of the transport and sent to a work camp near Treblinka. He escaped from there, returned to Sandomierz and told me he had seen you, that they had pushed you into a hut and that you were still alive. From that moment I knew you were in the Treblinka death camp. I went to Warsaw, taking a few portraits and pictures of saints along. Father printed up a little card saying that I was his agent, that he accepted orders for portraits and sold holy pictures. With all this I went to Siedlce and from there by train to Kosow. The last leg of the trip, as far as the Treblinka area, I made by wagon. The peasants did not want to put me up for the night, and warned me of the rapacious Ukrainians who guarded the Treblinka camp. It was a very dangerous area to wander around in, they said. In a village very close to Treblinka, I noticed a strange and sickening odor. The peasants pointed toward the forest and said there was a death camp behind it and that the odor was coming from decomposing, rotting bodies."

"When it became clear that I could get no closer to the camp, and that I could not find accomodations of any kind, I returned to Warsaw, hoping you were alive just the same."

Mother then asked the question I dreaded: "Did you see your sisters there?"

Having deceived Father, I now deceived Mother the same way: I knew nothing about my sisters, I said. Mother hugged me anew with each passing moment, never taking her eyes off me. She continued whispering: "Samek, Samechek". Only then did it truly dawn on me that I was no longer Katzap of Treblinka. Visions of my dear friends from the camp raced through my head. Alfred, the reverend, Merring, Choronzhitzki and others would never know moments of joy such as these. Perhaps it was an inner yearning for my parents which had kept me going, spurring me to survive the hell of Treblinka at any price. My awareness that they appeared to be alive gave me the strength to endure.

Mother continued whispering to herself again and again in disbelief: "You're alive, you're alive." Then again came the terrible question: "Are you sure you didn't see them?" I shook my head. A glimmer of hope appeared in Mother's eyes. In mine was the sight of my sisters' coat and skirt, next to one another, in the sands of Treblinka.

I spent another few days in Father's flat. Each day, toward evening, we faked my departure for the night. Father would shut the door firmly, for everyone to hear; then he would open it carefully and I would sneak in for the night. In the morning I slipped out quietly, and would return and ring the front bell for public consumption.

One Sunday, Mother came by and took me for a visit with the widow of a noted Polish writer named Galinski. At her house I recognized a journalist who had worked for an evening newspaper in Warsaw before the war. He invited me over the next day to his office, where he introduced me to an elegantly dressed elderly man with white hair and a long mustache. The latter, introducing himself as Henryk (in fact, he was Salo Fischgrund, an activist in the Bund in prewar Cracow) bombarded me with questions about Treblinka. When he asked if I had papers, and I showed him my documents, he wrinkled his nose and offered to arrange new photographs. Finally he asked at length about my father. From that day on, a blonde girl named Zosia would periodically visit our flat on Grojecka Street with a thousand zlotys for me – relief funds for Jews in hiding on the Aryan side.

I began to see Father's portraits in the display windows of the shops which handled sacred goods in Warsaw. A standard version was Jesus with a hand pointing at his heart, from which translucent white and red straps emerged. Father made a relatively good living, and I helped him arrange commissions as best I could. One day, standing in front of one of these shop windows, I noticed two women who stopped beside me, engaged in conversation: "Here our Lord Jesus is so beautiful." "But His clothes are too tight."

Once I understood their intent, I introduced myself as a painter of holy portraits who, together with his professor, lived at 104 Grojecka Street. The women clapped their hands in joy and cried: "You are heaven-sent, sir. We have come especially to order a picture of Jesus for the Church of St. Stanislaus in Siedlce."

We took a streetcar to Grojecka Street and mounted the stairs to Father's flat. Entering his room and observing the canvases of holy pictures strewn here and there, they said the Finger of God had sent me to them. I thought it was not a mere finger but the mighty hand of God which had sent these two women to us. Their advance payment was generous. The painting was to be entitled "Jesus, I Believe in You." Their only request was that the work be "solid". By this, I noticed, they were referring more to high-quality wood and canvas than to the artistic element of the work, as if good wood or canvas determined the qualiity and value of art.

When Father sketched them his own, unconventional Jesus, they shook their heads in dissatisfaction. They wanted Jesus to look the way he did in the shop windows – a popular figure, not a pretentious one. Father, seeing no point in arguing with them, now produced the kind of Jesus they wanted, and the deal was finalized. As the work proceeded, we had a very lively correspondence at first; the matrons from Siedlce literally bombarded us with letters, recalling another detail each time. Once they asked Father to produce a Lord Jesus who would give blessings not with two fingers as Father had portrayed him, but with the whole hand. On another occasion they insisted that Father change the color of Jesus' hair. Though the golden sunrise hue which Father had originally chosen intensified the beauty of Jesus' face, the matrons, visiting us often during the work and overseeing every detail strictly, now wrote us to the effect that the Lord Jesus must be not a redhead but a pure blond. I found these continuous modifications a tremendous nuisance, since I had to pose anew each time.

The most important person in any building during the occupation was the gatekeeper. His conduct spelled life or death for the tenants, and he was a constant menace for Jews. He knew exactly which tenants were registered in the population registry and which were not; he knew who visited whom, and everyone's place of work. Everyone tried to be on good terms with the gatekeeper, for his good will was often the sole obstacle to a tenant's arrest. He could stop German gendarmes or collaborating Polish policemen at the house entrance, and, by engaging them in noisy conversation, warn a tenant that they had come to arrest him – giving him time to escape.

Father and I felt secure where we were. The landlady was often invited to visit, and had seen my father's holy pictures. The frequent visits of our two female customers, who praised the beauty of Professor Penkoslawski's paintings at length, left us in better circumstances and diminished our fear of being fingered as Jews.

One evening, sneaking back to Father's flat before the police curfew set in, I ran into the landlady. She invited me into her flat and began to spew complaints about her husband, an older man. Pointing at the wall, she moaned that he had recently begun pulling the holy pictures (quite a collection) off the wall, whereupon she would hang them up again. I laughed to myself, observing how these people had created a hell in their own home and were dwelling in it.

From our talk I learned that her husband was an Adventist. He had in fact pressured me on occasion to become one of those fanatic examiners of the Holy Scriptures. Not wishing to insult him, I promised I would visit the church with him. One Sunday I went along with him to the church, at 56 Jerusalem Avenue. The problem now was how to patch things up with the landlady, who, as a devout and zealous Catholic, did not care for our joint venture.

I procured a slab of chocolate and, while her husband was off at prayer, visited her at home. We had a friendly chat, and she updated me as to her marital woes. In mid-sentence she grabbed my hand and, with seeming nonchalance, pressed it to her large breasts. Our talk ended in bed, under the holy pictures.

During the passing weeks and months, the problem of personal security robbed me of sleep and peace of mind. It was a life of emptiness, disorder, endless tension and tremendous fatigue. Like many other Jews, I always had the feeling of being under surveillance; I might be recognized at any moment – by a woman I had known, or by an acquaintance from bygone times who, for any reason, might hand me over to the first German he'd encounter, denounce me to the Polish police, or force me to pay him off – because I had succeeded in living. In the moral world of the Nazis' collaborators, my very survival was a matter of exceptional impudence.

My hair had begun to return, and I measured its progress each day by the millimeter. I began to comb; being able to tug at the new hair improved my state of mind. Now I could walk about with greater freedom, even removing the green cap.

One day as I strolled at leisure around Warsaw, I noticed a girl – blonde, blue-eyed, tall and statuesque. Badly wanting to meet her, I asked her how I might reach Zlota Street. With a delightful smile, she answered that this was her destination, too. On the way she told me she was studying in a trade high school, that these courses – like others – existed during the occupation, and that she was rounding off her education with private study. We reached Zlota Street altogether too quickly; shyly, I asked her out. The young student accepted with a naughty smile, and we decided on a time and place for the next day. As we parted, she gave her name: Hanka Kursa. Subsequently we met almost every day, and the world suddenly seemed more beautiful; I had something to look forward to upon awakening each morning.

Just then our landlady caught me spending the night in Father's room and demanded that I either register with City Hall at once or leave the premises. The first choice was no choice; my false documents did not tally with City Hall's official records. In contrast to my father's papers, which were issued by City Hall on the basis of a false birth certificate, my *Kennkarte* was an absolute and uncorroborated fake. My options closed, I decided to find shelter for the night and chose a manhole housing the wires of a regional telephone exchange, protected by a metal lid. I climbed in, pulled the cover down, and spent the night on a blanket in a maze of phone lines. Father knew of my whereabouts; early the next morning, he pounded on the cover with a cane to indicate that that the coast was clear.

Riding a streetcar with Hanka one day, I ruminated about the good life I was living at the moment. When the depressing thought of the approaching night came upon me, however, I felt a need to confess: "Hanka, You really don't know a thing about me, apart from my name, and you never ask for anything else. I am a fugitive Jew, I was in Treblinka..." Before I could finish the sentence, she yelled: "Jump!" I leaped from the streetcar; Hanka followed. Seeing no one around, she approached and began to yell that I was insane. How could I be so reckless as to speak about myself in a crowded streetcar? Was I sick of living? Did I want to be caught?

I told her how I lived, of the nights in the jungle of subterranean phone lines, in the ruins of houses blown up during the battles.

Without interrupting me, Hanka took me to her home and introduced me to her mother as her boyfriend from the underground. The Germans were after me; I could not sleep in my house. Might I spend the night with them? Asking no questions, Hanka's mother laid sheets and blankets on a sofa. I spent a tranquil night in a soft, clean bed.

One day I took the streetcar to a meeting with a man I did not know. I was referred to him by an acquaintance of my father's, who had been a journalist before the war. We were to meet in St. John's Cathedral at 9:00 a.m., on the left-hand side of the chapel. I would recognize the man by his mannerism of alternately and repeatedly standing up and kneeling. I was told to kneel to his left and whisper "My God, my God, my God."

I entered the cathedral at exactly 9:00. In the pastoral quiet, a mass was being held at the main altar for a very small congregation. In the gloom I saw a man of medium height, who kneeled, straightened up and kneeled again several times. I pushed my way to a position between him and two women at prayer. I kneeled, placed my hand on the railing, and whispered the agreed-upon message. The man at my side also rested his hand on the railing and furtively touched mine. A moment later he rose and turned to the exit.

I hurried after him, covering a considerable distance this way until we reached the old section of Warsaw. He entered one of the houses and descended to a basement which was equipped as a tavern. The odor of pickled cabbage and vodka filled the air. The man had selected a table near the door leading into the kitchen — a strategic location, I saw, which would enable a getaway in case Germans suddenly came upon the scene. I immediately sensed, too, that he was a regular customer here. The proprietor, with a fawning smile, brought us two bottles of vodka and a plate of pickles. The man filled his glass and poured it down his throat in one gulp. I did the same. This done, I could study him.

He looked like a simple Warsaw laborer: a dark cap over a bald head, a thick grey mustache under his beak of a nose. His blue eyes had gone glassy with booze, and large scars plastered his neck and the area around his mouth.

When we had downed all the vodka, he asked me to tell about myself. When I took off my hat to introduce myself, he gaped at its fresh pate of peach fuzz. I gave him a brief account of my recent life. When I came to the escape from Treblinka, I noticed a flash of astonishment and disbelief in his calm, glassy eyes.

"Did you break out during the rebellion?" he asked.

"How do you know there was a rebellion there?" I asked. He replied that his people in Malkinia had given him a full report. When I asked him out of curiosity who he was, he disclosed only a *nom de guerre*: Skala (Polish for "rock"). He asked me if I knew how to shoot, and ordered me to report at 4:00 the next afternoon to a grocery store in the court of a certain house on Jerusalem Avenue. A woman in a black beret would be waiting. My instructions were to ask loudly for half a liter of vodka and some pickled salty fish; I should repeat this order several times.

Did I have papers? he asked. When I said they were not good enough to enable me to register at City Hall, he promised me that the woman I was to meet would take care of everything. Finally, he warned me that if by chance we should meet anywhere and at any time, I must treat him as I would a total stranger. When I offered to pay for the food and drink, he refused, saying that everything was covered, and walked out.

I went to the secret rendezvous the next day. Seeing nothing but normal traffic in the street, I stepped through the doorway of the specified house. A crowd of customers pushed about the tiny grocery, placing orders vociferously. Considering wartime conditions, the shop was rather well stocked. After hesitating for a moment, I shouted my order – my signal for the anonymous woman in the black beret – over the heads of the customers. I repeated it several times. No one cared.

At my side was a woman who noticed my unsuccessful efforts with something which looked like pity. I was in a strange situation; I saw no woman in a beret, and stood there helplessly without knowing what to do. Suddenly the woman beside me rose on tiptoe and kissed me on the mouth, as if we were old friends. Seeing my amazement, she said: "You see it's full of people here. Why wear out your throat for nothing more than pickled salty fish? What you really need is a bottle of vodka." Ignoring the crowd and the commotion in the shop, she asked someone in the back to take down a half-liter of vodka and pass it to me over the customers' heads.

The pleasant and energetic woman, whose name was Stefa, now pushed me out of the shop and led me to a nearby house. Here we entered a little workshop, where her father made rubber stamps. It was next to their flat, and Stefa's room was next to the main door. She offered me a drink and a few delicacies, and while I downed them she bombarded me with questions. Was I Jewish? I did not look it, she ruled with expertise. Did I have a weapon, and did I know how to use it? How was I making a living? I told her I got along by selling my father's paintings, and anything else that came my way.

When I finished the story, she reached into a leather purse she had laid on the floor, pulled out a blood-caked rag, and unfolded it to reveal a German handgun – a Parabellum. She handed the weapon to me, recounting haw she had been stopped by German gendarmes on her way to our meeting. When they opened her purse and saw the bloody rag, they shouted "*Raus!*" in disgust and let her go. Her fears, fortunately, had proven unfounded. As I lit her a cigarette, she leaned toward me and rested a hand on my leg. Smiling innocently, she asked: "How are you doing with women? Bet you haven't had any in awhile." I embraced her and covered her mouth with hot kisses.

When I stood up to leave, she reminded me that the handgun would be mine for a few days only.

"During that time", she said, "you've got to get a handgun of your own."

"How?"

"Very simple: the 'hands up' method. You wander around Warsaw, looking for a German who's just walking down a quiet side street, and you grab his weapon. The first gun you confiscate will be yours; all the rest you give me. You need a girl for this work. Can you think of one, or should I find you one? It's best to find your own."

I told her I would think of someone but had to be sure. Now she added another admonition: "Don't kill Germans without good reason, for they shoot hundreds of innocent people for every casualty of their own."

"Shoot only in self-defense. If you don't obey these instructions, the AK will mark you for execution." The AK, I knew, was the rightist Polish underground.

I still had some questions: "Where am I? In which underground? In whose name am I acting? Who was the 'laborer' who sent me to you?'"

"He was our commander, and you're in *Polska Armia Ludowa* – the Polish People's Army, or the PAL. Our people have leftist leanings."

I parted from Stefa in a hearty mood, headed for my rendezvous with Hanka and took her to Skaryszewski Park. There I gave her a brief account of my meeting, mentioning that I needed a girl for my activity. She offered her services at once.

I well remember our first operation in Warsaw. I was very tense, keeping my nerves under control only by tremendous willpower. We saw a German stumbling in our direction, as if drunk. We pretended not to see him and conversed intensely. As he passed directly beside us I whipped out my handgun and hissed in German: "Hands up". Stunned at the ambush, the German sobered up rapidly, began to tremble, and obediently did as told. Hanka approached him from the side and stripped him of his pistol. As she backed off from him, she smiled; we gave him a kick to let him know the surgery was over. As he turned his back and stalked away, we fled.

Within a few moments we heard a big commotion and the German screaming at the next streetcorner. We blended into the crowd and, serenely, continued our walk. Finally we entered a restaurant and ordered pork patties and vodka. The glasses clinked in our trembling hands.

It was early March, 1944. The reports in the German press were better all the time. They spoke of a movement of troops to predetermined positions, and a deliberate shortening of lines at the front. Reading between the lines, we knew the *Wehrmacht* was cracking under Red Army pressure; this, for all of us, augured the end of the war. Now the Germans went around Warsaw setting up loudspeakers (which local residents called "yapping dogs"), over which they broadcast their victories on the eastern front. Occasionally the Polish underground succeeded in sabotaging the network, choking off the barrage of lies and providing some accurate news. These broadcasts, which always opened with "Underground Poland speaking", did wonders for Warsaw's morale.

One fine day that month, a convoy of heavy trucks with thick canvas covering pulled up at 84 Grojecka Street. One of them disgorged dozens of German gendarmes who burst into the court. A few minutes later they came out, leading more than thirty people – men, women and children – into detention.

That evening the gatekeeper of the raided building explained the event: the building served as the hothouse of a gardener, who built under it a shelter where Jews had taken refuge. The gardener's jealous mistress had denounced him to the Germans, who, finding the hiding place, arrested the Jews ... and the gardener together with his entire family. This story spread like wildfire up and down Grojecka Street. A few days later we learned that all the detainees had been shot behind the ghetto walls. Two of them were the Jewish historian Emanuel Ringleblum and his wife.

In the aftermath of this event, our landladies abruptly and vociferously ordered us out of their house. They needed the room for relatives from out of town, they explained. We had no choice but to pack up and start wandering again.

I crisscrossed Warsaw in search of new lodgings, approaching brokers and jotting down addresses in newspaper advertisements. One day I found a flat on Zurawia Street with one tiny room to let. The neighborhood was reasonable, the room was lovely and sun-drenched, and the landlady, an older women, was goodhearted. I liked her very much, as did Hanka, who accompanied me.

As we talked, it came out that the landlady was of noble stock. She told us of relatives whom the Germans had murdered, some at the front and others in concentration camps:

"Nearly one hundred members of my family have been wiped out during the occupation."

All this convinced me that the room was eminently suitable for us. Apart from the fact that it was warm and comfortable, the landlady appeared to be somewhat of a like mind; she, too, had tasted grief and suffering. Then this mature, cultured women commented: "We ought to put up a gilded monument to Hitler for having wiped out and murdered all the Jews." Disappointed and depressed, I walked out.

Hanka tried to console me: "Look at me. I'm Catholic, too, and just the same, I've become a partner in your fate."

We finally found a room with full conveniences in a large, elegant flat at 89 Natolinska Street; the landlady was the wife of a judge. We found a porter with a hand truck and loaded it with our possessions: my father's easel, a few portraits. Most of the space aboard was claimed by a paper mattress filled with straw. Hanka amused herself by photographing the moving operation.

Two weeks passed in our new accomodations, enjoying a comfort we had not known for so long. Thus far the landlady had not mentioned any need to register at City Hall, an omission we found most agreeable. We hoped to live out the rest of the war quietly. Mother visited every two weeks. Hanka moved in with me the first day; together we ran the household and, every few weeks, went out together on our "hands up" activities for the underground, which were not always crowned with success.

One day, after a failure of this sort, I stopped at a restaurant on Filtrowa Street for a cheap bowl of soup. An old man with long white hair was seated at one of the tables. I was stunned by his resemblance to a Treblinka prisoner named Wiernik.

I approached him: "Excuse me, sir, but have we met by chance?"

Obviously disquieted, he looked at me and answered in measured tones: "It could be. I'll join you in a moment."

I returned to my table, but our conversation there never took place. My acquaintance vanished like a shadow.

A few days later I encountered him face to face on Jerusalem Avenue, walking along pensively with an axe in his hand. Now I was sure I knew my man.

"Sir", I shouted. "Are you a carpenter?"

"Yes."

"Don't you recognize an old friend? Don't you remember?" I lowered my voice. "I worked in the *Tarnungskommando*." Then, in a whisper, I added: "In Treblinka".

Only then did his apprehension and suspicion melt away. After a warm and lengthy embrace, we shared with each other our experiences in the camp and following the escape. As we spoke, he mentioned that a book he had written – *A Year in Treblinka* – had been published by the underground.

One day, as Hanka and I walked down Nowy Swiat Street, we sensed someone following us. I sneaked an apprehensive look at the pursuer, ready to flee at any moment if the situation turned dangerous. The thought that detectives were on my trail gave me no rest. I felt the handgun in my pocket. Suddenly I heard the suspicious figure whisper my nickname from Treblinka: "Katzap, Katzap". I turned around in astonishment and saw a young man with blond hair, laughing. I recognized him immediately. It was Zygmunt Stravchinski, a Treblinka prisoner, one of the camp metalworkers – a good friend and much more. We entered the first doorway and kissed each other with joy. Though Hanka did not understand what had transpired, the three of us immediately headed for our flat, where we, together with my father, celebrated the unexpected reunion.

Events followed one another much more swiftly than we had thought. The new Red Army offensive brought masses of Russian soldiers to the outskirts of the Polish capital. The dull thud of artillery shells reached our ears with increasing frequency. Squadrons of Russian planes appeared overhead. The streets of Warsaw were increasingly clogged with convoys of the wounded and war-weary; wagons hitched to horses collapsing with exhaustion passed through day and night. Filthy, unshaven and deathly-tired German soldiers sweated in broken-down cars. Nothing remained of their previous arrogance and pride; now they felt the war in their bones. The people of Warsaw took to the streets and, smiling, contemplated the remnants of the haughty Wehrmacht. Jokingly, they called the procession "Hitler's funeral".

The final act of the drama approached. No one, however, imagined the devastation it would bring upon Warsaw.

35

The Warsaw Uprising

In tense anticipation we in Warsaw awaited the Red Army offensive as it developed to the east. The echoes of the Russian artillery and Katyusha missiles reached our ears as the inferno bore down on the Polish capital.

On the afternoon of August 1, 1944, the sustained wailing of air-raid sirens engulfed Warsaw in terror. An air raid, everyone thought at first. Observing the street, I noticed groups of people racing down the sidewalks, pedestrians fleeing in confusion and several figures hurrying toward Koszykowa Street. Several minutes later we heard bursts of machine-gun fire from that direction.

Tensely curious, I bid my father a quick goodbye. Though I also thought it time to part from Hanka, she insisted on joining me. I pulled a pistol and two grenades from my bed, and the two of us ran into the street. One needed no inside information to realize that a rebellion had broken out in Warsaw. Young people ordered passersby to take shelter in house entrances. Armed rebels raced by from every direction, hugging the building walls straight to Koszykowa Street, where the action was taking place. Ukrainians were firing from the windows of a house which had once accomodated a Czech diplomatic representation. I leaped into the entrance of house No. 13 and joined the attacking insurrectionists. A young man beside me, wearing a red-and-white armband, was shooting. Suddenly wounded, he fell to the sidewalk. As the rifle fell from his hand, another youngster grabbed it and took over the position. Two girls with Red Cross armbands loaded the casualty onto a stretcher and whisked him out of the firing zone into the house.

We raced across the street to the front of the house from which the Ukrainians were shooting. Covered by a hail of rebel gunfire, they could not look outside and see us. Though we were exposed to German gunfire from Avenue of the Roses, the Germans' response was weak and ineffective. We advanced along the facade toward the entrance; once we approached the opening, I threw a hand grenade inside. Immediately after the explosion, our group of six dashed into the entrance corridor. Apprehensive of being fired on, I hurled another grenade. The Ukrainians inside stopped shooting. We burst into a ground-floor room, stumbling over the bodies of several Ukrainians on the way. As I ran, clutching my revolver, the door of one of the other rooms opened and a Ukrainian carrying a rifle stepped out. I gunned him down without a moment's thought. Upstairs we still heard sounds of combat, then, a very short time later, complete silence. Though we could hardly believe it, we had taken the house with no losses on our side. We looked outside. The rebels across the street shouted to us. Among them I saw Hanka, who waved joyfully.

Meanwhile, the pace of gunfire from the direction of Avenue of the Roses, in the Germans' quarter, stepped up. As it turned into a shower of lead, we gave up any thought of leaving the building. The apartments were packed with weapons, and we wanted to get the arsenal across the street to the rebels there. Shouting, we asked them to throw us a rope, and, using it, we passed the guns. The only weapon I reserved for myself was what we called a "sprayer" – a submachine gun. I donned a German helmet, attaching a white strip to the back to indicate that I was not a German.

Once night fell, we abandoned the building and left our conquest in the hands of other rebels. "Who are you?" one of the fighters asked. "When I saw that a revolt had broken out," I replied, "I joined the group of fighters closest to me." He ordered me to go to a house on Natolinska Street and report to the rebels' commander.

The commander, wounded and bedridden, was busy giving orders to insurrectionists who had gathered around him. Approaching his bed, I immediately recognized him as the young man who had fought next to me until he was wounded. Was I a member of the AK, he asked, or a volunteer? "A volunteer", I answered. When he asked for my first and last names, I thought it over for a moment and reached the conclusion that, if I were killed, it would be better that my real name was known. "Samuel Willenberg", I answered. When I noticed the curious stares of the company, I added, "I am a Jew, and I was at Treblinka." No one said a word. The commander ordered my name added to the roster of rebels in the Seventh Company under Lotacki.

Because the right side of Natolinska Street ran alongside the Germans' quarter, we were afraid that the Germans would take it over. We therefore had to evacuate the civilians living there. This done, the rebels also left the area, taking up new positions on the left side of the street. We erected barricades, sealed the ground-floor doorways and windows, and positioned guards at first-floor apartment windows down the full length of the street. Our suspicions were well-placed; the Germans swept onto the right side of the street, across from us, and incinerated one house after another.

I had not seen my father for two days. Hanka told me that he had left our apartment and moved to our side.

The other side of the street had become a wall of flame. Suddenly, amidst the crackling of burning buildings and the thunder of shattering windowpanes, we heard the sound of a piano from a first-floor apartment. Someone was playing a Chopin prelude. The wonderful music went on and on, as if the pianist were oblivious to the menace he faced. As the flames reached the first floor, the music stopped. Even so, no one appeared at the window to ask for help. The mysterious musician went unidentified to his fiery death.

We took up new positions a few days later. Now we barricaded Koszykowa Street and fired from there at the German soldiers who had been shooting at us from their quarter. Beside me lay a delicate and intelligent young man who called himself Andrzej. Though we had just met, we immediately became as close as brothers. During the short periods of quiet between exchanges of fire, we conversed like old friends of many years' standing. Unfortunately, our friendship was not destined to survive. We had liaison girls who periodically brought coffee to the positions, and we would quench our thirst during momentary lulls in the fire. Now, as I edged toward the coffee, I heard Andrzej call out in joy, "*Igo, ra...*" That was all he had time to say. A bullet whistled, and Andrzej fell as silently as if he had fallen asleep. A large bloodstain spread across his shirt; he was dead before we could reach him. Moving his body aside, we opened up with a furious and unrestrained fire on the Germans. Second Lieutenant Lis, once a prisoner in Auschwitz, leaped into the middle of the street and began to spray the German side with his little Sten gun. We had to drag him away from this dangerous position by force. With Andrzej's death, I lost one of my closest friends.

As the fighting intensified, we found ourselves being moved from place to place. I was reassigned to the Baptists' house on Redeemer's Square. There we shot at the Germans with redoubled fury, for we saw how the Ukrainians, stones in hand, would break the heads of the unarmed wounded.

The battles dragged on for weeks, and grew fiercer with each passing day. We dug into our assigned positions and held on. In general, one of us would shoot while his comrade slept under the windowsill.

One day, while occupying a position on Marshalkowska Street off Redeemer's Square, we saw a crowd approaching us with fluttering kerchiefs, pleading with us to hold our fire. Afraid that the German tanks were advancing behind them, as had happened before, we waited in great suspense. Men and women, children and the elderly began approaching our positions. There were no tanks in pursuit. Aware of how difficult our food situation was, the Germans had sent us these additional starving mouths to feed. They meant to starve us into surrender.

We were rocked by heavy artillery fire from the suburbs and distant neighborhoods. Chaos broke out as mortar shells caused devastation to property and heavy loss of life. Batteries of very heavy artillery, known as "Big Berthas", shelled us with barbaric cruelty from positions along distant railroad tracks. By day, the *Luftwaffe* systematically strafed street after street. Lovely buildings, palaces, factories – all were slowly reduced to heaps of ruins and piles of stone and sand. Tremendous fires raced out of control throughout Warsaw;

clouds of grey-red smoke towered skyward. By night, flames illuminated the city sky.

Now the Germans torched the houses at 22 and 24 Sixth of August Street, let the ruins cool down a bit, and began to set up attack positions. Had they succeeded at this, they would have cut off the houses between the Sixth of August and Koszykowa Streets from the center of the city. We decided to take these two houses to foil their plans. Following very heavy battles and great losses, we succeeded.

Life in Warsaw proceeded during the siege according to a certain routine. Man, it seems, can adjust to anything. The population of Warsaw got used to daily air raids, artillery shelling, and an endless game of musical chairs in their accomodations. Life was worth much less now than in times of peace. Most people accepted their state at face value and were ready for death at any moment. On Krucza Street trade began to boom in food, dollars, and goods of every possible kind. There was no shortage of quick-fingered entrepreneurs who picked through the cellars of burnt-out amd bombed-out buildings for anything of value. New tragedies developed: children lost their parents, mothers lost their children, the elderly collapsed from exhaustion and malnutrition, medical services and drugs were unavailable. These harsh conditions allowed the fringes of society and the underworld free play; drunkenness spread everywhere, including the ranks of the AK.

One day, after a watch of several hours from my position at the window, I stepped back to a small room to rest a bit. On the way, I passed another room in which I noticed a group of rebels, also at rest; they belonged to a faction which attracted the lower elements of Warsaw society. Looking in, I saw them drinking clear booze from large glasses. They offered me a glass of the precious liquid. As I downed it in a single gulp, a strange taste filled my mouth and my throat went sore. "What is this?" I gasped. The fighters, laughing, answered, "Pure alcohol, home-made." Possessed of this information, I fell into a deep sleep.

I was awakened by a chorus of strange groaning and wailing from the next room. I opened the door onto a frightening sight: six men lying on the floor in various strange positions, frothing at the mouth, eyes rolling ceilingward. I ran to our headquarters on Marshalkowska Street and summoned a doctor. Reaching the room, the physician had nothing to do but verify their deaths. He smelled the remaining liquid in their glasses and determined that they had consumed denatured alcohol. We shrouded the bodies in blankets and, that very day, gave them a military burial.

My guard duty completed, I went to visit Hanka, who – one of the rebels informed me – was looking for me urgently. I crossed Mokotowska Street and headed for a house from which, I knew, a tunnel led to my destination. Still on the street, a group of underground members with whom I was familiar called me: "Igo, come with us". We went out and caught some "pigeon breeders" – Germans who would mount the roofs of houses we had taken and snipe at passersby on the street. Their operations terrorized the population, which had the impression that they were everywhere. People "saw" them everywhere, whether they were there or not.

We climbed some wooden steps to a third-floor apartment on Mokotowska Street. A young member of the underground rifle in hand, stood in front of the door and saluted us as we approached. In the gloom inside, we found a very old woman bent over and trembling with fear; in the kitchen doorway we noticed two young girls, their frightened eyes flowing with tears.

The old woman turned to us and said in fluent Polish: "Honored sirs, we are not your enemies. My husband and I are Poles of German origin. We hate Hitler as you do. The two girls here are not German; they are Jews who are hiding with us."

I looked in curiosity at the two sobbing girls. The rebel sentry, whom I knew as Kazik, was aware that I was Jewish. "Igo," he said, "Go speak to them in your native language." I started a conversation with the two young girls using the stammering Yiddish I had learned in the ghetto plus a few words in Hebrew. The sound of familiar speech put a ray of hope into their eyes. They were not from Warsaw, they explained; after losing their entire family they had fled to this house and taken refuge with these ethnic Germans.

Looking at the other rebels with distrust, one of them said: "We're afraid of them." I assured them that my comrades would do them no harm. As we discussed this, one of the fighters came up to me and said: "Igo, tell them to take care of this house, because I want to live here after the war." I looked at him in astonishment. At that moment a picture flashed through my mind: mobs of people standing in the town square of Czestochowa, demanding the right to move into the houses of the Jews who had been sent to Treblinka. I repeated my comrade's request to the young girls, together with a hint that it should not be taken too seriously.

The safety of the tenants assured, I hurried to my rendezvous with Hanka (whom we called "watch-hand"). I found her in one of the rooms of AK headquarters, agitated and enraged.

"Igo", she said, "A bunch of characters from NSZ (National Armed Forces, a wartime antisemitic group) are here, and they plan to shoot you. They know you're Jewish. They came and threatened me; they were angry at me for consorting with a Jew."

I found this unbelievable. That very day, as I was at my position shooting at the Germans, a shot came from behind me and whizzed past my ear. Turning around in horror, I caught a glimpse of a rifle barrel disappearing into an opening in the building from which we observed Redeemer's Square. I was stunned at the thought that my comrades in arms – after all we had gone through together, after all the battles we had fought as partners – were out to kill me because I was Jewish.

An AK liaison girl now reached my position. She proved to be Aniuta Orzech, a daughter of the head of the Bund in Warsaw, and she brought me an AK newspaper called *Barykada*. I updated her on the latest happenings and described everything I had gone through. "Igo", she replied, "Everything that's happened to you is your own fault; you did not have to admit you were Jewish. Hundreds of Jews are fighting with the AK while posing as Catholics. I, too, do not admit to being Jewish."

Emotionally, I interrupted her: "But you've got to see, Aniuta, that it was after we took the Czech legation building. I disclosed my identity to a platoon commander who was wounded next to me in the common cause. I did not want to fall in battle under an assumed name."

Aniuta did not let me finish. "Unfortunately, Jews who fight with the AK fall in battle under various names – just not as Jews."

Melancholy and bitter from the day's events, I walked down Marshalkowska Street toward Hoza Street. Sadly I observed the terrible destruction which intensified from day to day. Warsaw was being reduced to dust under relentless bombing from ground and air. Houses burned from one end of the street to the other; skeletons of incinerated hulks were collapsing all around. One could hardly maneuver in the rubble-filled streets. So many civilians were killed that there was no time to bury them. People performed improvised burials wherever they could; temporary crosses sprouted in the courts of houses, gardens, the street, and public parks.

I was worried about my father; I had been out of contact with him for almost three weeks. I knew he was living near the center of the city but I had no access to that area during the battles. Then, at the entrance to one of the houses, I noticed the silhouette of an elderly man. Pursuing the disappearing form into the house... I found my father. He motioned to me that he was still posing as a mute. In view of my experiences the previous day, I agreed that this was best. He pulled out some paper and wrote: "Even now they should not know I am Jewish". He was sorry that I had abandoned him and had gone out to fight. "I felt it my duty", I explained, "to fight the Germans after all they have done to us, after they murdered and annihilated our people. Hanka told me they'd evacuated you together with everyone else who lived on Natolinska Street. I thought you'd find somewhere to live together with all the others. As you see, I am always fighting with the AK. You'll see, everything will be over soon."

"What will be over?" he wrote.

To spare him unnecessary sadness, I said, "The rebellion". He looked at me and continued to write: "Have you seen what Marshalkowska Street looks like? The Germans want to do there what they did in the ghetto. They want to destroy Warsaw, they want to destroy the population. The Russians, on the other side of the Vistula River, are doing nothing to liberate the city. They are waiting, it seems, until the Germans kill all of us and leave nothing but rubble where Warsaw once stood."

We reached a first-floor apartment where a single man had given my father a corner. His bed was in the kitchen at a window opening onto the court. No one was at home; we could speak freely.

"Father", I protested, "why didn't you go down to the cellar like everyone else in the building? It's much safer there. Here, above ground, a bomb can fall at any moment!"

"I prefer being buried here to being buried alive in the cellar", he answered. Then he asked me to refer to him only as Father, not Professor as before; he wanted everyone to know that I was his son. He was secretly proud of me for fighting the Germans.

Visiting him again a few days later, I heard someone on the street call my name. I turned around and saw Stefa, who had put me in touch with the Polish People's Army, running toward me. After we embraced, she asked me, "Where are you? What are you doing?" Noticing my armband, she said in astonishment, "Fighting with the AK? Have you gone mad? Why aren't you in the PAL?"

I briefly described how I had reached the AK, mentioned my platoon, and added, "Now, after all the combats we fought together, my comrades want to kill me simply because I am a Jew. I cannot understand this hatred. Is it because they feel guilty for not having helped us when they still could have saved Jews and prevented their deportation to the gas chambers of Treblinka?"

We stood amidst the devastation of once-magnificent Marshal-kowska Street. Stefa was plainly stunned by my story. "Igo", she said, "they're not all like that. Come with me to our headquarters, PAL headquarters. It's not far."

We entered the corridor of an ultra-modern house and proceeded from there to the cellar, a cavernous room of concrete. A cloud of cigarette smoke blurred the forms of sitting and standing officers. In the deafening noise, I could hardly follow Stefa's words.

Just then the "simple laborer" I had met in the church, my first link with Stefa, appeared at a side door of the cellar. The officers in the room snapped to attention; one of them gave him a progress report on the fighting in Zoliborz. The general, as he proved to be, listened to the report and looked from one man to the next. Noticing me, he cried, "And you, for heaven's sake, where have you been all this time? From the moment the rebellion broke out I've been asking Stefa about you, and she didn't know a thing."

Gesturing at me theatrically, he turned to his officers: "I hereby introduce you to one of the men who snatched weapons from Germans in the streets of Warsaw before the rebellion."

After some hearty greetings, he led me by the hand to his room. On the way he turned to an old woman in the cellar: "Auntie, bring us something to drink." As the woman procured some vodka and barley cakes, the general complained that he had more officers than enlisted men.

"Most of our men are fighting in the suburbs of Warsaw, with the Germans between us. We are downtown, where the population has never had leftist leanings. Here we have one incomplete brigade and a company of gendarmes; we are presently organizing a new brigade from the survivors of the Syndicalist brigade who reached us through the sewers from the old city. We're in a tough spot. Not only are we surrounded by Germans, but the AK people hate us too. They think we're Communists. As you know, we are the fighting arm of the Polish Socialist Party. In AK terms, however, all leftists are enemies. They didn't even want to let me know when the rebellion would begin; the sons of bitches were afraid I'd pass on the information to the Russians, who are close by."

He asked me where I was fighting. I told him briefly about the battles in which I had taken part, not forgetting to mention the time I had come under fire from my "comrades". Concentrating intensely, he heard me out with no comments of his own. Then he summoned a short, thin man with major's insignia, and introduced him to me as the Chief of Staff of the Polish People's Army.

Wasting no time, he said, "Write a letter to General Monter of the AK and inform him that Ignacy Popow, known as Igo, belongs to our army. Now that he has found his company, we must return him to his original organization under the agreement between all the militias in Warsaw. After you write the letter, let me sign it, And you" – he motioned to the major – "should also sign it as Chief of Staff." He ordered me to appear the next day before Commander

Czemir, and informed me that I was to begin my official service in the Polish People's Army with the rank of sergeant.

The letter in hand, I ran to AK headquarters on Ujazdowskie Boulevard, near the Square of the Three Crosses. The staff officer ordered me back to my AK platoon and back into action, promising to process my demobilization from the AK through a special liaison officer. If I continued to fight in their ranks a little longer, I replied, there wouldn't be anyone to demobilize; I would have been shot by then for being Jewish. After waffling for a moment, the officer handed me the demobilization papers.

We organized the Syndicalist Brigade and took up position in the Imperial Cinema building. At first we were a mere handful: Lieutenant Czemir, Sergeant Jordan (a mathematics teacher and a Jew), a doctor and his wife (who were Jewish, too). Others joined as time passed, including my old friend Wiernik from Treblinka. Our brigade comprised about a hundred men all told. The PAL also began to publish a Syndicalist newspaper at the time.

Each night we set bonfires up and down Wilcza Street as we awaited Russian airdrops of supplies and arms. Nothing happened the first few nights, and we nearly lost all hope. Then we heard the sound of an airplane engine, followed by silence. We understood that the pilot had cut his engine. A few moments later, several heavy bags fell onto the road. Their contents – *pepeshas* (submachine guns) and biscuits – became our brigade's equipment.

Zosia, a liaison officer in the ZOB (Jewish Fighting Organization) before the rebellion, met me one day with money from her organization for my father and me. Noticing my rebel uniform and sergeant's insignia, she asked me to intervene on behalf of her brother, who had been taken prisoner by the AK. I talked it over with General "Skala", who gave me a force of three men armed with *pepeshas*.

As we crossed the Square of Three Crosses on the way to the Czerniakow area, the Germans launched an attack on the Institute for the Deaf and the Mute, where the rebels had taken up a front-line position. Fighters in one of the groups racing to the aid of the attacked asked for our help in repelling the Germans. Joining them, we headed for Ksiazeca Street, the thoroughfare leading to Czerniakow. As we advanced, we hugged the walls of buildings as protection against the sniping of the SS soldiers under Dirlewanger, whose platoons were staffed exclusively by criminals.

We crossed the street under heavy SS fire and leaped into ditches which afforded some protection from the bullets. Advancing along the ditches and between destroyed houses, we reached the cellars of the clinic. We climbed to the upper stories and opened fire on Dirlewanger's men. After an hour of combat we repelled the attack, whose goal it had been to drive a wedge between Czerniakow and central Warsaw.

Continuing to Czerniakow, we located the AK headquarters and walked in. There we found a haughty colonel in prewar uniform sitting at a desk, with two young women in revealing clothing standing on either side.

Addressing the Colonel, I demanded to know the meaning of the AK's action in imprisoning a member of the PAL. Did it have anything to do with his being Jewish?

The colonel could hardly control his rage. "That Jew was an informer for the Gestapo!" he exploded.

"On what evidence do you base your verdict, sir?" I asked.

"We caught this Jew with a *Volksdeutsch*. He was living with her."

"Colonel, sir, didn't it occur to you that this Jew might have been hiding from the Germans together with the *Volksdeutsch*?"

"We found lists of all the Jewish informers in Warsaw in his possession", the Colonel answered in a triumphant tone of voice.

He reached into a desk drawer and withdrew a document with a long list of Jewish names. I examined it carefully and, returning it to him, asked:

"By the way, does the name Willenberg appear on this list as well?"

"Yes, sergeant", he answered. "Is that perhaps someone you caught on your sector of the front?"

"No", I said coolly. "There was no need to catch Willenberg. He is standing in front of you, Colonel."

Noting his obvious embarrassment, I informed the Colonel that his document was a list not of Jewish informers but of Jews who had successfully fled the ghetto to the Aryan side and had been helped by the Jewish assistance organizations. My father's name was also on the list for this reason. Then I requested to know the whereabouts of the Jew who had been imprisoned. Looking at me cynically, straight in the eye, he said he did not know.

I understood there was nothing more I could extract from him, and strode out of the room with the three soldiers who had accompanied me. Immediately after us came the two young women. One of them caught me on the stairs and whispered:

"I once knew an artist named Willenberg from Czestochowa." I said I was his son.

The second young girl whispered, "I am Jewish, too. I'm the granddaughter of the the chief rabbi of Czestochowa, Rabbi Asch." I asked her if she knew what had happened to the young Jew who had been taken prisoner. "They shot him", she answered sadly.

Disappointed at the failure of my mission, I returned with my soldiers to the brigade. When I reached the corner of Marshalkowska Street, I heard overhead the familiar shriek of an artillery shell. The shells being used were so powerful they toppled tall buildings and made craters meters deep. They were now being fired at six-second intervals. In between came the terrifying wails of missiles which we called "cows". One explosion followed another, and a layer of dust and lime from the shattered buildings covered Marshalkowska Street from end to end.

Shaking with fear, I realized that the shells were landing in the area where my father was living. I immediately ran in that direction. Dodging the heaps of ruins, I tortuously made my way to No. 60. Its entrance was blocked by rubble from the upper stories. Jumping over pieces of masonry strewn at the entrance and in the court, I succeeded in reaching the stairwell and, clambering over bits of wall and broken glass, approached the door of my father's apartment. Fearfully, I forced it open. I gazed into the room and saw him... lying on the bed, covered with a blanket which was powdered with a white layer of dust.

"Father!" I cried.

He opened his eyes peacefully and pointed at the ceiling in a gesture of despair.

"The shell", he said, "stopped there."

Finding him well and unhurt, I became enraged: "I told you many times that this would happen. I've asked you to go to the cellar with everyone else who lives here, but all along you've stubbornly insisted on remaining above ground because you were afraid of being buried alive in the cellar. What more are you waiting for? Isn't it enough that part of the building is destroyed?"

His expressive blue eyes sparkling, Father said: "Very well; I must go down to the cellar. One thing you should know, however; I shall begin to speak. Everything is coming to an end anyway, so why should I suffer and pose as a mute? I'll say that I went into shock after the explosions and recovered my ability to speak."

I helped him into the cellar, where his neighbors made room for him.

When I visited the next day, my father's neighbors congratulated me on his recovery of his voice. I demonstrated great emotion and joy at the great miracle, and found Father, charcoal in hand, sitting on the steps leading to the cellar, surrounded by the other apartment dwellers. Swiftly he sketched the head of Jesus on the ceiling, with a cross in the background. On the arms of the cross he wrote, "Jesus, I believe in You." As he completed the picture, his neighbors went into a state of near-ecstasy. They believed the holy head of Jesus would protect them from the peril which threatened them all. (The sketch, by the way, is still there.)

Word of the joyous event spread like lightning (the cellars of the houses in the area were connected, forming a subterranean "street system" of sorts). Though accounts of the actual event varied, they all agreed on one thing: a master painter had produced a head of Jesus as a way of expressing gratitude to him. Father did not go hungry during those days, for his grateful neighbors always invited him to join them in their frugal meals. One day, I found a box of candles and gave it to my father. The electricity blackouts, which had become part of life since the outbreak of the rebellion, had made candles a genuine treasure; Father would exchange them with his neighbors for whatever he needed.

It was then that food shortages became a serious problem in Warsaw. Headquarters ordered us to requisition sacks of barley to feed the men at headquarters and in the field. After locating the barley in the warehouses of the Haberbusch brewery, we looked for helpers to transport them. We let our search for volunteers become public knowledge, stressing that any civilian who would help would receive half the barley he could carry. As Warsaw had been overtaken by hunger, we found more volunteers than we could use, despite all the danger involved.

We marched in a long file (about eighty people in all) to northern Warsaw. We were able to cover most of the distance through the cellars, which were linked by tunnels. Civilians stationed in the passageways by house committees guided the volunteers through the underground labyrinth.

The narrow openings and passageways were hard to navigate. The cellars were home to many families. We marched noisily past them, as they lay on mattresses which they had spread on the ground. They paid no attention; they were already used to it.

We came to a trench along the road linking the southern and northern sections of central Warsaw. It was a rather shallow trench, for it ran atop the concrete roof of a railroad tunnel. Furthermore, the Germans had it covered. As we crawled along it to the center of the boulevard, they opened up with a murderous fire. Mortars and shells exploded over our heads and fell into the street. One shell landed in our trench, killing two of our men and wounding another four. We crawled to the casualties and pulled them to the other side of the boulevard, where their wounds were bandaged.

We continued to advance in a column to the Haberbusch warehouses. The whole area was under German fire, though the rebels took control from time to time after vigorous attacks. During those moments we were able to extract sacks of barley from the storerooms. The area commander, spotting us, ordered us with a motion of his hand to take shelter in some ruins close by until the German fire halted. I did not consider the ruins a secure refuge from the shells. Looking for a better shelter for my men, I advanced on Prosta Street toward one of the burnt-out houses. Behind a wall there I noticed two men, who fled as I approached. I took them for Germans at first, since the Germans had positions in the area. I ordered them to halt, threatening to fire on them if they moved. They stopped in their tracks and raised their hands. As I approached the men, revolver cocked and ready, I saw that one of them had a typical Semitic face. Why were they running away from me? I asked. Their faces radiated tremendous fear. One of the men asked in a trembling voice: "Sergeant, sir, what do you want of us?"

"I want nothing of you. I just don't understand why you ran away from me when I approached you." Taut from head to toe, I studied the man with the Semitic face at length, and asked:

"Are you Jewish ,sir?"

Their bodies quaked; their faces reflected insane fright. Noticing all this, I said they had no reason to be afraid, for I, too, was Jewish. They gaped at me in total disbelief. I uttered a few Hebrew words to put them at ease. Did I belong to the AK? they asked.

"No", I answered, "I am in the PAL. But tell me just the same, why are you so frightened?"

In wordless reply, one of the men moved away and indicated that I should follow him. We reached 10 Prosta Street. There I confronted a mass of corpses of civilian men, all barefoot. My escort then led me to a cellar filled with bodies of women and children.

Shaken by the sight of the slaughter, I asked, "What happened here?"

My escort, halting and embarrassed, began to explain: "When the revolt broke out, we took shelter from the shelling in a cellar we found in the burnt-out ruins. Yesterday I noticed some men in battle fatigues and AK armbands entering the shelter. When we saw them, we hid, my friend and I, behind a burned-out wall. A little later we saw the rebels leading the Jews out and dividing them into two groups – men on one side, women and children on the other. On the pretext of looking for weapons, they made a body search and confiscated their watches, valuables and money. Then they took the men out to the street and ordered them to take off their shoes and line up against the wall. A lieutenant ordered the men shot to death. The rebels then returned to the yard and put two soldiers in charge of the women and children. They dragged the women and children into the cellar. A few moments later we heard the women screaming. The rebels were raping them. And a little later... a burst of gunfire. The rebels emerged and left the scene."

"Once they were gone, my comrade and I went into the shelter and saw what you've just seen. A few hours later, a bunch of rebel soldiers from the Chrobry Platoon came from Zlota Street. They asked us what had happened, wrote up a report and read it to us."

The miserable man, sobbing now, continued: "It said that some Jews had killed other Jews for loot."

I suggested that the two Jews join us, but they refused, explaining that they had to bury their dead. We shouldered our sacks of barley and returned to the brigade.

That afternoon the Germans stepped up their fire, raining hundreds of mortar shells. The center of Warsaw was one mass of flame, its tall buildings reduced to heaps of rubble.

I returned to the PAL's underground headquarters. There General "Skala" noticed me, pulled me into his office, forcibly seated me, withdrew a bottle of vodka from under the table and poured me a full glass.

Astonished, I held the glass and studied the angry commander. Finally, very slowly, I began to drink, unable to understand why he would give me as expensive an honor as a glass of vodka was in those days.

"Drink!" he barked, cutting off my ruminations. Then again, with an enraged cry:

"Drink, for heaven's sake. Faster!"

I upended the glass and emptied its contents down my throat. As I placed the empty glass on the table, the General said:

"Stefa is dead. This morning, while running orders to Major Ketling of the Dubois Brigade, she was hit by a mortar shell and burned to death."

Stunned by the terrible news, I felt tears flowing down my cheeks. The General's eyes were also wet.

As in a film, my mind's eye replayed our first meeting in the grocery store. I recalled her radiant figure, the big handbag in which she placed the pistols I had seized from Germans. She would risk her life, walking the streets of Warsaw, to deliver those handguns to this address or that.

Now, for a long while we sat silently, honoring her memory.

36

Surrender

It was early October, two months since the beginning of the Warsaw uprising. The capital of Poland had become a heap of ruins. Radio broadcasts from England lauded our courage and shed crocodile tears for the fate of the civilian population. The words did us no good and did not even make us feel proud. Our only hope was from Praga, across the Vistula River, where a giant Russian army had dug in. The Russians' cynicism, however, had become fully evident to us by this time. They watched the Germans slaughtering a civilian population and destroying beautiful Warsaw, and did not move an inch to help us in our struggle.

Despite all our troubles with the AK, and considering their great sacrifices, we were stunned to hear that the AK, under General Bor-Komorowski, had surrendered to the Germans. We all felt cheated. It was as if all our sacrifices had been for nothing.

Hurrying to PAL headquarters, I found all the commanders and officers discussing the surrender in rage. I looked for General "Skala", only to be told that he had gone to AK headquarters to meet with General Komorowski, with whom he wanted to reach an agreement under which the PAL fighters would be attached to the AK and go into German captivity as AK soldiers.

"What's this?" I asked in astonishment. "We want to be taken prisoner?"

"Yes, it is better to be prisoners than to have the Germans gun us down as looters and thieves", Colonel Burza answered. "They've evacuated everyone in the area for fifty kilometers around. There isn't a soul within that radius. Where can one escape? There's no one to give you shelter!"

General "Skala" returned and went into another room with Major Rog-Mazurek. Impatiently we waited for the results of his deliberations with General Komorowski. Deathly silence reigned. Then General "Skala" strode in. He turned sad eyes on each and every one of us, as if wanting to remember us forever. In a whisper, he said:

"The AK refuses to equip us with soldiers' documents. They told us sarcastically that, as prisoners, our PAL documents are good enough."

The General added mockingly: "They just forgot one small detail. The writ of surrender was signed by the AK alone. From that moment we became gangsters and looters – outlaws. They'll shoot us if we surrender. From the AK's point of view, we're Communists; they do not recognize us as the Socialists we really are. To these nationalists, all leftists, even the Syndicalists, are Communists. We've got to solve the problem by ourselves."

"I think some of us have to stay in Warsaw and keep fighting until the others, in civilian clothes, have left with the rest of the civilian population. We must try to keep away from the camp in Pruszkow, because the Gestapo sends people to concentration camps from there. It isn't true that there's no civilian population within 50 kilometers of Warsaw; we know that life goes on in most places as it did before the insurrection. Every enlisted man will get ten dollars, every officer, twenty. Everyone who took part in the revolt automatically goes up one rank. I suggest that all the Jews who fought with us stay in Warsaw, for their own safety."

"I appeal to all our comrades in arms, if you encounter our Jewish comrades after they've left Warsaw – help them under any conditions."

Silence.

Climbing out of the cellar headquarters, we found it was drizzling outside. All around there was a strange tranquility; the firing and the wailing of shells had stopped. People in rags went about the rubble in search of their relatives. Railroad and trolley cars had been overturned in the streets as barricades. Trenches connected the buildings. Bomb craters had filled with water and the sidewalks were covered with the rubble of buildings, a tangle of electric cables and fallen street lamps. A cratered moonscape littered with the burned-out skeletons of buildings – this was Warsaw, the capital of Poland.

I went to the house on Marshalkowska Street where my father was staying. Entering, I found him with Hanka. They stopped their conversation when they saw me.

Father turned to me: "What now, are we starting this business all over again? Again wandering to unknown places? I am not worried about myself. In the worst possible circumstance I shall become a mute again. They won't harm me; no one will accuse me of taking part in the revolt. But I'm worried about you. You are young; the Germans will seek and catch people like you. Perhaps you had better hide in the ruins of Warsaw. I don't know where you'll be safer."

"Father, I am bringing news from our headquarters. A surrender has been signed, and the Germans have ordered the civilian population of Warsaw to leave. About a million people will have to leave and wander about, who knows where. I just hope they won't set up a new Treblinka. Now I think you must leave Warsaw with everyone else. Hanka and I will stay here, and we'll join the crowds as the traffic picks up – in civilian clothes, of course. We must think about provisions for the way. We have between us thirty dollars. Hanka will stitch up some backpacks for the trip, and I will bring my good and trusty friend."

"Who?" Hanka asked in astonishment.

"My submachine gun, and a Parabellum handgun I have. I'll look around the Brigade headquarters; perhaps I'll find some leftover hand grenades. We must also bring clothes, blankets and sheets. With this equipment, we'll leave Warsaw."

Hanka interrupted me. "Igo, what route are we going to take? I noticed that Redeemer's Square is full of gendarmes who size up and examine every passerby, and you're well known in this area. The best thing to do is to head south on Zelazna Street and join up with the crowds of evacuees there."

We decided to leave at sunset; the darkness would help.

We set out on October 6, the last possible day. It was drizzling; the whole world was enveloped in greyish fog. Defying logic, we brought our weapons. Hanka concealed the flat submachine gun in her bag; I had two hand grenades and a handgun in a pocket. My knife, with which I never parted, was strapped to my leg.

We saw no one until we reached Filtrowa Street. Warsaw was dead to the world. In the morbid silence, our very steps caused us to tremble. The black shadows of the charred ruins, the rubble-strewn streets, and the crackling flames soaring from nearby neighborhoods, added up to a sad and fearsome spectacle.

At Filtrowa Street, we blended into an endless convoy of refugees. No one realized that we had climbed out of the ruins. Along the street, at regular intervals, German soldiers clutched their rifles and, with equanimity, contemplated the river of humanity streaming past them.

It was a nightmare: hundreds of thousands of marching refugees – destitute, begging, pleading refugees. Before reaching the railway station, the starving masses raided the fields round about in search of tomatoes which had ripened but had not been picked. Suddenly a voice called out: "Igo!" There, facing me, was Zygmunt Strawczyński, my good friend from Treblinka. His ruddy face beamed with joy at the unexpected encounter.

"Igo, let's walk together", he said.

"If you're not afraid of walking with an arsenal, you're welcome to join me", I answered. Seeing that he missed the point, I told him to touch my pants pocket.

Having crossed the fields, we reached the railroad where a train of half-open freight cars stood. A pushing, raucous mob surrounded us and blocked our way. Suddenly a German soldier pushed his way through, approached us, and addressed me in fluent Polish: "Igo, are you really still alive?"

It was the cook of the AK. In the very first days of the rebellion, he had reported to our company and introduced himself as a Silesian and a deserter from the *Wehrmacht*. After the AK interrogated him, he was appointed cook. Now he stood before me, smiling, in a German uniform.

A lightning thought struck me: this meeting could cost Hanka and me our lives. He knew me as a Jew and Hanka as an AK liaison runner. I extended my hand to him and, simultaneously, tripped him with my foot. As he fell to the ground, I threw myself on top of him and stabbed him, while Hanka stifled his cries by gagging him with a rag. In the darkness, the crowd surged and shoved without letup. Everyone tended to his own business and was oblivious to anything else. Once I was sure he was dead, we blended into the masses and leaped aboard the waiting train.

The train began to move, leaving behind a crowd which grew with every passing moment. Standing in the open car, I noted the settlements we passed and spotted a little town named Wlochy. The lights in its houses proved General "Skala" correct; there was still civilian life in the Warsaw area, there was still somewhere to hide. The train crept on, the drizzle intensifying the darkness. People around me who knew the area said we were approaching Pruszkow, where the Germans had set up a camp for the Warsaw evacuees in cavernous halls which had once served as repair shops for railroad cars and locomotives.

Pressed against Hanka and Zygmunt in the railroad car, I whispered, "Let's jump!"

It was after midnight. Everything was deathly quiet and dark. We did not know if the German gendarmes were patrolling around the tracks, but we knew it was time to escape. I jumped first. Feeling the gravel underfoot, I ran alongside the train and grabbed Hanka as she leaped. The two of us landed heavily on the gravel and lay quietly until the train had passed by. Suddenly we heard footsteps. We lay there motionless, in mounting fear, until we saw it was Zygmunt approaching.

37

After the Surrender

The three of us crossed a fence and found ourselves on a road parallel to the track. We heard the rhythmic pacing of an approaching army patrol, and we were immediately pelted with gunfire. There was no time to think.

"The submachine gun!" I shouted at Hanka. Soundlessly she handed me the weapon, which, I knew, had about thirty rounds. I pressed the trigger and fired a long burst in the direction of the shots.

Surprised by the unexpected attack, the Germans scattered to either side. They seemed to have no idea as to our numbers or our arms. We took advantage of their hesitation and fled into an alley bordering the fields, running in the mud to the limit of our strength. We sank into wet ground, wallowed in ankle-deep mud and water, vaulted fences, and eluded the peasants' houses.

We reached Jozefow at dawn. Soaked and exhausted, we knocked at one of the huts and asked for some water. It proved to be the residence of workers in a sugar factory. They and their families shared the hut in terribly crowded conditions – ten to twenty people in each little room, with no conveniences. Just the same, they put a room at our disposal and allowed us to stay a few days. Our plan was to reach the Kampinos forest and join the partisans who were active there.

Again and again the laborers asked us to describe the Warsaw uprising, and, though they knew we had weapons and were aware that there were German police in the vicinity, they were not afraid. They only asked us to be careful.

One morning I saw a German gendarme marching together with a civilian carrying a shovel. The two were leading a man along, whom I identified him as a Jew who had been a lieutenant in the PAL. Suddenly the German stopped and, from behind, shot the lieutenant in the head. He fell and rolled into a gully at the side of the road. The civilian approached the corpse, pulled the shoes off his still-warm feet and began to dig a grave. He did not trouble himself to dig deeply; a few scoops of his shovel opened a shallow trench. He gave the body a shove and covered it with a thin layer of soil.

I watched the scene in terror and, without thinking, raised my submachine gun. Hanka yanked it away. Behind us we heard the voices of laborers who had witnessed the event. "It must have been a Jew", someone said. "The Germans kill Poles in the forest to the west."

That evening we reached a decision, we had to clear out of Jozefow and try for the Kampinos forest. Though Zygmunt would have had us stay on a little longer – a nice young Polish woman was tending very warmly to all his needs (he married her after the war) – he decided in the end to set out with us. That evening, the sky in the distance was red from the inferno in Warsaw. The Germans, we understood, were razing the city to the ground to revenge themselves on the various Polish resistance movements.

We left hospitable Jozefow and headed for Blonie. As we made our way along the difficult route, Zygmunt grumbled all the while about our having left Jozefow. He regretted our decision to terminate the quiet and tranquil days we had spent there. I tried to explain to him that we had no choice; we could no longer exploit the warm hospitality of the laborers, stuffed into their little rooms, and the neighboring village was off limits because the German gendarmes were quartered there.

Even as we talked, a trio of German soldiers materialized from the bushes, submachine guns aimed at us. Hanka, the submachine gun on her shoulder under her wide coat, faced them and let loose. As the reports of the shots echoed into the forest, three bodies crumpled to the ground.

We leaped into the bushes and fled to the west. Reaching a river after an hour of running, we undressed in the reeds and bushes and plunged into the icy water. We climbed onto the opposite shore, shivering, and dressed quickly. Running north for several hours, we saw the distant houses of a town. As we approached it through the fields, we found it was Blonie. Throngs of refugees from Warsaw filled the streets and squares; here we felt safer.

Hanka was pale and complained of nausea. I joined a crowd at a pharmacy at the market square and noticed beside me an old man with a polite smile.

"How did you succeed in escaping that hell, Lieutenant?" he asked. Seeing my puzzlement, he hastened to explain: "I lived at 60 Marshalkowska Street, in the cellar where your father lived."

I asked him in excitement whether he knew what had become of my father, his neighbor. He said that he thought my father was in Okecie, not far from Warsaw, where he had headed with many of Warsaw's refugees. Whispering, he advised me to approach the local council for a referral to one of the villages in the area. I replied that I was not interested in settling down here, that our destination was the forests of Kampinos.

The old man objected: "There's no point in that. The Germans wiped out all the rebels in the forest. Their last resistance, which ended the battles, took place at the edge of Jaktorow next to Zyrardow. You'd be best off staying in this area for a while."

He persuaded us, and we headed for the local council house. It proved to be a spacious hall, with a wooden partition separating the public from the clerks.

At this point Zygmunt lost his composure for the first time. He placed himself behind Hanka and myself, flushing in agitation.

Trying to hide the tremble in my voice, I roared: "Where's the District Chief Clerk?"

As the crowd gaped, a secretary approached the partition and, voice quivering like mine, asked, "What is your wish, sirs?"

Without taking my eyes off him, I restated my demand with emphasis and great gravity. As I spoke, a side door opened, admitting a tall man with nervously flashing eyes. After he introduced himself as the District Chief Clerk, I turned to him and, looking him straight in the eye, barked: "We need a room with a separate entrance and electric light, in a quiet, calm village. At once!"

His expression changed slowly, fear yielding to the fawning smile of an indentured servant. Pressing my hand warmly and firmly, he leaned forward and whispered secretively: "Indeed, sirs, I have a room which is suited to your needs. It is in the village of Kopytow. That is where I live, and I can take you there after work. First of all, however, you must register yourselves as the law requires. Do you have documents of any kind?"

We handed him our false papers; he grabbed them and stamped them without so much as a glance. For the first time, then, we were genuinely government-certified.

We marched out and headed downtown. Suddenly Hanka burst into hysterical laughter: "*A room with electric light*", she roared again and again, rocking with mirth. "I never saw such a performance!"

Zygmunt, tensely scouting around, had no faith in the sincerity of the District Chief Clerk's offer. It was just a trap, he suggested. I expressed my opinion that this omnipotent bureaucrat's pants were probably wet through with fear by now. He knew the war was speedily winding down; he had to quickly find himself some merit, since he had undoubtedly served the Germans during the occupation. Now he had stumbled onto a golden opportunity to prove that he had indeed helped the Poles, and would be happy to exploit it.

"We can go to Kopytow without fear and without worry. But first, we need a good meal."

In Blonie, we exchanged our dollars for local currency and bought bread, sausage and a half-liter of vodka. The food and drink improved our mood. Calmed and sated we returned to the local council, where the District Chief Clerk was waiting for us with a horse-drawn wagon.

Reaching Kopytow, on the right side of the main road, we pulled up at a wooden farmhouse with a silo and various other farm structures in an adjacent courtyard. An old woman at the entrance of the house invited us in. We followed a narrow corridor to the kitchen, where a young, fair-haired young woman with a deeply creased face sat and friendly blue eyes. When the District Chief Clerk told her of his intention of putting us up in their house, she stood up and extended the hard, calloused hand of a laborer. "We're happy to have young people here", she said, and led us to an empty side room.

Zygmunt sized up the room. Apart from an electric light dangling from the ceiling, it was totally empty. He turned to our host and politely asked if they had any old furniture. Our host said he would look in the storeroom.

"But it'll still be empty tonight. You'll have to sleep on mattresses of straw which you'll bring from the silo", he added.

Not wishing to put him to trouble, I suggested we spend the night in the barn.

"There's no trouble involved. You bring your own straw and make beds in the room. But before that, come enjoy all this little house can offer you."

After a delicious hot meal, our host told us that the Germans had conducted a search and roundup of young people in the market just as he was leaving Blonie. "There's been talk about three Ukrainian collaborators getting killed near Jozefow."

Hanka stood up abruptly and poured me a shot of vodka. The daughter of our host stared at us as if sensing our connection with the story she had just heard. She turned to her father: "There are chairs and a table in the silo; there are also some boards which Father can use to make two beds..." Our empty room filled up with furniture that very evening; in the center, on a wooden crate, stood a metal heater, its long, twisting chimney encircling the entire room and spreading pleasant heat all around. Our host's daughter smiled at us, as if understanding our secret. Seeing that we were getting along well, she assured us that there was nothing to worry about and turned to leave. Shaking her hand, I wished her good night and thanked her for everything she had done for us.

We began planning an emergency exit the moment she left. The room had two windows facing the front of the house, and a door opening into the hallway. If the Germans raided the place, it would be hard to escape. We decided to dig a tunnel in the corner, beside a side wall against which the beds rested. This wall faced the fields, to which we would flee if danger threatened.

Early the next morning I pried up the rotten floorboards and started digging. Hanka scattered the soil in the silo. As we worked, we did not notice that our host had entered. He gaped at us and shouted in agitation: "Your digging may bring the whole house down! What is all this for? There's shelter in the silo; young people hide out there when they have to."

"And what if the police or the Gestapo make a surprise raid at night?"

"Even then there's nothing to fear", the peasant answered. "At the edge of the village our young men have an observation post, hidden in the bushes, where they watch for German police approaching in their cars. When there's danger they yank on a rope which rings a bell several hundred meters away from them. It's a tried-and-tested tactic. When they hear the bell, the Germans run toward it to seize whoever sounded the alarm. That gives the young villagers time to hide. But everything is usually quiet in our village."

We called off the excavation, lay our weapons in the pit and replaced the floorboards. The next day we decided to walk to the neighboring town, Milanowek, where I hoped to meet someone from the PAL. Zygmunt was ill at ease with the idea, but when he saw Hanka on my side, he too came along.

We set out at daybreak through paths and fields. On the way, opposite a farm compound, we came upon a wooden house flying a Red Cross flag. Hanka, we remembered, was not feeling well.

Looking for some help, we entered the structure, which had once been a barn, and climbed some very steep stairs to a spacious attic. Standing there was a beautiful, fair-haired girl in a white smock, who gave us a frightened look. A table nearby held various medicaments and a jarful of cotton.

Recovering her composure, the girl asked quietly, "Is one of you sick?"

Just then a short, middle-aged man stepped past a blanket hanging across the room. He, too, wore the white smock of a doctor.

"Morse!" I cried in joy.

Before us stood Dr Zielinski, the chief doctor of the PAL, a Jew like Zygmunt and myself.

Embracing, we bombarded each other with questions. He told us that he had left Warsaw via Pruszkow. After members of the underground had smuggled him out of the Germans' camp in

Pruszkow, he had come here and set up a Red Cross clinic, which was actually a way station for those heading to join the ranks of the partisans in the Kampinos forests.

Several days later I encountered General "Skala" in Zielinski's clinic. As we toasted each other with vodka, "Skala" told me that the chief of the Polish field police, Lieutenant Osa, had been arrested by the Germans after Ursula, Major Ketling's liaison, had informed on him.

Hearing that I was armed, General "Skala" ordered me to take part in an attack on Norblin's arms factory. The objective was the money in its safe. In horror I thought of my mother; she had been working in that factory. Was she still there? How could I encounter her in the middle of a raid without harming her?

The Germans brought cash to the factory for the payroll every Friday; so we were told by forced laborers from France who worked there. They also promised the General that they would try to get us into the factory premises in Glowno by way of a secure side road which bypassed the patrols.

We joined three other PAL fighters, all armed with handguns, and set out by train. Our "seats" were on the bed of a flatcar placed at the front of the train and pushed by the locomotive. The Germans, afraid that the railbed was mined, would use this tactic to minimize damage to the locomotive. The Germans allowed only Poles to ride this car, the idea being that the partisans would refrain from mining the tracks out of mercy for their compatriots.

We reached Glowno that evening. Three men awaited us, together with Sergeant Jordan. We headed for the factory, which as an important defense installation, was heavily guarded. Nevertheless, one of the French workers led us through a hole in the fence to the factory grounds. We headed for the office wing, where we would find the payroll office.

The Polish purser, seeing guns aimed at him, thrust his hands in the air and then opened the safe upon our order. We loaded piles of paper money into sacks, bound the purser and two clerks with rope, cut the telephone wires, and fled.

As we made our getaway through the manufacturing halls, I saw my mother and succeeded in exchanging a few words with her. We pretended to be strangers; our faces did not disclose what was happening in our hearts. Mother told me that Father was alive in Okecie. I gave her my address and rushed to rejoin my comrades. We retraced our steps from the factory and spent two days in Glowno, waiting for a cart loaded with straw which took the three of us back to Kopytow.

One gloomy night, as Hanka and I walked down a primitive track toward Dr Zielinski's clinic with our haul of some 450,000 zlotys, we sank into some snowdrifts. A strong wind blew snowflakes into our eyes. We heard the dull roar of artillery from the front at the Vistula River, and shots closing in on us from the Kampinos forests. An airplane passed overhead. Suddenly a light-bomb shredded the gloom of the night and, descending slowly from the black sky, illuminated the snowy scene. We fell to the ground to avoid discovery. Only after darkness had returned did we resume our trek through the deep snow, finally reaching the Red Cross station.

Following a prearranged code, we knocked forcefully on the door until Dr Zielinski (known as "Morse") appeared. We stepped into the heated room in relief, rushing to the lit stove to thaw our frozen limbs. The thought of spending the night in this cozy spot raised our spirits, and we decided to wait until morning to move on.

Before we could put down our packs, Dr Zielinski dispensed vodka for all of us and, glowing with satisfaction, gave us the good news: "The front has moved! The Russians have finally taken the offensive. They've breached the German defense line near Mogielnica and will apparently reach this place tomorrow. You must move on to Kopytow right now and defend the two bridges. The enemy must not be allowed to blow them up. I have learned that there are enough weapons in the village for the purpose. And now, please, get going. We'll meet after the liberation!"

It was the night of January 19, 1945. We bid the doctor a hearty farewell. If the frost was still a hostile force, we no longer felt it. The news warmed our hearts and mobilized our inner reserves when snowdrifts blocked our way. Our immediate task was to cross a railroad about half a kilometer away. It was guarded by Germans, and we were scared. Suddenly we heard a tremendous explosion. The railroad bridge, we knew, was gone.

We raced back to our flat, where we found Zygmunt with a group of young people. I ordered anyone with a weapon to come with me, and led the party to the Warsaw-Lodz-Berlin highway. Stopping just short of the road, we crawled forward and looked about. The road was clogged with endless convoys: cars, war material, soldiers marching frantically, horsecarts, ambulances – total chaos as the front closed in.

The thunder of artillery rose over the surging commotion on the road. From the east explosions ripped the night. We found an abandoned truck loaded with light arms, and equipped ourselves with rifles and large quantities of ammunition and hand grenades. We did not know the size of the enemy force facing us. However sizable it was, we had to keep it from crossing the bridge and blowing it up.

As dawn broke, two Soviet aircraft appeared overhead and circled over the bridge. I ordered my force to open machine-gun fire on the bridge and its burden of German soldiers. We also covered the road along its length, at the approach to the village, with light-arms fire. The very first volley produced a barrier of damaged enemy vehicles. A few soldiers tried to break through the wall of gunfire and race across the bridge. Just then the Soviet planes fired into the middle of the road which we had blocked. Though the Germans' first response was a sputter of aimless shots, the soldiers in charge of guarding the bridge from either side immediately bombarded us with strong and concentrated fire.

The exchange continued until nightfall. Then, without warning, the entire area was illuminated with light-bombs which had been launched from the other side of the railroad. White figures, hardly discernible in the snowy terrain, moved toward us. They were Soviet soldiers.

One of them addressed us in Russian: "Who is your commander?"

I stepped forward. In the dark I could hardly see the outlines of his face, which was enveloped in a fur hat embellished with a red star. When I identified myself as commander of the partisan unit, he extended a fur-gloved hand and shook mine warmly.

We stepped onto the road as enemy bullets whizzed all around. A few German soldiers had taken up position behind burning cars and overturned wagons and went on shooting. We, on our part, continued firing at the bridge. Hanka and Zygmunt were on the front line. The partisan unit fought hand in hand with the Soviet soldiers, and, after a fierce battle, the bridge was ours.

There we were – Hanka, Zygmunt and myself – on the bridge we had taken. Soviet soldiers passed by us and greeted us with joy: "Welcome comrades! For the motherland – onward to Berlin!"

A thought flashed through my mind: "Motherland?" For whom am I fighting?

Images passed before my eyes, the faces of people no longer alive. I, too, began to move toward Berlin, but not for my motherland. I had to avenge the blood of the murdered victims of Treblinka, the blood of my devastated people...

A voice roused me from my ruminations: "Igo, what's happened to you? Don't you notice the siren died down long ago?"

The gloom around me slowly disperses. Before me is a sun-drenched Tel Aviv street. Holocaust and Heroes Remembrance Day has begun.

Udim, Israel, 1984

Epilogue

The Treblinka camp was built mainly for Warsaw Jews. Already in the middle of 1941 there existed a forced labor camp, probably of local character, situated four kilometers away from the village of Treblinka and from a railway station bearing the same name. In the camp, among others, were local peasants imprisoned for such offenses as non-delivery of quotas of agricultural products. Jews were also imprisoned there. The location was ideal for realizing the German plans – reasonably distant from Warsaw (about 100 kilometers) and Białystok, secluded and with organized manpower. In May and June 1942 the necessary, preparatory work was carried out. The main buildings, three hermetic gas chambers, were erected by the Schoenbronn firm of Leipzig under the supervision of Obersturmführer R. Thomall.[1] On July 23 the first railway cars with Jews deported from Warsaw entered a specially prepared railway siding linking the main line with the camp loading platform.[2] The author of the present memoirs found himself inside the camp only toward the end of October 1942, after more than 300,000 persons had been put to death there. In the period July 23 – September 21, over 250,000 Jews had been

---

[1] Yitzhak Arad, BELZEC, SOBIBOR, TREBLINKA: THE OPERATION REINHARD DEATH CAMPS, Bloomington 1987; Martin Gilbert, THE HOLOCAUST: THE JEWISH TRAGEDY, London 1986, p. 37.

[2] Among the authors of works devoted to Treblinka, only Ryszard Czarkowski (CIENIOM TREBLINKI, Warszawa 1989) is of the opinion that the camp began to function several months earlier.

deported from Warsaw itself and gassed in the camp. The immensity
of the crime surprised the murderers, headed by the first Treblinka
commander, Dr Imfried Eberl, and surpassed their organizational
capacities. Unimaginable chaos ensued. A witness, Oskar Berger,
quoted by Arad, wrote: "When we were unloaded, we perceived
a frightening spectacle. Hundreds of human corpses were lying
everywhere. Heaps of parcels, clothes, valises lay all entangled. SS
men, Germans and Ukrainians were standing in the barrack corners
and shooting blindly into the crowd. Men, women and children were
all falling, blood-stained. The air resounded with shouting and cries
of despair. Those who had not been wounded by shots were forcibly
driven in the direction of an open gate, had to jump over the dead
and the wounded in order to reach a small square surrounded by
barbed wire."[3] The movement of the trains was so intense that the
Germans decided to send back to Warsaw uncleaned railroad cars. In
August Globocnik and Wirth inspected the camp. The inspection
resulted in a sharp criticism of Eberl's "work" and his replacement
by Obersturmführer Franz Stangl, hitherto the commander of the
Sobibór camp. For several days the transports were suspended and
the camp "tidied up". On September 3 the death machine was again
set into motion. Altogether, the hell of Treblinka engulfed the lives
of about 760,000 Polish and 130,000 foreign Jews.

The author of the present memoirs stayed in Treblinka II camp
from October 20, 1942 until the prisoners' rebellion on August 2,
1943. After a successful escape, he went into hiding in Warsaw and
took an active part in the operations of the armed Polish underground
until the final encounter with the Germans during the Warsaw
Uprising. These memoirs were written in 1948. However, only in
1986 did the complete Hebrew version of the memoirs, entitled
"Rebellion in Treblinka", appear, a year later its English translation,
and in 1988 a Spanish one. The origin of the essential framework of
these memoirs is very interesting. It is, in a way, characteristic or
typical. In 1948, one of the employees of the Łódź branch of the
Central Committee of Polish Jews interviewed our author. It was an

---

[3] Arad, p. 84.

87 page long interview, kept now in the archives of the Jewish Historical Institute in Warsaw.[4] This fact certainly strengthened Willenberg's conviction that it was absolutely necessary to preserve for the future generations the record of his camp experiences. Comparing the two versions, we can ascertain that the sections devoted to Treblinka are almost identical.

Thanks to the JHI narrative we become much better acquainted with the author's fate under the German occupation before his "resettlement" in Treblinka. It is worthwhile describing, even in brief, for it is most likely that the experience then acquired hardened the young Willenberg to such an extent that he succeeded in surviving the later, hellish experiences.

The outbreak of the war surprised Willenberg in Radość, near Warsaw, where he was spending his vacation together with his mother and two sisters. At that time his father was working in Opatów on the restoration of the local synagogue. The chaos of the first war days, fear and misgivings about its outcome made him first enlist in Otwock in the volunteer militia and then, on September 6, 1939, march east with others, in the direction of Ryki and Lublin. While on the march, he joined a routed company of the 66th Infantry Regiment and, together with it, found himself beyond Chełm Lubelski. There, when he was already a soldier, a Russian attack surprised him. He then felt perplexed, for the fact that his mother was a Russian woman, who converted to Judaism only after marriage, strengthened the temptation to remain in the Russian zone. On September 25, Willenberg took part in his first clash in the war, not with the Germans but with the Russians. He was severely wounded and saved by local peasants. Even though, as he relates, "they came in the evening to strip us of our clothes, boots," when they saw he was still alive they took him, together with other wounded, to a cowshed from where, after the Russians had temporarily withdrawn, he was moved to a field hospital. He spent three months in the hospital, which from a certain moment was guarded by Germans. He succeeded in escaping from the hospital

---

[4] ŻIH (Jewish Historical Institute) archives, Memoirs 247, minutes recorded by Klara Mirski.

to Radość though his wound, only partly healed, was still festering. The Willenberg family did not remain there for too long. German repressive measures, in particular the mass execution in Wawer, impelled them to leave for Opatów. In the ghetto of Opatów the Willenbergs did not belong to the "elite". Nonetheless they somehow made ends meet. The father painted small pictures which Samuel would sell on the so-called "Aryan side", "to peasants, in exchange for sugar, butter, coffee". His older sister earned some money by giving private lessons and his mother, by giving injections.

In 1942 news reached Opatów about the suicide of engineer Czerniakow and the beginning of the "resettlement" from Warsaw. There was talk about the extermination of the Jewish people but nobody wanted to believe it, for it seemed inconceivable that such a crime could be perpetrated in the 20th century (ŻIH narrative). Shops started opening in Opatów and Willenberg registered for work at the Starachowice smelting works but stuck it out there for only three months. "Thanks to the disinterested help of a Pole, Karbowniczek, the whole Willenberg family obtained Aryan documents." In order to hide, the family had to disperse all over Poland. The father went to the Siedlce area and the mother and sisters went into hiding in Częstochowa. Samuel traveled throughout the General Government in search of a hiding place. Tragically, one of the neighbors denounced the sisters to the Germans. They were arrested and the mother tried, in vain, to free them from prison. Disheartened, Samuel decided to return to Opatów and to leave everything to chance. Even though the niece of the head of the local Judenrat offered to intervene on his behalf to obtain a place in a labor camp, he would not avail himself of this opportunity. Most likely on October 18, 1942, at a railroad station near Ożarów, he was shoved onto a train going to Treblinka together with the majority of Opatów Jews. After two days of murderous travel they reached their destination. In his memoirs Willenberg describes what happened to him later.

As we know from the memoirs of Treblinka survivors, the rebellion in the camp did not entirely succeed. The insurgents failed to liquidate the German and Ukrainian gun emplacements. Only a hundred inmates were able to get across the wire entanglements surrounding the camp.

Barely forty of them survived the war. But the insurgents were able to burn down most of the camp buildings. Despite the reconstruction attempts made by the Germans, Treblinka virtually ceased to exist. After August 2 only two transports of Jews were directed to the camp. At the beginning of September, 13 inmates succeeded in making their escape from the camp. The rest, about one hundred, were brought by the Germans to Sobibór at the end of October. On November 13, in the fields of Treblinka, the last execution took place, that of a group of 30 inmates used to obliterate the traces of the camp. On its site the Germans set up an agricultural farm and transferred it to a Ukrainian family for cultivation.

For Samuel Willenberg, the moment when he crossed the camp fence marked the beginning of a new period in his life. As before, his main concern was to hide from the Nazis and to live to see the liberation. From that time he would again hide among Poles. The experience he had acquired until then led him to believe that it would not be an easy task.

The issue of Polish-Jewish relations during the Occupation was undoutedly a most sensitive one during the entire postwar period.

The few researchers, both Poles and Jews, who have hitherto expressed their views on the subject, have only been able to outline the matter and put forward some of the most fundamental questions. It must be stated that our knowledge of Polish-Jewish relations during the Occupation is very limited. The memoirs of Jews hiding on "the Aryan side", unpublished until now, provide us with some means of enriching our sources of information. To a Polish reader, accustomed during the past forty years to hearing only opinions presenting the Poles as a nation of heroes, as the nation most afflicted by this war, such memoirs will be a hard pill to swallow. Nevertheless, there exists a rich collection of memoirs containing descriptions of events in which Poles adopted a hostile attitude, often a very active one, towards Jews who were hiding.

Despite the suggestions of some Polish researchers, hostility displayed toward Jews was not characteristic solely of a marginal group of extortionists. "Grot" Rowecki himself clearly stated in a telegram sent to London already in 1941 that "the overwhelming majority in the country is anti-Semitic".[5] The gamut of attitudes that could be recognized as anti-Semitic in the Occupation reality is undouptedly very wide. For a person of Jewish origin hiding from the Germans, a manifestation of such an attitude was every refusal on the part of a Polish acquaintance to put him up, even for one night, whether the person seeking shelter knew the reason for the refusal was ordinary fear or some deeper resentment. Jakub Karpinski very aptly remarked that "during the German occupation the level of terror was different for the two sides".[6] Awareness of their extreme danger undoubtedly determined the way in which Polish Jews perceived and judged the behavior of their neighbors.

Doubtlessly the most complete testimony from that period, describing the condition of a Jew hiding "on the Aryan side", is the essay of Emanuel Ringelblum, "Polish-Jewish relations during WWII".[7] Ringelblum wrote his essay in specific circumstances, hiding in his bunker in a garden at Grójecka 84. Abviously, at the time, he could not keep orderly notes. It is most likely he was also in a great hurry. Therefore, one could hardly expect a cool and objective appraisal of the reasons guiding the various characters.

Ringelblum's judgment on the attitude of the Polish population toward persecuted Jews is very harsh. Only a few "good souls" or, as Artur Eisenbach explains, the progressive and democratic elements of Polish society urged the Polish population to hide Jews. On the whole Polish society acted with indifference or downright hostility. In conversations among Poles about the occurrences in the ghetto there prevailed, in general, a tone of anti-Semitism and satisfaction that Warsaw had finally become "Judenfrei". Ringelblum sought the reasons for this hostility in the prewar anti-Semitic campaign of national-democratic and Sanacja groups. The publisher of the work, the outstanding historian Artur Eisenbach, wrote in a similar vein. These negative sentiments were magnified to an extremely high degree

---

[5] Quotation from Jan Tomasz Gross: "Ten jest z ojczyzny mojej... ale go nie lubię", "Aneks" 41-42 (1986), p. 29.

[6] Jakub Karpinski, "Asymetria", "Aneks" 41-42 (1986), p. 10.

[7] Warszawa 1988.

by the occupiers' propaganda machine, putting the blame for the war exclusively on the Jews. Moreover, the extermination of the Jews enabled the Polish lower middle class to take over a large part of the Jewish property. To be sure, it was this class that had a decisive influence on forming the public opinion. On the other hand, according to Eisenbach, "the attitude of the rural population toward the Jews depended on the sentiments prevailing in the respective area with regard to the Jewish population before the war". Fear and prejudice, as well as the passivity of the Catholic clergy, caused the peasants' reactions to be mostly negative. Nonetheless, Ringelblum noted in his work many examples of heroic help extended to the persecuted and murdered Jews, from the Council of Aid to Jews, "Żegota", to individual help, given also by some clergymen. He most sharply criticized "the government circles", which, in his opinion, "did nothing to save at least these remnants of Polish Jewry".

Among the fugitives from the ghetto who frequently met with a refusal of help, were many keen observers of the society on whose good will they had become dependent. Most often they could not grasp why they were constantly rejected and why they could not extricate themselves from the trap of isolation. In her memoirs, Maria Nowakowska noted: "Those Jews who got out of the ghetto, who obtained 'Aryan' documents, who had where to live, should have saved themselves. They could and should have lived afterwards as peace-fully as non-Jewish Poles, as Polish Christians did. Why were there to be found such dregs of society that, for the sake of destroying one Jew, sent to death, at the enemy's hands, entire Polish, Catholic, brotherly families?... Why could not those Poles who did not intend to denounce or blackmail a Jew they had seen keep it secret? Why did they share this information with others? Why were they not discreet? After all, nothing was asked of them so much as silence, as not whispering to others who were just as friendly toward Jews, who carried on with their whispering until the Gestapo got wind of it. If they had simply remained silent, almost all the fugitives from the ghetto would have saved themselves... After all, no German did at first distinguish between a Jew and a Pole, a Slav... Now that I die a dozen times a day because I am a Jewess, I want a plain, straightforward answer coming from the heart, not from the brain".[8] Also those who had a hiding place would remark that "Warsaw streets were not hospitable to Jews during the war. To this tens of reasons contributed all of which made no difference whatsoever to people whose only desire was to find refuge. One had to fight one's way through the streets of Warsaw, permeated with openly manifested anti-Semitism and full of German agents, to the privacy of homes that could offer relative safety... Most needed of all was money, money and once again money."[9]

Someone who had no money could at times reckon on the help of Polish acqaintances. But only educated and assimilated Jews had such possibilities. Very eloquent is the testimony of Professor Marian Malowist[10] who was saved by Polish friends from the university and colleagues – teachers from Kreczmar's school. But the majority of Jews did not have Polish acquaintances. In support of this theory one may quote Professor Malowist: "When I was already a teacher, I polled our students, in cooperation with an Aryan colleague. We asked the Jews: 'What Poles do you know? What Polish streets do you know?' We posed identical questions to the Poles. It turned out that my Jewish girl students did not know a single Pole except the janitor, that they actually did not know anything about this society. The results among the Poles were identical." According to Malowist, this was quite a common occurrence. Even at such exclusive university seminars as those conducted by Professors Handelsman and Czarnowski there was no social intercourse between Jews and non-Jews. Neither did any "Aryan" come to the ceremony when a doctor's title was conferred on Malowist.

It was easier to hide for those who, like the husband of Maria Steczko, had a "good Aryan appearance" that could "throw the best sleuth hound tracking Jews of the scent". Others, who were better

---

[8] Maria Nowakowska, "Moja walka o życie", AŻIH, Memoirs 142. This work – memoirs of a Jewess hiding among Poles – was printed in Warsaw in 1948. Unfortunately, the fragments quoted by me were omitted in the printed version.

[9] Archives of ŻIH, Memoirs 121-B.H."Przesiedlenie w zaświaty", compiled by W. Pawlak.

[10] "Res Publica", 7 (1988), p. 43-52.

off, coped with the circumstances in a different way. Benjamin Muenz's son-in-law was "very well operated, which also cost a dozen or so thousands, whereas his daughter underwent a nose operation that changed her physiognomy".[11]

Nevertheless, about 20,000 Jews were hiding in Warsaw alone, on the "Aryan side", as we learn from numerous authoritative testimonies. Most often they themselves covered the costs connected with hiding. A proper place, together with board, could cost as much as 20,000 zlotys monthly. Only in rare instances could they find cheaper lodgings. Very few were able to find any employment. In consequence, the decisive factors were a so-called good appearance and adequate financial reserves. Persons who did not meet these requirements could either seek the help of underground organizations or hope to be fortunate enough to meet a person of high moral principles, ready, for the sake of higher ethical reasons, to run the mortal risk connected with hiding a Jew. In memoir literature we find at least as many examples of such attitudes as examples of hostile attitudes or conduct. In most complete fashion they were compiled in the anthology prepared by Władysław Bartoszewski and Zofia Lewinowna, "Ten jest z ojczyzny mojej".[12] Nevertheless, both the above mentioned authors and Teresa Prekierowa,[13] author of a monograph on the Council of Aid to Jews, "Żegota", clearly state that the aid possibilities on the part of the Polish and Jewish underground organizations were very limited. At the beginning of 1944, "Żegota", the "Bund" and the Jewish National Council supported financially about 12,000 persons.

The wave of blackmail, extortion and denunciations could not be overcome by the counteraction of the Polish authorities in exile and the underground organizations in Poland. The Prime Minister of the London government, Władysław Sikorski, resolutely condemned the

---

[11] AŻIH, Nar. 476.

[12] Kraków 1969.

[13] Teresa Prekierowa, "Konspiracyjna Rada Pomocy Żydom w Warszawie 1942--45", Warszawa 1982.

German crimes perpetrated against Jews. Similarly, the government-in-exile's delegate to Poland came out on several occasions in support of the Jewish cause. The same holds true for the National Council in London and for Polish political parties active in the underground in Poland. Definitely most significant was the activity of the Information and Propaganda Bureau of the General Command of the Land Army (AK), and that of the Information Bulletin (Biuletyn Informacyjny KG AK) directed by Aleksander Kaminski.

Polish underground military organizations tried to actively oppose the wave of blackmail and denunciations directed against Polish citizens of Jewish origin. In the Warsaw area the effect of these efforts was extremely modest. In his statement made at the Jewish Historical Institute, Kazimierz Moczarski, who headed the Information-Investigation Section (code name "Magiel") at the Government Delegation to Warsaw, gave information about only five cases known to him of investigation of "Jew hunters", and about separate proceedings concerning 12 employees of the German criminal police, "who constituted a special, secret group of Gestapo men dealing with the rounding up of hiding Jews".[14] The files of these cases were delivered by Moczarski's section to the prosecutor of the Central Special Court, "Alfi" Sakowicz. Teresa Prekierowa gives in her work details of several judgments on blackmailers, passed by the Underground Struggle Direction and published in the "Information Bulletin".

But it is a fact that the majority of Jews who were in hiding during the Ocupation and survived the war, bear a bitter grudge against Poles for not having done all they could to save the maximal number of their brethren, and for the circumstance that quite a large number of Poles could be found who actively supported the occupying power in its war against the Jewish people. For the sake of truth and reconciliation, no effort should be made to weaken these testimonies by pointing out, among other things, their uniformity and homogeneity. A much more honest attitude would be to try to understand the nature of this phenomenon.

---

[14] AŻIH, Nar. 5830.

The statements of Jan Tomasz Gross[15] in his article, "Ten jest z ojczyzny mojej... ale go nie lubię", published in "Aneks", may serve as a good starting point. According to Gross, Polish patriotism under the Occupation, directed against Germans and Russians, did not entail giving up hostility toward Jews. Let us add that the same held true for the "patriotism" of the Lithuanians, Letts and Ukrainians.

Willenberg encountered the anti-German underground quite accidentally but joined it as a very active member. Thanks to complementary information, drawn from his narrative deposited at the Jewish Historical Institute, we know that he acted as intermediary in bringing arms from Rembertów and even graduated from an underground officers school. An armed Jewish underground in Warsaw was virtually non-existent after the suppression of the ghetto uprising. From among the soldiers of the Jewish Fighting Organization, only a handful had survived, and, until the Warsaw Uprising, they remained very deeply underground. The AK practically did not accept Jews in its ranks, also in view of the additional risk. For persons like Willenberg, who desired to actively fight the Germans, their only chance was to make contact with armed organizations of socialist and communist groups. It is obvious that these organizations did not conduct military operations comparable with those of the AK; they were, nonetheless, very attractive to young people. By chance, Willenberg found his way to PAL, an organization that has remained very mysterious until now, even though 45 years have elapsed since the end of the war.

In the wealth of material kept at the ŻIH archives, there are only a dozen or so narratives of Jews who were in Warsaw during the uprising. Some of these testimonies came from persons fighting in insurgent units. Company Sergeant Jakub Smakowski fought in an AK unit in the Old City.[16] Efraim Krasucki[17] fought in the same quarter, in a SOB unit. He noted after the war: "In our company in the Old City there were a dozen or so Jews with a conspicuously

15 Gross, p. 24, 33.
16 AŻIH, Memoirs 145.
17 AŻIH, Nar. 1539.

Semitic appearance but nobody took any notice of it." In the memoirs of Jewish survivors, the Old City occupies an exceptional place. On August 5, 1944, the "Zośka" battalion of the AK, supported by an AL platoon, while conducting an operation aimed at maintaining contact with Wola, captured the site of the Gęsiówka concentration camp, located on the ruins of the former ghetto. An additional result of the operation was the liberation of a group of over 300 Jews imprisoned there. Some of them had been transferred to Gęsiówka from Pawiak prison immediately before the outbreak of the uprising. After a few days, in view of repeated German attacks, the majority of the liberated prisoners moved to the Old City. Thanks to the memoirs kept at the ŻIH,[18] it may be said, with great probability, that the above group, composed almost entirely of men, was placed at the disposal of the AL command in the Old City. The Polish--speaking Jews formed a fighting squad in the 3rd Platoon of the 3rd Company of the 3rd AL Battalion commanded by Zbyszek Krukowski (code name "Kruk"). The rest were formed into an auxiliary unit, commanded by Jan Fotek (code name "Wieczysław"). In the sources the unit is named the AL International Auxiliary Service Brigade. This group was commanded directly by Fotek's second-in-command, Dr Stern, a Czech Jew. Fotek himself, after the war, estimated the effective force of the brigade at approximately 250 persons. During the fighting, about 50 perished. After the fall of the Old City, about 30 succeeded in hiding themselves among the civilian population and about 40 passed through sewage canals to Żoliborz. From the memoirs of Dr Bronisław Elkan Anlen[19] we learn that some Jews also managed to reach the City Center. Also in the Old City, a group from the former ŻOB (Jewish Fighting Organization), several fighters headed by I. Cukierman, cooperated with the 3rd AL Battalion.[20] This group also made its way to Żoliborz at a later date. The sources do not

---

[18] Concerning Gesiowka – T. Berenstein, A. Rutkowski, Bull. of the ŻIH, 62 (1967); AŻIH, Nar. 5678, 6752, 6760, 6687-6690.

[19] AŻIH, Memoirs 259.

[20] AŻIH – Nar. 6752, narrative of Jan Fotek; Mem. 114, memoirs of Jozef Zysman about the bunker on Promyka St.

always provide us with detailed information about the fate of the Jews from Gęsiówka. For example, a Greek Jew, Jacques Otidell, noted[21]: "Our joy. Two months of revolution. Ten Greek Jews were incorporated into Nalec (?) battalion. Our struggle around the Bank of Poland. Then the surrender of the Old City. The escape through canals to the City Center... The remaining 14 Jews split up into groups and took different routes." Also in the Center, in Wola and Mokotów small, sometimes organized, groups of Jews fought. Wacław Myzia noted in 1948 that many Jews "took an active, armed role in insurgent operations, mostly in the ranks of the KB, PAL and the AK 'Parasol' Battalion."

To conclude the presentation of authoritative sources relating to the fate of the Jews hiding in Warsaw during the uprising, I have decided to present several fragments of narratives confirming the fact that many anti-Jewish sentiments, dating back to an earlier period, were extant despite the new, common and so cruel experience. Two of narratives are directly linked to events that took place in the neighborhood of the Haberbusch brewery.

The author of the first narrative is Stefan Sendlak (code name "Stefan")[22], an activist of the PPS (Polish Socialist Party), who during the war was a member of the Aid for Jews Council. During the uprising he performed the duties of the deputy delegate to the 3rd District of the City of Warsaw – Town Center North. His scope of observation in the matter that is of interest to us, was, before and during the uprising, wide enough so that we may trust his opinion. He tersely characterized the Polish attitude toward Jews in the period preceeding the uprising: "The anti-Semitic agitation of many years' standing, conducted by nationalistic and clerical groups, was effective. It resulted in the psychosis of catching Jews in the streets, extorting ransom from them and delivering them to the Germans." Similar situations occurred also during the uprising. At the end of August 1944, "seven Jews, among them two women", were brought to the delegate of the 3rd District and charged with spying. The reason for

---

[21] AŻIH, Nar. 2033.
[22] AŻIH, Nar. 3973.

the accusation was the "Aryan" documents found on them. The persons, identyfied as Jews, were released, but were given proper passes to move to another district "for fear that a similar incident might happen to them again". The same section of the Government Delegation Office conducted an inquiry into the mysterious disappearance of a certain Jew taken to barricade construction works on Śliska St. Suspicion arose that he had been murdered. Such incidents were probably quite frequent, for the activists of the Aid for Jews Council, who were operating in the City Center – Fajner, Arczynski, Miller – nominated Fajner to undertake efforts with the Government delegate with the aim of "repealing decrees issued by the Germans that deprived the Jews of their rights". "The Jewish population, however", writes Sendlak, "began to avoid making contact with the Aryan population." Indeed, a kitchen was set up by Jews for the Jewish population only, on Mariańska St. near the Rzym bar. Incidents, and even provocations, were a frequent occurrence. Cwilich, a member of the "Bund" perished "for he had been deceitfully drawn into an ONR organization on Mokotowska Street. In the course of his work he communicated with the members of this organization until, at one of the meetings, he was murdered." The Delegation itself actively helped groups of hiding Jews. "After the suppression of the uprising, two Jewish groups, numbering about 20 persons, could not leave Warsaw because of their appearance. They hid among the ghetto ruins. The Delegation of the 3rd District supplied them with food, within the scope of its possibilities."

In the course of the evacuation of the civilian population, after the collapse of the uprising, fear of being spotted by Germans or by hostile Poles prevailed among Warsaw Jews. At any rate, quite a few testimonies of people who for this reason had decided to remain in devastated Warsaw, have been preserved. Dawid Zimler[23] wrote in 1945 about his companions in hiding, that most of them "were already resigned to their fate and simply

---

[23] Quite a few memoirs of Jews hiding in the ruins of Warsaw after the suppression of the uprising have been preserved. M. Grynberg published fragments of several of them, but omitted the interesting narrative of Dawid Zimler (AŻIH, Nar. 470).

wanted to go to the Germans and give themselves up". However, they constructed a "bunker" at Pańska St. 31, and 42 persons found shelter there. The majority were killed in a clash with Germans combing out the ruins. Only ten persons remained alive. Nevertheless, many Jews who had been hiding succeeded in leaving Warsaw, together with the Polish population, just as the author of these memoirs did. At any rate, a socalled "good appearance" always favored a lucky escape or played a decisive role in it. Dr Bronisław Elkan Anlen[24], an inmate of Pawiak and Gęsiówka, saved by soldiers of the Baśka battalion, wrote an interesting account. The attitudes of the generally very young AK soldiers of the above mentioned battalion were, according to his description, most diverse. Some of them treated the liberated Jews in a very friendly manner. Anlen wrote: "Some of the former prisoners, who were directly made to join the insurgents' struggle, also in the armored platoon, received the insurgents' uniform – German camouflage battle dress – thus ridding themselves of the concentration camp striped clothes." But, despite this, incidents occurred. A young officer, "seeing the liberated prisoners, shouted in a tone I would describe as contemptuous and violent, full of disappointment: 'What the hell, only Jews? Dammit, they didn't kill you off?' After a moment he called out: 'Are there no Communists among you? (...)' Three German Jews who kept together and were speaking German to one another, were immediately treated as Germans disguised in striped clothes, and shot." The insurgents also used the released Jews to bury the shot SS men. It seems that while they were doing this work, comments by the insurgents were heard: "You're doing a good job, you did it to our folks." Also a certain Jew, "Filip", was shot after his collaboration with the Gestapo had been proven. This execution caused general panic among the prisoners, which was strengthened by the widespread opinion that "since all those Jews are alive, they surely collaborated with the Germans." At any rate, in Anlen's view, extending help to and cooperating with persons of Jewish origin was not, in

---

[24] AŻIH, Memoirs 259.

public opinion, a praiseworthy activity, and people engaged in it were even boycotted by their neighbors. In the Old City the liberated Jews were contemptuously called "the Beduins from Gęsiówka".

Much more tragic incidents occurred, such as the murder of a group of persons of Jewish origin in the cellar of a house on Prosta Street, described by Willenberg. It is absolutely unquestionable that the reported incident indeed occurred. Willenberg, however, did not mention it in his testimony of 1948. His description is corroborated by other source material, and the manner of its presentation rules out the possibility of a later borrowing. The most detailed description of the incident, however, was given by Jonas Turkow in his memoirs, published in Buenos Aires in Yiddish, in 1949, under the title "In kamf farn lebn".[25] According to the information he gave, 14 persons from the families Gutman, Bursztyn and Szeinfeld were murdered in the cellar of the house at Prosta 4, on September 10, 1944. Four men whose names are known were saved. It must be added that two of them, Henryk Herszbein and Adam Bursztyn, were also mentioned in Willenberg's memoirs. According to Turkow, the perpetrators of the murder were Lieutenant "Okrzeja" and the two Mucha brothers, solidiers of the "Chrobry II" unit. Szeinfeld, a dentist, did not perish with the others, but after reporting to Captain Hal about the murder. After a visit to the latter's quarters, situated at Ceglana 7, he was sent back, together with some soldiers, and disappeared. Turkow did not say in his memoirs from which survivor he had received such comprehensive information. He himself visited the site of the murder in January 1945 and found in the cellar some objects left by the victims. The ŻIH archives contain testimony signed by Henryk Bursztyn,[26] probably a cousin of Adam Bursztyn in which the incident is described in a very similar manner. According to this testimony, the murder was perpetrated by a group of eight to ten soldiers of the "Chrobry" unit, commanded by a lieutenant. The person who wrote down the narrative pointed out that "in already liberated Warsaw,

---

[25] The book is available at the ŻIH library.

[26] Nar. 1106. S. Willenberg siggests it is the narrative of H. Herszbein. It is possible, of course, that the person who wrote it down made a mistake in the names.

Adam Bursztyn removed the remains of his relatives from the cellar and buried them in the Jewish cemetery in Warsaw, on Okopowa St." The whole incident is indirectly corroborated by the testimony of Dawid Zimler[27] who, during the uprising, worked as a barber in the insurgents' barracks at Pańska 5. One day, under the pretext of checking his documents, he was taken to a lieutenant or captain waiting outside the building. Zimler continues: "The captain winked at the soldier, which meant that he was to finish me off. He gave the order: 'Go to Haberbusch; you'll get wine and sweets there.' I knew what it meant. I refused." Zimler managed to survive by a sheer miracle, thanks to the intervention of another military man. Interestingly he persuaded the officer with the argument that it is "a shame and dishonor to us Poles to kill a Jew who for several years has been hiding from Hitler's thugs." Summing up, it seems that we may unhesitatingly accept the murder described by several persons as an authentic but undoubtedly incidental occurrence.

All the examples of attitudes and behavior, bearing a definitely anti-Semitic character, have been selected and presented in this essay in order to make better known the truth about Polish-Jewish relations during the Occupation. We may, of course, conceive that they could be used to intensify further mutual feelings of prejudice and distrust. Nonetheless, these testimonies do exist and cannot be passed over in silence. The same holds true for hundreds of testimonies speaking of help extended to hiding Jews by individual Poles and some organizations. Polish-Jewish relations have never been exemplary and we need not forcibly try to prove the contrary. But we may expect that a new generation of historians, not burdened by the memory of the tragic war experiences, will enrich our knowledge of what really happened between the two nations in the last chapter of their common history.

Andrzej Zbikowski

---

[27] AŻIH, Nar. 470.